ORDINARY PEOPLE IN PUBLIC POLICY

Also by Richard Rose

The Postmodern President: the White House Meets the World
Taxation by Political Inertia, with Terence Karran
Ministers and Ministries: a Functional Analysis
Patterns of Parliamentary Legislation, with Denis Van Mechelen
Voters Begin to Choose, with Ian McAllister
Public Employment in Western Nations
The Nationwide Competition for Votes, with Ian McAllister
Do Parties Make a Difference?
Understanding Big Government
Understanding the United Kingdom
United Kingdom Facts, with Ian McAllister
Can Government Go Bankrupt? with Guy Peters
What Is Governing? Purpose and Policy in Washington
Managing Presidential Objectives
Northern Ireland: A Time of Choice
The Problem of Party Government
International Almanac of Electoral History, with T.T. Mackie
Governing without Consensus
People in Politics
Influencing Voters
Politics in England
Must Labour Lose? with Mark Abrams
The British General Election öf 1959, with D.E. Butler

Edited by Richard Rose

The Welfare State East and West, with Rei Shiratori
Fiscal Stress in Cities, with Edward Page
The Territorial Dimension in United Kingdom Politics, with Peter Madgwick
Presidents and Prime Ministers, with Ezra Suleiman
Electoral Participation
Britain: Progress and Decline, with William B. Gwyn
Challenge to Governance
Elections without Choice, with Guy Hermet and Alain Rouquié
New Trends in British Politics, with Dennis Kavanagh
Comparing Public Policies, with Jerzy Wiatr
The Dynamics of Public Policy
The Management of Urban Change in Britain and Germany
Electoral Behavior: A Comparative Handbook
Lessons from America
European Politics, with Mattei Dogan
Policy-Making in Britain
Studies in British Politics

Ordinary People in Public Policy

A Behavioural Analysis

Richard Rose

Sage Publications

London · Newbury Park · New Delhi

SAGE Publications Ltd
28 Banner Street
London EC1Y 8QE

SAGE Publications Inc
2111 West Hillcrest Drive
Newbury Park, California 91320

SAGE Publications India Pvt Ltd
32, M-Block Market
Greater Kailash - I
New Delhi 110 048

British Library Cataloguing in Publication data

Rose, Richard
    Ordinary people in public policy: a behavioural analysis.
    1. Political behaviour
    I. Title
    320′.01′9

ISBN 0-8039-8135-X
ISBN 0-8039-8136-8 Pbk

Library of Congress Catalog Card Number 89-62000

Typeset by Sage Publications
Printed in Great Britain by Dotesios Printers Ltd, Trowbridge

Dedicated to
the memory of my mother,
who would have understood

Contents

Tables and Figures

Tables

Figures

Acknowledgments

This book brings together two analytic traditions that are often kept apart, the study of political behaviour and the analysis of public policy. While the subject matter is public policy, the perspective is that of amateurs in government, that is, ordinary people. Having done intensive research about political behaviour and about public policy, it is appropriate to write a book that joins the two concerns. If one holds that government should serve the ends of individuals rather than individuals being servants of the state, it is also important to think of public policy from the 'underall' perspective of ordinary people.

Most studies of political behaviour concentrate upon ordinary people in electoral situations, but for most people voting is an occasional action of limited personal significance. People do not expect the outcome of an election to alter the public provision of such household benefits as education, health care and social security. Elections are interruptions too in the daily activities of high-level politicians and civil servants, whose daily priority is to deal with what goes on inside government, and inside their particular department. There is thus a puzzle about the significance of government for ordinary people – and of ordinary people for governors.

This book is a sequel to a study that I wrote about *Understanding Big Government*; it is about understanding little people in a society with a big government. While doing research on the growth of government I began to wonder: What happens to ordinary people when government grows? One set of answers was encouraging: the more that government does, the more ordinary people benefit. From this it followed that if the growth of government stopped, then ordinary people would be frustrated by not receiving expected benefits of public policy. However, politicians on the right have argued that as government grows it reduces the capacity of individuals to look after themselves; hence, anything that stops its growth would be socially desirable. Subsequent chapters show that we live in a mixed society in which public policies are important, but not all-important in everyday life.

Because ordinary people are concerned with many things outside of politics – earning money, talking with friends, and caring for their family – the focus of this book is broader than government departments, or elections. To understand how ordinary people think about public policy we need to consider questions of economics and social psychology as well as politics. Policymakers need to do so too, for economic constraints limit what government can spend money on, and winning elections is a social psychological art. This book seeks to integrate ideas from different social sciences in ways that illuminate activities rather than cloud them in jargon. This also reflects the way in which ordinary people think about public policy.

In preparing this book, I have drawn upon decades of research spanning many countries and several continents. The experience has provided insights into what is common to ordinary people in many lands, and also into differences caused by national contexts. The ideas are meant to be widely applicable; the evidence is drawn primarily from Britain and America, the two countries that have taken the lead in the social scientific study of political behaviour and public policy.

The references at the end of this volume show that the author is not an ordinary person, for ordinary people do not write so much about politics. Over the years I have written many books and articles about public policy and about political behaviour. Here I have drawn freely upon these works, which are cited as appropriate in the text. Writing this book has made me think afresh about a number of issues, secure fresh evidence, and update and polish some previously published ideas.

Original research reported herein has been supported by grants from the British Economic & Social Research Council, the Anglo-German Foundation, the Volkswagen Foundation, the Japan Foundation, and the Wissenschaftszentrum Berlin. Through the years many individuals in the Centre for the Study of Public Policy at the University of Strathclyde have been helpful, most recently, Ms Anne Shaw and Ms Isobel Rogerson. Chapter 3 on elections draws in part upon work undertaken with Professor Ian McAllister, and chapter 6 on taxation upon work with Dr Terence Karran.

Richard Rose
University of Strathclyde

Introduction

Bringing Ordinary People Back In

> Just as small-scale humanly comprehensive groupings are essential, so are large-scale humanly incomprehensible ones.
>
> Henry Kariel

If politics is about people, what is government about? Most books about government start with the view from the top, describing how it appears from the point of view of Presidents or Prime Ministers, or from the ethereal perspective of those who play at being philosopher kings. Ordinary people are not deemed relevant to the affairs of state; the world within government is divorced from the activities of ordinary people. Yet the public policies of government employ millions of people and spend billions to provide benefits important to ordinary people in childhood, in a working lifetime, and in old age.

If government is about activities on a scale incomprehensible to the ordinary person (Kariel, 1969: 52), then what are the lives of ordinary people about? The conventional political science response is to analyse ordinary people in their role as citizens, and more particularly, as voters. But this gives a distorted view of the significance of elected officials in an era in which bureaucracies on a scale that is humanly incomprehensible deliver most public policies. Defining ordinary people as voters also gives a distorted picture of the significance of government for people who may be more worried about their spouse or children or about buying a house than about problems that concern a diplomat or a politician trying to improve his or her television image.

In a modern society, no individual can live alone on a desert island outside the reach of government. Societies of 6, 60 or 240 million people depend upon the institutions of the modern state to exist as a social system. To understand the society in which we live today it is necessary to comprehend both face-to-face human relations that are the stuff of everyday life *and* the large-scale impersonal institutions of government that provide the foundation and framework for our everyday activities.

In a modern society most people concentrate upon what is closest at hand; for policymakers, this means concentrating upon the big numbers that turn up in government budgets. When policymakers turn their attention to individuals, the person that they think of first can be themselves.

An elected official is a self-employed entrepreneur, responsible for his or her own career. If a civil servant is to have promotion prospects, he or she must show above-average qualities. However, the work, the friends and the family closest to an ordinary person are remote from centres of government. It is rational for ordinary people not to follow closely what policymakers do, for most people lack the information or expertise to make informed judgements about the large-scale humanly incomprehensible concerns of national government.

The purpose of this book is to bring ordinary people into the study of public policy by examining the extent and also the limits of the impact of public policy upon ordinary lives. The success of government depends upon what people make of its programmes to educate youths, maintain health, promote economic wellbeing and provide social security in old age. Yet there are limits to what government can or should do. To treat government as the sole source of individual wellbeing is to reduce the plurality of social institutions upon which individuals depend for welfare to a single monolith. Equally, there are limits upon the influence that ordinary people can have upon the practice of government. In the contemporary world issues of public policy are no longer simple matters that can be decided in an assembly of citizens, as in ancient Athens, or by a town meeting. Nor can electronic technology substitute for the human skills inherent in the practice of politics.

The underall view of ordinary people

No one is ordinary to himself or herself; each individual is a unique personality, and each ego has a unique set of concerns. Following the philosophy of Marx (Groucho, that is), a person can proclaim: 'Take care of me, I'm the only one I've got.' Each individual necessarily has an egocentric view of the world, starting from his or her personal circumstances and experiences. If we are to understand the significance of public policy, we must understand how the actions of government appear from what Fesler (1949: 10) once described as 'the underall position of the ordinary citizen' as well as from the overall view of politicians in the nation's capital.

Ordinary people can be defined as those who share the characteristics and views of a majority of persons in society. As individuals, ordinary people have little political weight; collectively, democratic government is meant to represent the views of this majority. Ordinary people are in the middle in many senses; they are not among the rich, the powerful and the very well educated. But they are also not representative of minorities. In the words of an American pundit, ordinary people are unpoor, unblack and unyouthful. The median individual in society is likely to be on the

border line between the working class and the middle class. Ordinary people have shared in the benefits of mass affluence; most are now home- and
car-owners, but ordinary people are not capitalists in the entrepreneurial
sense. Usually more than one income is needed to support the life style of
the ordinary family. If ordinary people often complain about taxes, they
also benefit from the policies of government.

While policymakers are people, we live under a government of laws,
not individuals. The modern state is impersonal, subject to laws and
bureaucratic procedures ensuring that such public services as education,
social security benefits, refuse collection and transportation are routinely
delivered to people who depend upon these everyday public services.
Individuals who devote their working lives to making public policies
by definition are atypical: only a handful of the population can sit in a
national legislature, occupy a high post in the civil service, or represent
leading pressure groups. Making and administering policies is a full-time
job, different from but as time-consuming as being a lawyer or a doctor
or managing a supermarket or running a farm. While a surprisingly large
portion of the labour force works for a public agency, most do so as
employees, not policymakers. From the underall view of ordinary
citizens, government is something that goes on over their heads.

Traditionally, the study of politics was the study of the great ideas of
political philosophers and the actions of men in important positions of
government. The great books of political philosophers set out stimulating
ideas about the meaning and justification of political activity – but their
dialogue has been over the heads of the ordinary citizen. The study
of great men implies that history is made by a select few, kings and
generals, or presidents and prime ministers. This is an elitist assumption
out of harmony with the assumptions of mass democracy, and the role
of women in society. It also ignores the importance of impersonal social
and economic forces, such as markets and classes, that shape the world in
which we live.

Studying the constitution and institutions of government is necessary
to understand the legal authority and limits of legislatures, executives
and courts. A constitution concentrates narrowly upon fundamental forms
and procedures of government at the centre. However, the institutions of
government that most immediately concern ordinary people are not at the
centre, but in what is called the periphery or provinces, where most of
a country's population lives. It is in the community that public officials
must deliver such basic public services as police protection, education,
roads, and health care (Rose, 1985).

The behavioural revolution in political science has contributed greatly
to understanding the activities of both governors and governed. We now
see public policies as reflecting not only formal institutions and laws, but
also the motives and actions of individuals who shape policies to their

political ends. Equally important, the behavioural revolution focused attention upon the outlook of the mass of the population. Thanks to sample survey techniques for studying public opinion we are now able to view politics 'from the point of view of the actor' (Campbell et al., 1960: 27). We no longer need infer what ordinary people think by reading the speeches of Winston Churchill or Franklin Roosevelt or by watching John F. Kennedy or Margaret Thatcher on television. Instead, we can ask ordinary people what, if anything, the words and actions of politicians mean to them.

The development of the study of public policy in universities and think tanks has shifted the focus of the study of government. Public policy concerns what government does rather than who governs or how institutions work. As well as learning a variety of social science concepts, students of public policy must also come to grips with substantive problems that face government, such as providing police and fire protection, financing health, education and social security programmes and defending the nation's security in an uncertain international system.

Research trends in public policy and in political behaviour have tended to lead in opposite directions. Public policy research demonstrates the importance of government actions for the lives of ordinary people. How could it be otherwise when government collects upwards of two-fifths of the national product in taxes, employs a large proportion of the nation's labour force and is responsible for a host of major social programmes? However, political behaviour research emphasizes that ordinary people do not invest much time, effort or thought in political participation, as this term is conventionally defined, that is, voting in elections, discussing politics with friends, or attending political meetings (cf. Dalton, 1988). How could it be otherwise when there are only 24 hours in a day and ordinary people have so many concerns at home and work that must be attended to first?

What you see depends upon where you sit. Public officials define their work in terms of the problems immediately before them, the 'fires in the In tray'. A Treasury official will see economic problems, the head of a social security agency will see the need to avoid poverty among the elderly, and an educationist sees problems in schools. The recommendations that officials put to elected office-holders will be conditioned by their own departmental expertise. For example, in reaction to the 1962 Cuban missile crisis, President Kennedy's Department of Defense officials were primarily concerned with military implications, State Department officials with the diplomatic implications, and the President's White House staff had to consider the President's personal political stakes too (Allison, 1971).

What you write also depends upon where you sit. University-based social scientists are affected by their identification with professional academic disciplines. Political scientists see the political dimension in problems facing government, economists think in terms of the costs and benefits of alternative policies, and sociologists often identify with those who are the recipients of major spending programmes. Concentrating upon one aspect of a public policy problem is consistent with the division of labour between academic disciplines. But most public policy issues are undisciplined, simultaneously involving political, economic, administrative and social problems (Rose, 1976).

Ordinary people are left with the task of integrating the disparate concerns of policymakers and social scientists. From the underall position of the ordinary citizen, the policymaker's concern with political tactics and techniques of public management is less important than children learning to read and write at school, or social security benefits providing an adequate income in retirement. The academic's speculative interest in what government might do differently is less immediately important than popular concern about what is happening to public services here and now.

Relating public policies to ordinary people

The growth of government has required the participation of ordinary people. In a pre-democratic era, keeping matters of state in the hands of aristocratic governors also meant keeping government small. A government only concerned with defence abroad and law and order at home was a small government. Few people would be directly affected by it, and people would pay little in taxes to finance the minimal activities of the Nightwatchman state. Government has grown by providing social benefits for the great majority of citizens, and it has expanded further by raising the standard of public programmes. By providing benefits to every family, government has become important in the lives of ordinary people. Because costs are proportional to benefits, taxation has simultaneously risen, so that today public taxes claim a substantial portion of the average family's income.

What counts most to ordinary people is not the programmes that traditionally concern political elites, such as diplomacy, defence or macroeconomic management of the economy, but programmes providing education, social security, health and housing. These public policies of everyday concern to ordinary people are often deemed beneath the dignity of leading politicians. No one with political ambitions sees a job as school superintendent, health administrator, or social security actuary as the height of his or her career. The big-spending social programmes are not important enough, as status is measured in politics (cf. Rose, 1987: chapter 4). Yet sewage treatment, health care, education, and social security are of great importance to ordinary people.

This book is a behavioural analysis because it integrates the everyday activities of ordinary people with the public policies of government. Understanding ordinary people requires a wide-angle vision that includes but also extends beyond the political system. While citizenship is important, it is not all-important. While most people think that free elections are important, they do not give much time to their role as a voter. The primary concerns of individuals usually involve face-to-face relations in the family, with friends, and at work. Many of the everyday concerns of individuals – health, a secure income, and education for children – are matters of concern to government too. While ready and willing to benefit from public policies, most people do not see government as the source of their wellbeing. Most people believe that their income is secure if they work harder or better, that education can be achieved by children studying more, and that health is a matter of individual diet and exercise.

This book is about public policy because it examines how the major outputs of government relate to the lives of ordinary people. These outputs can be described by the claims that they make upon the public purse. The biggest-spending programmes are extremely diverse: social security, defence, education, debt interest payments, health care and support for the economy. To produce these programmes, government must mobilize three principal resources: laws, money and public employees (Rose, 1984). We cannot generalize about government from evidence of a single programme; it is important to consider how public policies differ as between concerns with social welfare, a healthy economy, or public order.

Government provides the means not the ends of wellbeing. Attention must also be given to the use that ordinary people make of the programmes produced by government. From this perspective, the ultimate outcome of public policies is not measured by public expenditure data, by numbers in public employment, or by the construction of new public buildings. These are only inputs to the process of education, health care or social security. In a behavioural analysis we need to think of public policies as inputs to the lives of ordinary people.

To put flesh on this simple model of ordinary people in public policy requires ideas that are relevant both to ordinary people and in government. Ideas give meaning to what would otherwise be mere prose description or quantitative data. We must see the big-spending social programmes of government in relation to such qualitative political priorities as civil and political rights. We must also relate political concepts to non-governmental institutions in society. We cannot understand the welfare of ordinary people by thinking only about the welfare policies of the state. Ordinary people find the market and activities in their own household important too as sources of welfare.

Good ideas must meet the test of evidence; as T.H. Huxley once noted, the great tragedy of science is 'the slaying of a beautiful hypothesis by an ugly fact'. Statistics – in its original sense of facts pertaining to the state – provide a means for evaluating whether interesting ideas actually offer a valid description of how ordinary people are involved in public policy. The chapters that follow present tabular information drawn from sample surveys of popular attitudes and behaviour, and from government reports about the resources allocated to public policies. At times statistics are only rough indicators of how ordinary people make use of public policies. Yet it is better to have a rough measure than none. As the noted mathematician, John Tukey, has said: 'Far better an approximate answer to the right question, which is often vague, than an exact answer to the wrong question, which can always be made precise' (quoted in Banks and Textor, 1963: 7).

Social science starts from the assumption that human behaviour tends to follow common patterns, and that nations have much in common too. Many politically salient differences of class, race or gender create divisions within a country and link people with the same social attributes across national boundaries. In principle, ideas about the role of ordinary people in public policy should be relevant to any country with a government based upon free elections, and sufficient economic wealth to maintain a variety of costly public programmes. Marshalling evidence from both Britain and the United States avoids the fallacy of treating the experience of a single nation as evidence of universal truths, or alternatively, regarding the political behaviour of a country as unique because of unconscious ethnocentrism.

Chapter 1 examines national pride and patriotism, two of the most ambivalent links between ordinary people and national governments. The legitimacy of government depends in substantial part upon people identifying with overarching symbols of the nation; national identity is meant to be a symbol of unity above the electoral battle, and independent of the ups and downs of the government's management of the economy. However, pride and patriotism are not independent of a country's historical experience. Two world wars have shown that pride can be turned into aggressive patriotism, and defeat in war has shown countries such as Germany and Japan that pride goeth before a fall.

Contemporary public policies collectively provide private benefits that are of continuing importance in everyday life. Chapter 1 shows that the ordinary European household today receives more than two major social benefits from government. An elderly couple receives a pension, and treatment by the national health service. A couple with growing children will rely upon state schools, and a teen-age member of the family may be drawing unemployment benefit. At some stage in the life cycle, everyone is likely to depend upon public education, health care, social security and other social services as well. In the United States the proportion of the national product spent on social benefits is not so great as in Europe, but the greater wealth of American society means that the actual value of spending on social benefits can be higher.

In democratic theory, voting is the critical link between ordinary people and government. An election gives each person an opportunity to hold elected representatives accountable for their actions and to express a preference about who should govern. Chapter 3 demonstrates that voting is also a link between political behaviour and individual experiences accumulated through a lifetime. Influences upon voting include actions by government and political parties as well as social influences that are relatively remote from government in time and space. Hence, the functions of elections for government – choosing governors, influencing policies and affirming legitimacy – are different from the function of elections for individuals.

In the practice of public policy, elections are not the only signals giving direction to government. Chapter 4 considers the significance of four different sources of direction: laws, expert values, money and votes. Laws mandate how public officials must act, and they entitle ordinary people to claim many benefits from government, for example, a free education or a pension in old age. The values of experts often decide the specific content of public policies; in health care, for example, the specialist knowledge of doctors greatly influences the way in which ordinary people are treated. Ordinary people may vote with their pocketbook if they do not find public services satisfactory, for example, buying a car to drive to work if public transport is found inadequate.

Money matters in government, for most policies that affect the everyday life of ordinary people are costly to provide, and the costs as well as benefits of social policy tend to be proportionate to the numbers receiving them. Economists claim an interest in public policy, because economics is about the efficient allocation of scarce resources to the greatest benefit of society. Chapter 5 emphasizes that while economic analysis is often relevant, it is not sufficient to determine public policies. One reason is that economists often disagree on political as well as professional grounds. Another is that elected officeholders have the final say in deciding what government does.

Taxation has traditionally been one way in which government's influence has been widely felt, for the ability to extract money from ordinary people is one of the defining characteristics of the modern state. It is also a necessary condition for government providing many and costly benefits. Unlike many activities of government, taxation depends upon compulsion, not voluntary choice. It represents the dues of citizenship. Politicians may seek to maximize the benefits of public policy, but citizens want to minimize the costs. Without a steady and large flow of tax revenue it is not possible to increase public spending on popular benefits. Chapter

6 explains how government resolves conflicting pressures of taxing and spending by collecting tax revenues vicariously.

In a mixed economy a significant fraction of earnings is left to every citizen as take-home pay, that is, earnings after the deduction of tax. When government spending rises rapidly or an economy moves into recession, then taxes are likely to rise or earnings fall; this can create a squeeze on take-home pay, or even leave a worker with a reduced after-tax income as the price of increased public spending. Insofar as maintaining consumption is the object of the ordinary individual, chapter 7 shows how ordinary people can get by through relying on three economies – the officially recorded economy, the unofficial shadow economy, and the non-monetized household economy. While much journalistic attention has been given to tax avoidance in the shadow economy, this chapter documents the much greater importance of the household economy, where no taxes are due because goods and services are produced without money changing hands.

Only in a totalitarian society would the state be the sole source of welfare. We live in a mixed society, in which total welfare is the sum of activities by the state, the market, and the household. From the top-down perspective of the public budget, the growth of government appears to absorb more and more money, and leave less and less scope for the market or the household economy. Insofar as this may be true, then any cut in public spending will reduce total welfare in society. But chapter 8 demonstrates that this is not the case: the growth of the economy has not crowded out the market and the household as sources of welfare. In some cases the production of welfare by the market and the household has increased. The overall welfare of ordinary people reflects the benefits of what is obtained from all three sources.

Insofar as ordinary people rely upon government for social benefits and security in hard times, then what do we expect when government faces difficulties in meeting the costs of large and expanding social programmes? Prior to the onset of world recession in the mid-1970s, many theories assumed that politicians had to buy the allegiance of ordinary people by promising and delivering more and more benefits. But ordinary people did not react to recession by making society ungovernable. Chapter 9 examines the outlook and expectations of ordinary people in out-of-the-ordinary economic circumstances; the views of ordinary people about work and politics often differ from what is assumed by the abstract logic of either capitalism or socialism.

Consent, not cash benefits, is the first political priority of citizens. When the central tenets of freedom and democracy are threatened, politics is important to ordinary people. Most people would find it inconceivable to be denied such civil rights as the equal protection of the law, the right to vote and freedom of speech. Yet such rights could not be assumed in every

European country a half-century ago, and many black Americans were denied civil and political rights. Northern Ireland is a standing exception to generalizations about civil rights and the legitimacy of government within the United Kingdom. Chapter 10 shows what ordinary people want is government by consent; once that is assured ordinary people look beyond the realm of politics for satisfaction in life.

1

The Private Benefits of Public Policy

There is no such thing as society; there are only individual men and women, and there are families.

Prime Minister Margaret Thatcher

In contemporary political debate the words public and private are often treated as opposites. Politicians on the right treat the private sector as desirable, and the public sector as the source of much that is wrong in society. By contrast, politicians on the left treat the public sector as the source of benefits, and regard private motives as undesirable evidence of self-seeking. Although there is agreement that one label is good and the other bad, left and right disagree about which is which.

With characteristic vigour, Margaret Thatcher has stated an extreme view of the importance of private actions, private motives and private responsibility. When she proclaimed – There is no such thing as society; there are only individuals – the Prime Minister was explicitly rejecting the idea that any collective entity, whether government or society, could deal with the needs of individuals. Mrs Thatcher declared:

All too often the ills of this country are passed off as those of society. Similarly, when action is required, society is called upon to act. But society as such does not exist except as a concept. Society is made up of people. It is people who have duties and beliefs and resolve. It is people who get things done. (quoted in Atticus, 1988)

President Ronald Reagan put the point very simply when he campaigned with the slogan: Government is not the solution; it is the problem.

The anti-government ideology of rightwing politicians is contested. Social democrats argue that government is desirable as well as necessary for individual wellbeing. In a democracy the public sector can be considered another name for individuals acting collectively; the endorsement of government by the electorate is said to justify the presumption that government does what the people want. The idea that individuals can live without the collective institutions of society is dismissed as absurd: schools, hospitals and pension funds are necessarily social institutions. The purpose of democracy is to enable the mass of the people to give direction to government so that it can provide benefits for the great mass of individuals.

Concepts of the individual and of society are not so much in conflict as complementary. A society consists of millions of individuals, and government is obligated to recognize individual rights and claims. Yet there are severe limits upon what an individual can do on his or her own: the family, hospitals, business corporations, universities, trade unions, insurance companies and broadcasting firms are familiar examples of ways in which collective organizations make provision for individual needs. Even though government is not the only collective institution or the sole source of collective services, it is critical in maintaining the order required by every major social institution.

In the 1980s rightwing politicians succeeded in winning elections, but lost the battle of the budget. After a decade in which politicians such as Margaret Thatcher and Ronald Reagan have scored great electoral success, government remains big. Moreover, the bulk of public spending is not on the traditional responsibilities of the state, such as law and order and national defence, but upon public programmes that provide private benefits, such as education, health and a pension in old age. While these benefits could be purchased by individuals in the market from private enterprises, in fact they are produced by public agencies. This does not mean that government has taken over all responsibility for individual wellbeing. The first part of this chapter distinguishes between thinking in terms of the outputs of public policy, and thinking of individual wellbeing as an output of a network of relationships in which ordinary people are at the centre. The second section describes the extent to which government has evolved from providing a limited number of collective goods to financing what the right attacks as an unending number of private benefits.

Policy as output and input

From the perspective of policymakers, public programmes are the output of government. The political struggle to define purposes, introduce legislation, mobilize resources and shift directions culminates in the production of programmes that are meant to provide defence, education, health care, and other collective and individual benefits. However, from the underall perspective of ordinary people, the outputs of government are only inputs to their individual wellbeing. The output of individual wellbeing depends only in part upon what government does; it is also influenced by inputs from other formal and informal institutions of society. It also reflects what individuals do on their own behalf.

Programmes as outputs. In its long history of use in English the term 'policy' has acquired many different meanings. It can refer to an issue or problem for discussion, as in the terms education policy or industrial policy. It can refer to a statement of intention or goal, for example, party policy or the President's policy. A third usage is to refer to the means that government uses to secure its intention, for example, a policy to reduce the pollution of rivers or to train the long-term unemployed. Given so many meanings, it is better to restrict the word policy to use as a general reference to the activities of government.

The term *programme* best describes the specific outputs of government. Analysing government in terms of programmes puts the purposes of government first. Government is not just about winning votes, administering files or extracting taxes; it is also about mobilizing resources in order to produce goods and services of use to ordinary people. Instead of thinking of government as producing a single output, such as power or popularity, or reducing it to a single measure, such as public expenditure, we should see government as producing programme outputs directed at such things as pensions, crime, education, health care and transportation.

Programme outputs are the product of public sector organizations that mobilize three major resources – laws, money and public employees (Figure 1.1). To view government simply as a set of institutions ignores the fact that organizations are, in the Greek origin of the word, an instrument or means to an end. The term agency captures this sense, for a school or a hospital or a department is an agent of the lawfully expressed purposes of an elected legislature and executive. Students of public administration are inclined to generalize about agencies, attributing common characteristics to central government departments, local authorities and nationalized industries. But ordinary people do not think of government agencies in terms of legal attributes; instead, agencies are identified by their outputs. The social security ministry is the agency paying pensions; an education authority is an agency for teaching young people; and the post office is the agency that is meant to deliver the mail.

Three different types of resources are mobilized by public agencies.

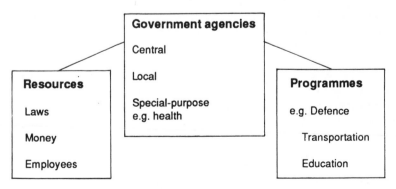

Figure 1.1   *Programmes as Outputs of Government (Rose, 1985a)*

Laws are a monopoly resource of government; private agencies cannot make and enforce laws binding upon everyone in society. Laws also provide positive direction to public agencies, expressing the will of elected politicians about what government ought to do. More than that, laws set out the procedures by which officials are expected to act, and what ordinary people are entitled to receive as benefits. Money is a second important resource of government. The capacity to collect taxes is a necessary condition of the growth of government, for without such revenue government could not adopt laws entitling people to receive pensions or other cash benefits, nor could public agencies hire the teachers, policemen or nurses needed to deliver major programmes. Thirdly, public employees are important, for most programme outputs cannot be produced simply by enacting a law or paying out money. Education requires teachers as well as laws compelling children to go to school, unemployment benefits are only paid after officials verify that individuals are legally eligible, and military defence requires soldiers, sailors and air personnel.

The resources mobilized by government are not hoarded; they are combined to produce programme outputs. Programme outputs are what ordinary people experience as the palpable evidence of what government does. Outputs constitute the benefits that justify the costs of contemporary big government. From a programme perspective, the money that government collects in taxes is not a burden imposed upon citizens but a boon, financing education, pensions, health care and other programme outputs. Programmes are means to the end of realizing more or less clear political purposes, goals and values.

Focusing upon public programmes emphasizes the hundreds of different things that public agencies do, from controlling air traffic to running zoos. Variety can be found within a single organization: the Home Office in London is responsible for broadcasting, for prisons, for the welfare of animals, and for passports. The United States Department of Agriculture is responsible for rural housing as well as farm crop subsidies; it promotes the sale of American farm products in more than a hundred countries abroad and it supports an extension network of farm advisors in more than 3,000 rural counties within the United States.

To understand the outputs of government we must consider the variety as well as the scale of government. Most public employees, public laws, public expenditure and public agencies are intended to produce specific programme outputs. Politicians who rail against waste and preach the need for cuts in public expenditure learn, once in office, that there is no 'waste' line in the budget offering an easy target for cuts. Instead, the hundreds of lines in the budget refer to programmes that provide outputs of particular interest to specific groups of people: to the elderly or physically handicapped children; to university students or military servicemen; or to business firms or trade unions or to both. Any proposal to cut programmes will therefore mobilize a variety of interests to defend measures said to merit public support *because* they produce private benefits.

Programmes as inputs. From the perspective of the ordinary individual, government programmes are important but not all-important. If an opinion poll asks people whether education or health care or social security is important to them, the great majority of people would say yes. If asked whether government was important in providing education, health care or social security, most people would also say yes. But if the questioner persisted in asking whether public programmes were the sole resource upon which people relied for their wellbeing, then the great majority would say no.

Wellbeing refers in a very general way to a condition of individual happiness, health and prosperity. While the term appears vague, the manifestations of wellbeing are easily recognized. A person in good health is keeping well, whereas a chronically ill individual lacks an element of wellbeing. A person who has enough money to live in accord with his or her expectations enjoys material wellbeing, whereas someone always in debt does not. A person with lots of friends and people to turn to for help in times of difficulty enjoys social wellbeing, whereas an individual who is ill at ease with other people and lacks friends also lacks wellbeing.

The sources of individual wellbeing are multiple; public programmes are only one of a variety of sources. To some extent wellbeing reflects actions for which an individual is personally responsible. A person who is overweight and refuses to diet cannot be helped by government and, Margaret Thatcher would argue, should blame himself or herself rather than blame society for the consequences of obesity. Difficulties with members of the opposite sex will affect the psychological state of an individual; here too there are limits to what government can do to improve problems in boy–girl relationships. By contrast, the financial problems of unemployed people may be alleviated by income-maintenance grants from government or by its macroeconomic measures. The positive advantages gained from identification with nation and society can be boosted by a government taking actions that increase pride in country, or depressed by collective actions of which people feel ashamed.

A diagram of the causes of individual wellbeing will include public programmes as one among three major inputs affecting the lives of ordinary people (Figure 1.2). Social structure is important, insofar as wellbeing reflects an individual's network of social relations. There is a small but positive relationship between a sense of wellbeing and occupational class; higher-status people tend to a marginally higher sense of wellbeing. Belonging to a social group that has been the object of social discrimination, e.g. blacks, would reduce a sense of wellbeing. Feminists argue that

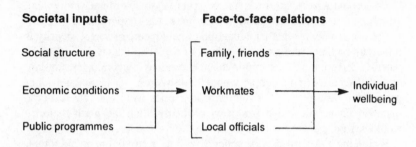

Figure 1.2   *Inputs to the Wellbeing of Ordinary People*

whether a person is male or female also affects wellbeing.

In the economy ordinary people are usually decisiontakers rather than decisionmakers; they are employees of large organizations rather than self-employed entrepreneurs. Responsibility for the wellbeing of the organization for which they work is in the hands of managers and agency heads. Its wellbeing will also be influenced by national economic conditions and trends in the international economy. When there is inflation, no individual can unilaterally protect himself or herself against its consequences, and rising unemployment makes it harder for a jobseeker to get a desirable job. The money that people earn reflects in part individual effort – but it also reflects whether the particular occupation or sector of the economy in which a person works is booming, and national economic conditions also influence what a person earns.

Public programmes significantly affect individual wellbeing, indirectly as well as directly. Major programmes of government are inputs directly affecting the wellbeing of individuals, families and communities. Parents look to government to provide for the education of their children, and to provide roads, parks and other community amenities. Safety at work is meant to be ensured by legislation, and a host of government measures promote employment opportunities. Indirectly government measures may affect the social structure, for example, housing programmes that segregate socially disadvantaged groups in inferior public housing, or laws seeking to prevent discrimination against minority groups.

From an individual perspective pervasive but impersonal social, economic and political forces are less significant than immediate face-to-face relations. Concepts such as class are abstract, whereas ordinary people are aware of those to whom they are supposed to defer, and whether or not neighbours are also friends. Whereas an individual cannot influence the structure of society as a whole, an ordinary person can do a great deal affecting immediate social relations. National statistics about marriage and divorce, or the probability of finding a spouse among a particular social group, are less meaningful to ordinary individuals than the choice of a particular spouse.

While a public official may view the economy as an aggregate of statistics, an individual is likely to concentrate upon a particular job or a particular employer. Earnings, job satisfaction and job security are immediately seen as a consequence of the particular firm for which a person works, and the people whom one sees on a daily basis at work. An individual wanting to earn more money is not likely to compare different economic theories in order to see which is most likely to make the economy prosper. Instead, he or she will look around for a different employer or change occupations in an effort to improve personal economic wellbeing.

Rules of fairness or equity limit the capacity of government to adapt programmes to individual concerns. Everyone who is entitled to a particular benefit is meant to be treated the same by a public agency. This is most evident in pension payments, where there are precise rules related to age and previous contributions to determine the amount of money that a person can receive. Public programmes can vary to some extent, for example in local government the political complexion, tax resources and skills of officials vary from one district to another. Service outputs can vary when services are provided by experts. A national health service can lay down that everyone has the right to medical treatment, but the actual content and quality of that treatment depends upon decisions taken by a particular doctor.

In a sense, any diagram of the causes of individual wellbeing risks over-simplification, for the processes that determine life satisfaction are complex in the extreme. Complexity makes it wrong to infer that the outputs of government produce individual wellbeing, or that an increase in the outputs of a particular programme will increase wellbeing by the same amount as outputs increase, or that cuts in a programme similarly reduce wellbeing. Even in an era of big government the totality of public programmes is one (but not the only) important influence upon the wellbeing of ordinary people.

From public goods to private benefits

When capitalism and laissez faire ideology flourished in the late nineteenth century, government concentrated upon the provision of public goods, such as military defence, public health and law and order. These are goods and services that provide benefits collectively; individuals cannot provide them for themselves and they cannot readily be sold in the market place since it is impossible to charge everyone who benefits – the problem of the 'free rider' (Olson, 1965). Government must provide public or collective goods essential in a modern society, and they can be financed by taxation.

The twentieth century has seen the growth of major collective institutions such as business corporations, trade unions, and non-profit institutions such as universities. It has also seen the development of collectivist ideologies such as socialism, which emphasize the importance of collective wellbeing. Simultaneously government has grown because it has greatly expanded the provision of private benefits, those goods and services that individuals can use for their personal benefit and that can be sold in the market place, for example, education, health care or a pension in old age. While these services are in principle marketable, government provides them without charge to individuals as part of the private benefits of public policy.

Growth and shift in public spending. Traditionally, government was a concern only of elites and administered by a handful of officials in the national capital. The state concentrated upon a few activities necessary by definition: protecting territory against foreign invasion, maintaining courts and order, and raising a minimum of finance for these purposes (Rose, 1976a). Ordinary people did not expect to benefit from the activities of the state; the local face of government was the tax collector, or the army's recruiting sergeant. Public officials were concerned with regulating or extracting resources from ordinary people, rather than providing individuals with services for their personal benefit.

In the era of laissez faire, governments did not spend much, and what was done related to the defining concerns of government – defence, justice, police, administration, and interest on debts incurred in financing past wars and expenditure (Table 1.1). While statistics from a century ago are sparse, so too was public expenditure. Government claimed only a small proportion of the national product in taxation, and once it had provided a few collective goods, it did not seek more revenue. In Britain, for example, the nineteenth century was an era of the growth of the economy; the size of government (that is, public expenditure as a percentage of the national product) actually fell. Because American statistics are not comparable, expenditure by the United States is omitted, but the same pattern is found in America too (Austin, 1986: 436ff).

The public provision of private benefits could satisfy diverse groups. Public health measures not only benefited poor people most subject to ravages of disease but also protected the well-to-do against deadly epidemics, and ensured a sanitary environment in middle class as well as working

Table 1.1   *Government Shifts from Public Goods to Private Benefits*
(percentage total spending on public goods)

	Traditional	(Year)	Current
Britain	81	(1840)	19
France	91	(1842)	32
Germany	69	(1872)	25
Italy	78	(1870)	29
Netherlands	87	(1870)	25
Sweden	76	(1865)	28

Source: Flora, 1983: Britain, 446f; France, 380f; Germany, 387; Italy, 402; Netherlands, 410f; Sweden, 428f. For earlier periods data are sometimes for central government only.

class neighbourhoods. Education benefited the children who received it, and also employers who could profit more from a skilled labour force. Social security benefits provided an income for those unable to work; it also removed from employers a humanitarian obligation to pay people who could not produce goods that could be sold at a profit. Popular benefits could be provided by governments that were not accountable to the populace; Bismarck's Germany pioneered popular social benefits in the hope that people offered private benefits would not demand the political right to influence public policies (cf. Flora and Heidenheimer, 1981).

Today, three-quarters or more of public spending goes for the public provision of private benefits. The activities of government are no longer confined to a few traditional measures of interest to kings and aristocrats; throughout Europe the bulk of public revenue is now devoted to financing programmes central to the lives of ordinary people, such as social security and health care. Since every nation's economy has grown greatly in the past century, higher tax rates in more affluent societies give government far more money to spend on these private benefits. Instead of four years of schooling in an overcrowded village classroom, the ordinary individual today can count on ten years or more of education in modern classrooms, and if the interest and aptitude is there, can continue to advanced study at university with tuition at the state's expense.

Private benefits dominate public spending. The single biggest programme of government today, social security, directly transfers money from the public purse to the pockets of ordinary people (Table 1.2). The purpose of social security is to ensure that everyone, whatever their age, employment or family circumstances, has sufficient money to live on. In a modern money economy, every family needs a cash income, and the biggest programme of government provides just that. In the average advanced industrial nation, health care ranks second in public expenditure for private benefit. Everyone wants good health and freedom from anxieties about paying health bills when ill. The public provision

Table 1.2 *Concentration of Government Spending on Private Benefits*

	Average for OECD nations (percentages)	
	Gross domestic product	Public expenditure
Private benefits		
Social security, services	14.1	32
Health	5.6	13
Education	5.5	13
Other	8.0	18
Subtotal	33.2	76
Public goods		
Debt interest	5.1	12
Defence	3.0	7
Other	2.5	6
Subtotal	10.6	24

Source: calculated from OECD data as reported in Rose, 1989.

of individual health care meets this popular concern. Education is the third biggest claimant on public funds. Since education is compulsory, everyone benefits from the public money spent to provide education free of charge to every youth. The value of this benefit is indicated by the tuition charged those parents who choose to have their children educated privately. Altogether, a host of programmes covering social benefits such as housing and commercial benefits, for example subsidies to farmers and to businesses, account for an additional portion of public spending.

While we talk about public policies, less than one-quarter of government expenditure today is devoted to public goods. Debt interest accounts for nearly half of what is spent on public goods. When governments were more frugal, debt interest represented the cost of borrowing to finance past wars. Today, the public debt increasingly represents the gap between what government spends on private benefits for ordinary people, and what ordinary people are asked (or want) to pay as taxes to finance these benefits. When the bulk of public spending is for private benefits, then a US federal budget deficit of $150 billion represents a preference for enjoying the private benefits of public spending now, and deferring payment until later. It also adds more than $10 billion to public spending annually, the cost of additional interest paid on each year's additional borrowing.

While conservative politicians may rail against government allegedly wasting money on the salaries of 'pointy-headed' bureaucrats, in fact the great bulk of public spending goes on programmes that are reasonably effective in improving and enriching the lives of ordinary people. This is most evident for social security programmes, which every month put cash in the hands of more than 10 million Britons and more than 30 million Americans. The purpose of these programmes is to raise the income of people with average or below-average incomes; cash in hand does just that. Money spent on health care is intended to prevent or cure illness, and doctors and hospitals are reasonably effective in dealing with most of the problems that lead people to seek medical treatment. Any politician who proposed big cuts in health expenditure on the grounds it was ineffective or wasteful would be signing his or her political death warrant. Nor are politicians likely to propose big cuts in spending on education; they even hesitate to close a particular school building when falling pupil numbers are an argument for doing so in the name of efficiency.

In theory it is not necessary for government to provide private benefits, and advocates of the market have been ingenious in devising ways in which individuals could make private provision for benefits rather than rely upon public expenditure. The simplest way would be to abolish the programmes that account for three-quarters of public expenditure today, and more than one-quarter of the national product. Doing this would make it possible for government to abolish income tax and social security contributions, immediately producing a big boost in the take-home pay of the ordinary person. But it would also cause a big boost in the cost of living of the ordinary individual. The family bill for health insurance on the scale of a national health service could claim up to 10 per cent of weekly earnings, and education fees would cost a family even more.

The radical upheaval that would result by confining government to late nineteenth-century collective commitments has prevented serious electoral politicians such as Margaret Thatcher or Ronald Reagan from repudiating public responsibility for financing private benefits. Proponents of the market have thus urged government to give individuals vouchers to spend as people choose for particular public services. An education voucher, for example, would have the value of current public spending on education. A parent could not cash the voucher; it could only be presented as payment for a child's education. Choice would be encouraged inasmuch as the voucher could meet the full cost of a state school education, or could contribute part of the cost of a private education, with the parents paying the difference. Notwithstanding the appeal of the voucher system to the right, in both Britain and America rightwing politicians continue to accept that public services should continue to provide major private benefits.

Government on the doorstep. Today, national government must be nationwide government; it can no longer be confined to elite concerns in the capital. Four of the six major programmes of government must be delivered nationwide. Education can only take place in schools in the community in which children live. Health care is delivered by doctors or in local hospitals rather than in distant legislatures or courts. While social security is centrally financed, payments are valued as cash in the hands of ordinary people to spend as they think fit. Law and order on the street and in the security of each individual's home are more important than national crime statistics. Only debt interest payments are made in the national capital and delivered to a relatively few institutions.

Nationwide delivery means that services must be provided where people live, and not just where government is centred in London or Washington. Complaints that government is top-heavy reflect the concentration of the media upon a few visible national politicians. In fact, government is bottom-heavy; the typical unit of government is a local school or a hospital providing services locally (Rose, 1988; 1985). While national laws and funding can entitle everyone to benefits, they are realized only when programmes are delivered to people where they live.The great bulk of public employees are not bureaucrats but local government employees delivering a service locally. Government has grown by reproducing or 'cloning' service-delivery units such as schools and hospitals. This process of pluralization is familiar in the world of retailing; it is the logic of McDonalds or of Marks and Spencer. Like successful retail chains, government agencies can claim that they are delivering private benefits for public purposes. Delivering public policies on the doorstep increases the confidence of ordinary people in government, because they can see what it is doing for them – and they approve. While Margaret Thatcher has consistently attacked the alleged waste and inefficiency of local government, going so far as to remove its power to levy property taxes, most British people still have more confidence in local government than in central government or the market (Table 1.3). When Britons are asked who is best at the job of delivering a variety of services, more than two-thirds normally endorse local government, and the proportion rises above 80 per cent having most confidence in local government to provide recreation and refuse collection. By contrast, only one-sixth on average think that national government is best at administering services and only one in ten have most confidence in the market.

In the United States Presidents Carter and Reagan, each in their own way, have railed against the alleged waste of public funds, locally and nationally. Since 1972 the confidence of Americans in local government has risen. When Americans are asked which level of government gives most value for money, local government ranks first, and state government comes second. In 1972 more Americans had confidence in the efficiency of the federal government than in any other layer of government. But since then the federal government has fallen in public esteem: only one-quarter think the federal government is best at delivering services (Table 1.3).

Everybody benefits. If spending on the classic public goods of defence and debt interest were to double, together they would still account for less

Table 1.3   *Popular Confidence Highest in Government Near at Hand*

Britain: Best at doing job (percentages)

	Local	National	Private	Don't know
Recreation	84	4	6	6
Refuse collection	81	4	11	4
Housing	65	8	18	9
Social services	63	25	4	8
Fire and police	62	29	2	7
Education	56	27	18	9
Average	68	16	10	7

USA: Level of government giving most for your money (percentages)

	1972	1976	1980	1984	1988	Change
Local	26	25	26	35	29	+3
State	18	20	22	27	27	+9
Federal	39	36	33	24	28	−11
Don't know	17	19	19	14	16	−1

Sources: Britain: Gallup Poll, *Political Index* 332 (April 1988), p. 9; USA: Advisory Commission on Intergovernmental Relations, *Changing Public Attitudes on Governments and Taxes* (Washington: S-17, 1988), p. 2.

of the public budget than social programmes today. It is by increasing the private benefits that ordinary people receive that government has grown. The justification for big government today is that it provides big benefits for big numbers of people through education, social security and health services.

No ordinary person would want to receive every benefit that government offers individuals, for some, such as unemployment benefit or hospital treatment, depend upon individual misfortune. Yet these insurance-type benefits are nonetheless appreciated when misfortune creates a need. Other benefits, such as education or a pension in retirement, are positive goods. While a few services, such as public transport, may be considered inferior to a private automobile, they remain for the most part a second-best solution.

The great majority of ordinary families are likely to want one or more publicly provided private benefit at some time in the course of a year. Nine-tenths of all British families regularly receive a major benefit from public services (Table 1.4). While the state is not the sole source of welfare in society, the family whose domestic welfare is unaffected by

Table 1.4   *Households Receiving a Major Private Benefit from British Government (percentage of population)*

	Household member receives benefit
Public transport	38
Pension	36
Regular treatment, doctor	35
Education	34
Housing	30
Hospital care, past year	29
Unemployment benefit	23
Personal social services	5
At least one benefit	90

Source: Calculated by the author from Gallup Poll survey, April 1984. Incidental benefits, such as occasional sickness payments or children's allowances, not included.

public services is the exception. The average British household actually receives 2.3 social benefits in the course of a year.

In the United States the proportion of families receiving private benefits from public funds is less than in Europe, but it is still substantial. The great bulk of American children attend public schools, and the great bulk of elderly in need of health care are treated by Medicare, and draw a social security pension. Low income families may receive publicly financed benefits, including health care, housing, or unemployment or supplementary income payments, according to circumstances. Altogether, the majority of American families today, young or old, receive a major private benefit from a public programme (cf. Rose and Peters, 1978: 257).

Because public programmes provide private benefits, ordinary people usually want public spending to increase. This is logical, for if education or health care is considered good and no charge is made for its use, then more or better education or health care is desirable in itself – and it imposes no specific charge upon the users. In Britain, more than four-fifths of people want more money spent on health care and pensions, and more than two-thirds want more money spent on education (Table 1.5). In the United States, notwithstanding attacks by the Reagan Administration on allegedly high levels of public expenditure, more than half of all Americans want more money spent on programmes to improve health care and education and to deal with problems of crime, drug addiction and environmental pollution, and there is a balance in favour of more spending on big city problems and the condition of blacks too.

Ordinary people are so accustomed to seeing government as a source of private benefits that its collective responsibilities now have a relatively low priority. When British people are asked whether they think more

Table 1.5 *Popular Views of Spending Priorities (percentages)*

	Too little	About right	Too much	Spend more (net)[a]
Britain				
Health service	84	14	1	83
Pensions	81	14	1	80
Education	69	23	2	67
Roads	57	27	5	52
Defence	8	36	45	−37
USA				
Improving health	67	26	4	63
Halting crime	67	23	4	63
Drug addiction	65	28	4	61
Environment	65	25	5	60
Education	61	30	6	55
Big city problems	38	33	13	25
Conditions of blacks	34	43	14	20
Welfare	21	31	44	−23
Space exploration	16	38	40	−24
Defence	15	40	40	−25
Foreign aid	7	20	68	−61

Don't knows omitted.

[a]Percentage saying too little being spent minus percentage saying too much.

Sources: Gallup Poll, *Political Index* 339 (November 1988), p. 8; 1987 National Opinion Research Center, Chicago, data calculated by Dalton, 1988: Table 6.3.

or less should be spent on defence, the largest group is in favour of cutting expenditure on defence. In America, people are against spending money on social programmes (that is, welfare programmes) targeted on the so-called 'undeserving' poor and against spending money on such examples of collective consumption as space exploration, defence, and foreign aid programmes that in the first instance provide benefits to foreigners. Ordinary people today approve of government as a source of private benefits, but many doubt that government always spends money well when it provides collective public goods.

2

Pride in Nation

Dulce et decorum est pro patria mori.
(Sweet and fitting is it to die for one's country.)

Horace, *Odes*

Patriotism is the last refuge of a scoundrel.

Dr Samuel Johnson

National pride is the psychological hinge that joins an individual's sense of self with the public community. Traditionally, pride in nation was regarded as natural and desirable; a patriot not only loved his country but was prepared to die for it. The two world wars of this century have shown destructive consequences of national patriotism. In reaction, patriotism today is often viewed with suspicion, or even as the vain boasting of a scoundrel. A fear has also developed that leaders could appeal to national pride for misguided and sometimes violent ends. Links between personal psychopathology and government policy – clear in the National Socialist Third Reich of Adolf Hitler and in Stalin's Kremlin – have raised questions about politics as the acting out of neurotic impulses. The mobilization of patriotic pride can be a means of encouraging aggression with deadly results.

The dichotomy between the self and the nation, 'the largest community which, when the chips are down, effectively commands men's loyalty' (Emerson, 1960), is dissolved in wartime. As Horace long ago noted, men will fight and die for the abstraction of a nation. The world of *la haute politique* seems very remote from the everyday world of ordinary individuals. Yet twentieth-century family histories bear witness to the devastating effects that international wars can have.

The movement of colonial countries to independence in the decades since the Second World War has been a recent reminder of the potent impact of nationalism and pride in nation. Regardless of ethnic or linguistic heterogeneity, dozens of Third World countries quickly made the transition to independence. Newly independent states have sought support by mobilizing a sense of national identification congruent with the geographical boundaries of the new state. Nation-building and pride in nation are seen as working hand in hand to reinforce each other. Concurrently, a variety of transnational loyalties – economic, professional and religious – have brought groups closer together across national boundaries, while separating them from some fellow countrymen.

The growth of the welfare state has given a new impetus to the identification between the individual and the state. In increasingly affluent societies public policies provide education for children, pensions for the elderly, and health care. The benefits of big government are expected to produce a positive, popular response from citizens. But worldwide economic difficulties have generated concerns about the capacity of government to do what citizens want. Whereas an economically prosperous and internationally powerful government is a source of pride and material benefits, an economically insecure state lacks the material inducements to 'buy' loyalty. Can pride in nation sustain political authority?

Are most people in fact proud of their country? National pride may differ between countries that win wars, thus having patriotism reinforced, and those where defeat can be a cause of shame. There can also be major differences within nations; educated persons, who are more cosmopolitan, may feel less national pride than persons who are less educated, and young people may differ from elders in their response to traditional symbols of patriotism.

Empirical answers to many questions about national pride can be found in a massive cross-national survey of values, organized under the aegis of the European Value Systems Study Group (Stoetzel, 1983: 299–330; Harding et al., 1986). It provides evidence about national pride covering 15 different countries from Europe to the Americas and Japan. In each country a nationwide sample of more than 1,000 respondents was asked a wide variety of questions about personal, social and political values, including pride in country. The result is a unique set of data for testing the extent to which national pride is common among countries; whether those who are proud of their country have a normal or neurotic outlook on life; and the character of the anti-patriotic minority.[1]

National pride: a source of unity

For an aggregate of individuals to be a society, people must share a consensus about a relatively few values. If people do not share any values in common, then the state continuously faces the danger of breaking up as a consequence of disagreements about national identity, and related matters of religion, language and race. National pride can be either a source of unity or a cause of division. Insofar as there is nearly complete agreement in the population about the central question of pride, then it is a unifying value. But because politics is about the articulation of conflicting views, then patriotism may become a controversial issue – as it did in the United States during the Vietnam War – or it may become a battleground on which nationalist parties fight each other in mutually exclusive claims for supremacy, as in Northern Ireland today, where Protestants and Catholics are each proud of their country, but give allegiance to different nations and political systems.

The measure of patriotism in the Values survey is direct and easily understood; each person was asked how proud he or she was of the country. Two positive alternatives (very proud, quite proud) were offered, and two negative alternatives (not very proud, not at all proud). The question avoided abstract theoretical phrases. The absence of any intermediate response between quite proud and not very proud forced people to take sides. The first two answers identify those who are proud of their country, and the latter two those without patriotic sentiment.

Pride is the norm. In every country surveyed the majority reported pride in their country; differences in national pride are a matter of degree not kind (Table 2.1). In the United States, 96 per cent report that they are proud to be Americans, and in Ireland, 91 per cent are proud to be Irish. In the median nation, Italy, 80 per cent report pride in being Italians. Even where national pride is lowest, the Federal Republic of Germany, those showing pride outnumber those who are not proud of their country by more than two to one. Nor is there any hesitation or doubt about national commitment. In the average country only 5 per cent say that they don't know whether they are proud of their country, a substantially lower figure of don't knows than is usual in public opinion surveys.

Table 2.1   *Extent of National Pride (percentages)*

	Proud	Not proud	Don't know
United States	96	2	2
Ireland	91	6	3
Iceland	89	9	2
Mexico	88	11	1
Britain	86	11	3
Spain	83	12	5
Finland	81	17	2
Italy	80	17	2
France	76	17	7
Denmark	71	22	7
Belgium	70	19	11
Sweden	69	25	6
Japan	62	31	7
Netherlands	60	32	8
Germany	59	29	12
Average	77	17	5

Source: This and subsequent tables calculated by the Gallup Poll (London) from original data collected in the European Value Systems Study.

An average of 17 per cent say that they are not proud of their country, and the figure is as low as 2 per cent in the United States. Even where the rejection of national pride is at its highest, in Germany, Japan and the Netherlands, a lack of pride characterizes less than a third of the population. In the median country, Italy, those who are proud of the country outnumber those who are not proud by a margin of nearly 5 to 1.

Although the majority of citizens express pride, the level varies across national boundaries. The proportion of Americans expressing national pride is more than half again as great as the 59 per cent of proud Germans. At least seven-eighths of Irish, Icelanders and Mexicans show pride in their country, compared to less than two-thirds of Japanese, Dutch and Germans. Differences cannot be explained in terms of levels of economic development, for all the countries surveyed except Mexico are advanced industrial nations in the Organization for Economic Co-operation and Development (OECD). Countries in which national pride is above average include many of the less affluent OECD nations, such as Ireland and Spain. Moreover, countries with very high standards of living, such as Germany and Sweden, rank below average in national pride. Pride in nation is not a function of national wealth.

National pride appears to be higher in countries that have had to fight for independence. In nations that were once colonies, there has been a need for conscious nation-building after independence. Past experience of being a subject part of another country can explain why countries as diverse as the United States and Ireland (both formerly under the English crown), Iceland (formerly part of Denmark), Mexico (a Spanish colony) and Finland (formerly under the Russian Czar) all rank above average in national pride. The positive effect of having to struggle for national independence appears to have lasted for more than two hundred years in the case of America, 'the first new nation' (Lipset, 1964).

Defeat in war is a blow to national pride. Germany and Japan rank low in national pride, because many Germans and Japanese still have a sense of shame about their country's role in launching and losing the Second World War. Defeat in war thus overrides the pride that was related to nineteenth-century German and Italian nation-building. Other countries ranking less high in pride include those that suffered military occupation in the Second World War, such as the Netherlands, Belgium and France, before emerging on the winning side following the Anglo-American landings in Europe. Nations that avoided military occupation or defeat in the Second World War are the six ranking highest in national pride.

Insofar as the political history of a country affects citizen outlooks, then those who have lived through such traumatic military experiences as wartime occupation and defeat should differ in their views from those who have had little first-hand experience of the deprivations of war, especially the generation born into the period of relative affluence and peace since

1945. Among victorious nations, experiencing victory could make older people more patriotic, just as in defeated countries older people may be relatively less proud.

In the majority of countries surveyed, pride in country is strongest among older people and least strong in people who were young children when the Second World War ended (Table 2.2). Elderly people who have known the ravages of war are more likely to feel pride in their country than their children or grandchildren, who have only read about war. However, the differences are limited, 12 per cent between the oldest and youngest generations. The differences are greatest in Japan (29 per cent) and France (28 per cent), both on the victorious side in the First World War but defeated in the Second World War. The effect of age is least in countries in which pride tends to be high, such as Ireland.

The decline in pride among young people reflects an increase in education. In 13 of 15 nations, citizens with more education are less likely to be proud of their country. The level of pride in a nation is on average 14 per cent higher among those with less education than it is for those with further education, a greater difference than that between generations.[2] Governments spending large sums of money to improve the education of youths will find that this has the unintended consequence of reducing the national pride of younger citizens as they become more educated.

Table 2.2   *Variations in National Pride by Generation*

	Percentage proud of country			
	Born 1916 or before	Born 1917–36	Born since 1937	Difference old–young[a]
Japan	83	69	54	29
France	92	88	64	28
Germany	75	66	48	27
Sweden	86	74	62	24
Britain	96	91	80	16
Italy	89	84	75	14
Belgium	79	71	65	14
Denmark	79	73	67	12
Netherlands	66	66	56	10
Spain	87	88	79	8
Ireland	95	91	90	5
Finland	81	84	84	−3
Mexico	78	88	88	−10
Iceland	80	88	92	−12
Average	83	80	72	12

[a] Proportion proud in generation born 1916 or before minus proportion proud among those born since 1937. No data available for USA.

While churches claim to address transcendental concerns, in many countries historically there has been mutual support between church and state. The Values study asked people whether they would call themselves religious. In every country surveyed, those who are not religious are less likely to be proud of their country. On average the difference is 11 per cent. Among the small group who classify themselves as atheists, pride in nation is lower still. As religious commitment has been in decline, this implies a small but noteworthy secular decline in national pride.

So pervasive is pride in nation that it would be misleading to conclude that the passing of generations or the growth of a more educated and secular citizenry will lead to a rejection of patriotism. The important point about social influences upon a sense of pride is that they are relatively weak. They reduce very high levels of pride, but do not make large sections of the population ashamed of their country. Even among younger people, an average of 72 per cent continue to register pride in country.

Because national pride is widespread, it is normal in both the literal and statistical sense. It is the norm to which all groups in society are expected to conform, or risk being labelled deviant. It is also normal statistically, in that the median person among the young, middle-aged or elderly, and among people of different levels of education and degrees of religious conviction is invariably a person who is proud of his or her country.

Natural not neurotic. The Second World War is a reminder that patriotism can have destructive consequences. The association of patriotism with an authoritarian personality (Adorno et al., 1950) makes it important to test whether a high degree of national pride is associated with characteristics that indicate patriotic people are anti-social or alienated from society. Does a very patriotic person substitute love of country for lack of affection in conventional face-to-face social relationships? Or are people who are proud of their country more likely to have desirable characteristics, such as being better integrated in society?

For the great majority of people the family is the centre of social life, the focus of affection, and of many different everyday activities. Emotional relations within the family are concrete, and thus very different from nominal (and shallow) attachments to such abstract concepts as Queen and Country (cf. Rose and Kavanagh, 1976). To measure social integration the Values survey asked: Overall, how satisfied or dissatisfied are you with your home life? Respondents could rate social satisfaction on a scale ranging from 1 (lowest) to 10 (highest). Across all nations surveyed, the great majority of people report a high level of satisfaction with their home life; the average level of satisfaction overall was 8 out of 10.

Comparing people most satisfied with their home life with those actively dissatisfied provides an appropriate test of whether or not patriotism correlates with more general anti-social outlooks. Those who place themselves at the dissatisfied end of the scale (points 1 to 4) are relatively few in number, 4 per cent of the total in Britain, and 6 per cent in Japan. Because they are deviant, they could feel differently about their country, and this is in fact the case.

In every country examined, people who are more satisfied with their home life are most likely to express pride in their country; those least satisfied have a lower level of national pride. The average difference in pride between socially integrated citizens and those who cannot get on with their immediate relations is 19 per cent. Yet even people who are strongly dissatisfied with their lives usually do not project this into anti-patriotic political ideologies. In the great majority of the countries surveyed, a majority of the small deviant group that felt dissatisfied at home still express pride in their country.

The sense of national pride is doubly secure. It is secure because it is usually high independently of specific historical experiences and the economic record of the government of the day. It is also secure because it is reinforced by an individual's most immediate and important face-to-face relationships. Just as individuals seek and gain satisfaction in their home lives, so too they are likely to take pride in the larger national community of which they are a part.

The anti-patriotic minority

Given the high degree of national pride in most countries, why does patriotism receive little attention in analyses of political systems? And why do those who challenge or deride patriotism receive so much attention in the elite media? To answer these questions we must consider the nature of the anti-patriotic minority.

While the percentage of persons who are not proud of their country is small, a small group can be substantial in absolute numbers. Projecting upon the national population the survey estimates in Table 2.1 indicates that upwards of 5 million Americans, 6 million Britons and 9 million Italians have no pride in their country. While such groups are a minority of the electorate, they are sufficiently numerous to attract attention in the political system.

A majority of those who are not proud of their country are informal opinion leaders; they make some effort to persuade friends or fellow workers to share their views. In the countries surveyed, an average of 55 per cent of those not proud of their country are active in trying to persuade others to hold their views, 7 per cent higher than the proportion doing so among those proud of their country. This difference is reinforced by the fact that persons who are not proud tend to be more educated, and thus more articulate. The proud majority is a relatively silent majority.

Those who are not proud of their country are also more likely to engage in unorthodox political behaviour. The majority of people in Western nations distinguish very carefully between lawful forms of expressing dissatisfaction with public policy, and unorthodox and unlawful forms of activity. For example, while a majority of Americans and Britons approve signing petitions, a lawful form of protest, only a small percentage approve damaging property or personal violence (see below, Table 10.3; Barnes, Kaase et al., 1979: 544f; Harding et al., 1986: 97ff). The patriotic and law-abiding majority are complemented by a small minority who are both unpatriotic and ready to break laws.

People who are not proud of their country receive a disproportionate amount of attention because they are adept at activities that gain media publicity. Since the media regard novelty as news, the minority status of those who attack their country, like that of individual Britons who criticize the Queen, makes them newsworthy. Since those without pride in their country are disproportionately young and well educated, they are capable of exploiting media publicity. A crowd of a few thousand carefully massed in a public place in the capital city, voicing anti-patriotic slogans intended to provoke an outburst from opponents, can receive television attention out of all proportion to their numbers at the ballot box. The 1968 student protests demonstrated how a youthful minority could command international attention. The politics of protest, unlike the politics of the ballot box, does not require a numerical majority to claim attention. If protesters organize as a faction within a left-of-centre party or as a separate party in a multi-party political system, like the Greens, they have a second source of leverage (cf. Lawson and Merkl, 1988).

While it is journalistically easy to describe a typical (*sic*) person who rejects patriotism – a young, well-educated atheist who feels alienated from society – such individuals are extremely atypical members of society. The people who are least likely to have pride in their country are a minority of a minority; they are not even a majority among students or on the left. Differences in pride within a nation are limited in degree, distinguishing between those who tend to be unambiguous in voicing pride, and those who usually but not always feel a sense of national pride.

Policy implications of national pride

The paradox of democracy is that it assumes consensus about the political system, but continuing competition between parties about who should govern and what policies should be pursued. Insofar as partisan divisions reflect differences in patriotic sentiments, then it would be expected that those on the left would be less likely to take pride in their country, because the left is dissatisfied with the status quo, and that those on the right would be proud, even excessively proud, of their country, as the right is expected to stand for traditional values, including patriotism.

In the countries surveyed, most people are actually in the political centre. When a national sample are asked to place themselves on a scale in which 1 is the furthest left and 10 the furthest right, the average person is slightly to the right of centre at 5.73 on the scale. The mean national respondent ranges from a right-of-centre figure of 7.53 in Mexico to a left-of-centre mean of 4.63 in Italy.

In view of the traditional claims of rightwing parties to endorse patriotism and of leftwing parties to deride much that is associated with traditional patriotism, those on the left should be less likely to show pride in their country. This is the case nearly everywhere. Among citizens who describe themselves as on the right, an average of 86 per cent show pride in their country. Among those who say they are on the left, two-thirds do so (Table 2.3). While citizens on the left are less likely to show pride in their country, a majority of the left nonetheless does show a sense of national pride in four-fifths of the countries surveyed.

Any party that is identified as anti-patriotic could not hope to win an electoral majority. Since the left is normally a small fraction of the

Table 2.3   *Left–Right Differences in Pride in Country*

	Percentage proud of country			
	Mean	Right (8–10)	Left (1–3)	Difference right– left
France	4.94	96	56	40
Germany	5.60	83	45	38
Spain	4.89	93	62	31
Japan	6.13	87	59	28
Netherlands	5.53	66	42	24
Denmark	5.77	71	48	23
Finland	5.69	86	64	22
Britain	5.70	96	75	21
Ireland	6.20	96	81	15
Sweden	5.39	74	61	13
Italy	4.63	84	71	13
USA	5.94	99	88	11
Mexico	7.53	91	82	9
Belgium	6.10	75	73	2
Iceland	5.85	88	92	–4
Average	5.73	86	67	19

[a] 10 is most rightwing; 1 is most leftwing.

population – as little as 5 per cent in Ireland and at most only 23 per cent in Italy – its views do not reflect the sentiments of most ordinary people. Even when there are disagreements about the wisdom or morality of a government action abroad, elected politicians with doubts are hesitant to express them, and party leaders do not want to voice criticisms that could be labelled as unpatriotic, for fear of the electoral consequences of this. Voicing doubts about the goals or tactics of international policy is possible; for example, British politicians disagree about reliance upon nuclear weapons and American politicians about the extent to which agreements with the Russians can be trusted. However, siding with a nation's opponents is regarded as unpatriotic, and when troops are in action, even voicing doubts can be regarded as suspect.

Important as the commitments of patriotism are, they are not uncritical or absolute. This is dramatically demonstrated by the response produced by the Values survey to the question: 'We all hope that there will not be another war, but if it were to come to that, would you be willing to fight for your country?' The answers show substantial variation between nations, ranging from a high of 82 per cent in Mexico to a low of 22 per cent in Japan (Table 2.4).

Pride in country does not necessarily stimulate a feeling of belligerence. In 5 of the 15 countries examined, less than half who expressed

Table 2.4 *National Pride and Willingness to Fight for Country*

| | Percentage willing to fight for country | | | |
	Total	Proud	Not Proud	Difference proud–not proud
USA	72	73	38	35
France	42	49	18	31
Britain	62	66	39	27
Spain	53	57	31	26
Ireland	49	51	25	26
Finland	75	79	56	23
Germany	35	43	22	21
Mexico	82	84	66	17
Netherlands	44	50	33	17
Japan	22	28	11	17
Denmark	59	64	48	16
Iceland	67	69	54	15
Italy	28	31	19	12
Belgium	25	28	19	9
Sweden	78	81	75	6
Average	53	57	37	20

pride in their country were also willing to fight for it. Equally, those who are not proud of their country are not necessarily pacifists. In four countries an absolute majority of those not proud said that they would be willing to fight for their country, rising to 75 per cent in Sweden.

Consistently, those who are less proud of their country are less likely to be prepared to fight for it; on average, the difference is 20 per cent. The difference is greatest where the numbers affected are least. Among citizens who are not proud of the United States, only 38 per cent say that they would be willing to fight for their country, but since this group constitutes only 2 per cent of the population, its significance is small. The trauma of the Vietnam War has not left a large residue of Americans who are unwilling to wear their country's uniform in wartime. The reasons for people hesitating about fighting for their country appear to reflect past experience of military defeat, as in Japan, Italy and Germany, rather than a lack of national pride.

The greatest influence upon national pride appears to be the actions of government itself. A government that persisted in a war that was both unsuccessful and shameful would give good reason to ordinary people to lose their sense of national pride. Military defeat is even more effective in disillusioning people about their country, and depressing the level of national pride.

National pride appears independent of the everyday failings of government, such as difficulties in managing the economy, failure in coping with social problems, or corruption in high office. While the events of Watergate and world recession were disillusioning experiences for Americans in the 1970s, pride in the United States remained very high. Where a national government has been created by the drive for national independence and nation-building, pride has been stimulated by the existence of an independent country without regard to what it costs to achieve or what it does subsequently. For example, Ireland achieved independence in the early 1920s at the cost of years of rebellion and civil war, and independence was followed by great economic hardship, leading to the emigration of a substantial portion of young people (Rose and Garvin, 1983). Yet people do not ask about the cash benefits of being an American or an Irishman; a sense of national pride is rooted in the political struggle to create and maintain an independent nation.

Notes

1. The analysis that follows draws heavily upon Richard Rose, 'National Pride in Cross-National Perspective', *International Social Science Journal* 37, 1 (1985), 85–96.

2. Differences in social structure, such as the varying importance of agriculture and the peasantry, make it impracticable to compare the impact of class cross-nationally. Insofar as there is a tendency of middle-class people to be more patriotic, because better off, this will be partially offset by higher middle-class levels of education.

3

Ordinary People in an Electoral Situation

Election is like baptism; it is essential but one does not want to spend one's life in the font.

Louis Napoleon

The right of everyone to vote is central in defining democracy. Voting gives an ordinary person the opportunity to register an opinion about how the country ought to be governed. It is the only way in which the majority of people may directly influence government; most forms of political participation are confined to a minority who take part in the activities of a political party or a pressure group. Casting a vote is as much and as little as the ordinary person does to take part in politics (Rose, 1989a: Table 6.2; Dalton, 1988).

Universal suffrage makes the views of ordinary people of immediate concern to politicians. But in an electoral situation, individuals remain ordinary people first, and are only secondarily voters. The outcome of an election is all-important in the career of an elected officeholder, but it is of limited significance to most people in the electorate. An ordinary person can paraphrase Louis Napoleon and argue that while the right to vote is absolutely essential, one does not want to spend all one's life marking ballots.

The ballot cast on polling day is not a permanent commitment to follow a particular party or leader. It is good for the moment, a judgement on balance in favour of one group or against another. An election *temporarily* links politicians and voters. Between elections, an officeholder may forget the views of those who elect him or her and an ordinary person can turn attention to work, to family or to leisure pursuits, ignoring what politicians say ought to be done. In the course of a four-year period, an ordinary person is likely to consider voting for (or against) more than one party.

The significance that we attribute to voting and elections depends upon whether we take the top-down view of candidates or view elections from the underall position of the ordinary individual (Rose and Mossawir, 1967). An election outcome is immediately important in determining who governs. Its influence is direct only in those few countries, such as the United States, that elect their national leader. In parliamentary systems an election determines who sits in Parliament, but the choice of Prime Minister and Cabinet is made by Parliament. The choice is simple when a single party has a majority, but it is subject to complex bargaining when several parties must maintain a coalition government. In every political system, elections are also intended to give some direction to public policies. But the information conveyed by ballots is only a rough judgement about what government has been doing and about the claims of its opponents.

Election, like baptism, is meant to confer a special status upon those who are elected. Granting ordinary people the right to confirm or reject those who govern helps to legitimate the authority of rulers. When ordinary people have a say in who governs, there is an implicit commitment to accept its authority and do what 'their' government says. This commitment is meant to bind those who vote for the losing party as well as those who support the winner. Dictators as well as democrats appreciate this. Most of the elections in the world today are elections without choice; they are held in one-party states where the authorities calling the election know what the result will be (Hermet et al., 1978). Elections enhance political legitimacy in a world in which election by the masses has replaced election by a Calvinist God as a token of authority.

This chapter looks first at the behaviour of ordinary people in electoral situations. Insofar as ordinary people are not specially interested in politics, then voting may reflect 'extra-political' influences accumulated through a lifetime of learning, starting with family upbringing. Alternatively, people may formulate durable political principles for judging parties, or simply make diffuse judgements about the performance of the government of the day. Secondly, the chapter considers the collective significance of voting in determining who governs and influencing what government does.

Reflecting a lifetime of learning

For the ordinary person, voting is both a duty and an opportunity. Voting is an obligation as well as a voice for a citizen; many countries even go so far as to make voting compulsory. Voting is also the one opportunity that an ordinary person has to influence who governs. The amount of influence that any one individual can have upon an election result is infinitesimal, but by casting a ballot along with millions of other citizens, an individual collectively becomes part of the result that determines the election outcome.

Whether to vote. Like everything else in life, voting requires effort. The effort required to go to the polls depends upon the extent to which election laws facilitate voting, or make it a relatively onerous task, thus depressing voter turnout. European laws facilitate voting; American laws do not. The likelihood of voting is also affected by the amount of interest that people have in politics; the lower the level of political interest, the less likely a person is to bother voting.

Western democracies vary greatly in laws affecting the ease of voting. Election laws can automatically enter every citizen's name on the electoral register, voting can be compulsory, election day can be made a public holiday and polling stations located close to where voters live. Where this is done, turnout rates can rise above 90 per cent. Where these conditions are not met – and the United States is extreme in the extent to which it creates difficulties in registering voters and thus disqualifying people before polling day – turnout can drop to about half of the potential adult electorate. Britain falls between very high turnout countries such as Italy and the Netherlands and the United States, where turnout, even at a Presidential election, is well below the international average. In Britain public officials compile the electoral register, thus ensuring that virtually every potential elector has the right to vote. But ballots are cast on a workday not a weekend or public holiday (cf. Crewe, 1981).

The character of party competition also influences the likelihood of an individual voting. When parties can mobilize support by appealing to strong ties of religion, language or class, then an ordinary person is more likely to vote, for voting expresses a social loyalty to class, ethnic or religious groups (Powell, 1982: chapter 6). Ideological polarization between parties offering conflicting world views can also encourage turnout by frightening voters into believing that the outcome will make a great difference to society. In such circumstances, a low turnout can be interpreted not so much as a sign of apathy but as evidence of citizens being sufficiently satisfied that there is not even a need to vote (cf. Lipset, 1960).

Participation in politics can take many forms; voting is only one form of participation. Those who are most motivated to vote are individuals for whom politics is a fulltime career, but these are extraordinary people, a small handful of the population. Survey researchers classify the adult population into five groups, ranging from those who are totally inactive, not even bothering to vote, to persons who are complete activists, taking part in election campaigns and community activities as well as voting (Table 3.1). In Britain, the average person is prepared to vote, but not to participate in other political activities. The proportion of Britons who say they do not vote is greater than those who say they are active in community affairs (Table 3.1).

The behaviour of Americans appears paradoxical, for while voting turnout is low in national elections, more Americans appear to participate in politics. One reason for this is that while political parties are weak, community organizations are extremely active in the United States, and this is regarded as a form of political activity. Secondly, talking about politics with others is regarded as a campaign activity, and this can occur

Table 3.1 *Extent of Political Participation (percentages)*

	Britain	USA
Complete activists (vote, take part in election campaigns, community activities)	8	23
Campaign activists (vote, campaign action)	7	7
Community activist (vote, community activities)	15	25
Only voters	50	27
No activities	20	18
Turnout, last general election	75.3	55.0

Source: Political Action Survey of Barnes, Kaase et al. (1979) as calculated and reported by Dalton, 1988: Table 3.4.

even in the absence of activities by political parties. In Britain political participation tends to be more organized, and such bodies as business and professional associations or trade unions vicariously represent individuals. Group loyalties are also more effective in mobilizing individuals to vote on election day than are the informal and tangential forms of political activity in the United States. Even though more Americans than Britons say that they are politically active, in fact turnout at Presidential elections is about 20 per cent lower than turnout at parliamentary elections in Britain.

How to vote? The question that an ordinary person faces in an election situation does not require a classroom answer; all that is needed is a mark on a ballot paper. An individual does not need to explain or justify the choice. In order to vote a person does not need a great deal of information about the candidates or parties. The action of an ordinary person will not be based upon a well-articulated political philosophy or a knowledge of party programmes. Nonetheless, it is a considered response, reflecting the cumulative experience of a lifetime of political learning, indirect as well as direct.

If we think of the actions of ordinary people in electoral situations as reflecting a lifetime of learning, this avoids the fallacy of reducing the causes of voting to a single explanation. Five different explanations of voting – childhood socialization, socio-economic status, political principles, the current performance of parties, and party identification – are proffered in the literature of electoral behaviour.[1] As Figure 3.1 shows, these theories are not so much alternative as they are complementary. In the course of a lifetime a multiplicity of influences can affect how ordinary people vote.

To test the lifetime learning model empirically, we need to proceed in the order in which events occur in the life of an ordinary person. This can be done statistically by using hierarchical stepwise multiple

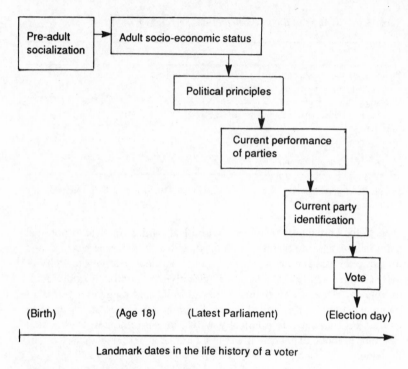

Figure 3.1   *Lifetime Learning Model of Voting*
(Rose and McAllister, 1986: Figure 7.1)

regression. In turn, it calculates the influence (statistically, the variance explained) of each element in the lifetime learning model. The effect of pre-adult socialization is reckoned before examining the influence of adult socio-economic position, which is calculated before testing how much more variance can be explained by political principles. If, for example, pre-adult socialization were all-important, then it would explain 100 per cent of the variance, but if class were all-important, then neither pre-adult experiences nor political principles would explain any of the variance (for details, see Rose and McAllister, 1986: 128ff). The model is tested with evidence from three British general elections, October 1974, 1979 and 1983, in order to identify conclusions that are consistent from one election to the next.[2]

Pre-adult socialization. Theories of political socialization emphasize that growing up in a family is primary, being first in time, and capable of dominating throughout a lifetime. Youthful political socialization is indirect, not direct; only a totalitarian society would think of people making babies for the sake of the party. In the home parents can indicate which political party they support, and a child can learn that the family identifies with a particular party without knowing anything else about it. Even if a child does not think about social class, the parent's class provides a class environment and affects a child's educational opportunities.

The influence of the family continues to some effect throughout a lifetime, explaining an average of 15 per cent of the variance in Conservative–Labour voting (Table 3.2). Father's party is consistently the most important early influence upon adult party choice. But its effect is limited, and in decline. Father's party explained 10 per cent of the variance in Conservative versus Labour voting in 1974, and 7 per cent in 1983. Parental party remains more important than parental class, which

Table 3.2 *Cumulative Determinants of Conservative and Labour Voting*

| Influences | Conservative vs. Labour (percentage variance explained) | | | |
	October 1974	October 1979	October 1983	Change 1974–83
I *Pre-adult socialization*	20	12	14	–6
Father's party	10	7	7	–3
Father's class	6	3	3	–3
Education	2	2	2	0
Religion	2	0	2	0
II *Socio-economic status*	10	12	13	+3
Housing	4	4	5	+1
Union membership	4	4	3	–1
Nation	0	3	3	+3
Current class	2	1	2	0
III *Political principles*	22	22	29	+7
Socialism	22	19	27	+5
Social welfare	0	0	2	+2
Racialism	0	2	0	0
Traditional morality	0	1	0	0
IV *Current performance of parties*	18	17	21	+3
Leaders	14	16	6	–8
Evaluation governing party	4	1	7	+3
Event evaluation[a]	0	na	1	+1
Campaign	0	0	0	0
Future expectations	0	0	7	+7
V *Current party identification*	9	20	3	–6
Total variance explained	79	83	80	+1

[a] Common Market in 1974, Falklands in 1983.

Source: Rose and McAllister, 1986: Table 7.3.

now explains only 3 per cent of the vote. Education and religion are of little consequence.

The electoral significance of pre-adult socialization has been declining in the past two decades (cf. Butler and Stokes, 1969). In 1974 pre-adult influences accounted for 20 per cent of the variance; in 1979 for 12 per cent; and in 1983 for 14 per cent. Nor is this surprising. Whereas the choice offered voters between the Conservative and Labour parties used to be relatively stable, today the parties are in flux. Since 1974 Labour has had four leaders and veered between centrist and hard left positions. In the same period the Conservatives have been subject to a radical change in leadership style under Margaret Thatcher, and to some extent in policies as well.

Socio-economic status. An adult's social position reflects individual efforts and choices as well as family background. The influence of this position is stressed in theories of class voting, which assume that an individual's occupational status is of pervasive importance in every aspect of life. As some people rise and others fall in relation to their parents' status, class can be an influence independent of the home. Occupation is not the only socio-economic influence upon voting. Trade union membership can stimulate a sense of solidarity with the left, and home-ownership can make a person more conservative. Region of residence can be significant, insofar as ordinary people are suggestible, wanting to vote like other people where they live.

Socio-economic status accounts for about one-eighth of the variance in the vote, but occupation, the conventional measure of class, is the least significant of the four socio-economic influences (Table 3.2). Whether a person owns a home or is a tenant of a municipally owned council house is the most important socio-economic influence, explaining 5 per cent of the variance, after controlling for the effect of pre-adult influences. Trade union membership and nation of residence (England, Scotland or Wales) each explained 3 per cent of the variance at the 1983 election, compared to 2 per cent for current class.

Together, pre-adult socialization and current socio-economic status account for about one-quarter of the variance of the vote. The relative importance of the two is changing. Voters today are less inclined to vote like their parents, and current socio-economic position is becoming more important. However, the combined effect of these influences upon political behaviour has declined from explaining 30 per cent of the Conservative–Labour vote in 1974 to 27 per cent in 1983.

Political principles. Since political socialization and socio-economic status leave nearly three-quarters of the variance in voting unexplained, there is great potential scope for political views to influence voting. However, a correlation between a person's expressed views on issues and party preference is not proof of issue-preferences determining voting, for loyalty to a party could be the cause of an individual adopting the views. Insofar as experience leads individuals to formulate relatively durable political principles, concerning such matters as the role of government in the economy, then these durable principles may influence how people vote at a particular election independent of family and social background.

The effect of four durable political principles can be tested; they are derived from a factor analysis of British election survey questions about enduring political attitudes (see Rose and McAllister, 1986: 118ff). The principle of socialism distinguishes views traditionally endorsed by Labour Party leaders, and rejected by the leaders of the consciously anti-socialist Conservatives. Approval of public provision of social welfare benefits is a second principle; attitudes toward traditional or permissive morality (abortion and sex on TV) a third; and views about racial equality a fourth principle.

Views about socialism consistently determine more than a fifth of the vote – but not in the way that Labour activists would like. The electoral force of socialism benefits the Conservatives much more than Labour, because the majority of voters are anti-socialist. Anti-socialist principles are the single most important influence upon voting, and their impact is particularly striking since influence is here measured after allowing for the effects of family background and adult socio-economic status. The views of ordinary voters about socialism explain as much of the vote as the combined influence of pre-adult socialization and current socio-economic position. Moreover, the influence of this political principle has been increasing. Other political principles are not important electorally. Support for social welfare cannot explain differences in voting, since virtually the whole electorate is united in favouring the welfare state. Views about traditional morality and race relations have little electoral effect because they divide both Conservative and Labour supporters.

Current performance of parties. In a search for novelty, journalists emphasize current events as the most important determinants of voting, for example, reporting a television debate between candidates as decisive. It is assumed that a lifetime of previous experience is of little consequence compared to the experience of the moment. In an election situation, ordinary people are expected to react to current events, deciding whether to punish or reward the incumbent government. The current performance of parties is much more immediate than childhood experience and more directly relevant to voting than socio-economic status.

At the start of each Parliament voters have already formed judgements about parties. This is shown statistically by more than half the division of the Conservative–Labour vote being explained by previous influences. During a Parliament the government is responsible for whatever happens to the economy, whether popular or unpopular, and it must also accept responsibility for both fortunate occurrences and mishaps. Often party leaders change during a Parliament and crisis events can also arise to stir the electorate; for example, the miners' strike in 1973 or the Falklands War in 1982. The events of a Parliament give a person some reason to think again about voting, and voting at by-elections and fluctuations in opinion polls indicate that many voters at least temporarily drift away from their normal party preference. In an election campaign, all parties seek to resolve indecision in their favour.

The voter's evaluation of parties during the life of a Parliament accounts for up to one-fifth of the variance in Conservative versus Labour voting (Table 3.2). The record of the Conservative government on unemployment, taxation, the cost of living and strikes accounted for 7 per cent of the variance in 1983. Expectations of a party improving the standard of living in the next four years, in part reflecting retrospective evaluation of past performance, accounted for another 7 per cent. In 1983 the collective evaluation of party leaders – Margaret Thatcher, Michael Foot, David Steel and Roy Jenkins – collectively accounted for 6 per cent of the vote, much less than in 1974 and 1979.

Transitory events and issues appear to have little direct importance on election day. The Falklands War was an important event in 1982, when it had positive consequences for the Conservative Party's morale and its standing in the Gallup Poll at mid-term. While it helped the Conservatives regain support lost during its mid-term slump, by the time of the June 1983 general election, it could add only 1 per cent to what voters had earlier learned about parties. Similarly, views about the Common Market had no independent influence on voting in 1974. After taking into account a lifetime of previous learning, the election campaign itself is a transitory event of limited influence upon voters.

Current party identification. Identification with a political party is sometimes cited as a fifth determinant of voting behaviour. If explaining variance in the statistical sense is the sole object of analysis, the ideal determinant (*sic*) would be highly correlated with voting because it was simply another way of measuring current party preference. To a substantial extent, party identification is such a tautology. A high correlation between party identification and party vote does not explain why a person votes for a given party; it supports the view that party identification and party preference are two different names for the same thing.[3]

The test of party identification as an independent influence is its impact upon voting after controlling for the effect of a lifetime of influences that determine both the voting behaviour and the party identification of ordinary people. When prior determinants are taken into account, party identification appears largely redundant, adding an average of only 11 per cent to the variance explained by pre-adult socialization, socio-economic status, political principles, and the current performance of parties.

Party identification is the only influence examined that is *not* consistently important. In 1983 it added only 3 per cent to the explanation of the Conservative versus Labour share of the vote. The spurious nature of a correlation between party identification and voting is emphasized by its high correlation with support for the Alliance parties; it appeared to account for 26 per cent of the Alliance vote in 1983, but this is only because other influences on Alliance voting are weak (Rose and McAllister, 1986: 133). The link between party identification and voting Alliance is tautological because the normal process of acquiring a party identification through childhood socialization could not operate. The Alliance did not come into existence until 1981. Thus, it was not possible for Alliance voters to develop a lifetime identification with that party, as is assumed in theories of party identification as an independent influence upon voting.

When tested across a decade of elections, the lifetime learning model gives a coherent and parsimonious explanation of the factors that differentiate Conservative from Labour voters. It can account for four-fifths of the variance in voting, an extraordinarily high degree by comparison with attempts to reduce voting to a single influence. While all five influences are of some importance, they are not equal in significance. Political concerns are more important than extra-political influences; political principles and the current performance of the parties explain more than 43 per cent of the total variance in the vote. This figure is particularly striking given that the regression model calculates their influence *after* allowing for the impact of pre-adult socialization and socio-economic interests. Moreover, voters are increasingly affected by these immediately political determinants. In 1974, 40 per cent of the variance was explained by political principles and the current performance of parties; in 1983, the proportion had risen to 50 per cent.

A reasonable electorate. The votes of ordinary people can be described as reasonable insofar as an explanation can be given for their behaviour, whether reasons take the form of clearly articulated opinions stated by ordinary people in response to survey interview questions, or an explanation that can be offered on their behalf by out-of-the ordinary persons such as political scientists.

When ordinary people are directly questioned about their reasons for voting, the answers are often vague. Moreover, the reasons offered should not always be taken at face value. For example, a voter may say that a party has the best policies and leaders to deal with the problems facing the country today. However, if the person has always voted for this party then the underlying reason must be a prior cause, such as pre-adult socialization. Similarly, a voter may explain a vote by reference to political principles, but if these principles can also be linked with socio-economic status, then class or housing may be the prior cause of holding principles that rationalize socio-economic interests. The reasons that we would regard as a convincing explanation of voting are not necessarily those that an individual would articulate.

The actions of ordinary people may be considered reasonable if a justification can be offered on behalf of a voter's choice. As John Plamenatz (1988: 9) has noted:

> A choice is reasonable, not because the chooser, when challenged, can give a satisfactory explanation of why he made it, but because if he could give an explanation, it would be satisfactory.

Reasons offered on a voter's behalf may or may not be like those that an ordinary individual would articulate in response to survey questions. Moreover, an explanation may be offered in the absence of any articulate opinion. For example, a person may have no interest in politics and reply don't know in response to a series of questions. But we would consider it reasonable if a person with little interest in politics voted like others in the same class or like neighbours in a housing estate, on the assumption that a party favoured by other people with whom the person identifies is also appropriate for that individual. The lifetime learning model shows that most voters are reasonable, because easily understood reasons can be offered to explain the voting of the great majority of ordinary people.

The collective significance for government

From the overall view of government, the vote of an individual is but a means to the end of constituting government. An election is not just an opinion poll of the preferences of voters. It is also a means of choosing a small number of people for the chief positions of government. A ballot does not record the views of voters with the detail of a public opinion survey; it simply records the number of people who support a party or candidate as best qualified to govern, or favoured as the lesser evil. Collectively, elections do three things: they confirm the rights and duties of individuals as citizens, determine who holds the chief offices of government, and sometimes influence policies of governors.

Confirming rights and obligations. An ordinary person does not think of himself or herself primarily as a citizen; other roles in society – spouse or parent, friend or employee – are likely to be more significant in everyday life. Yet when an election is called, everyone in a democracy expects to have the right to vote; the franchise is a badge of citizenship. Without the right to vote, a person is subject to authority but has no claim to influence those who wield it.

While the right of ordinary people to vote is today taken for granted, the struggle for universal suffrage took generations to achieve. In Britain the 1832 Reform Act began the process of establishing a modern basis for the franchise, but the majority of adult males did not gain the right to vote until 1884, and the principle of one man or woman, one vote for all citizens was not applied until 1950. In the United States, the suffrage was early granted to white males and guaranteed women by constitutional amendment in 1920; however, blacks in the American South only had the right to vote guaranteed after a series of civil rights demonstrations culminated in the 1964 federal voting rights act.

Rights also confer obligations. Ordinary people as well as philosophers can ask: Why should I do what government wants? An ordinary person can identify circumstances in which the actions of government appear to be contrary to the national interest, to an individual's self-interest, or to common sense. Yet public officials expect ordinary people to accept political authority whether or not a person agrees with the specific actions that government takes.

People obey laws even when they disagree with them because laws are made by people whom we elect. A popularly elected government is thought to deserve allegiance because it is the kind of government that people want. Coercion and tradition are no longer the chief basis for justifying authority in Western nations. If an ordinary person does not like what government does, dissatisfaction can be expressed by voting to turn the government of the day out of office. No other system of choosing rulers is considered desirable and practical.

Free competitive elections tend to make governments more moderate because a party wanting to win an election must make a broad appeal. Parties with what the French call a 'majority vocation' (that is, a desire to be the largest party in the country) tend to present programmes that appeal to a majority of ordinary people, rather than formulating policies and principles that appeal only to the minority active in party ranks. Free elections force politicians who want power to test their popular support with ballots, not bullets.

Free elections force politicians claiming to represent the people to put their claim to a popular test. In the postwar era ordinary people have used the vote to register no-confidence in extremist groups that have sought to rule without democratic accountability (Rose, 1983: 29ff). After years of dictatorship ordinary Spaniards, Portuguese and Greeks were given the choice in the 1970s between parties pledged to maintain a democratic regime and parties seeking to govern by non-democratic values; in each country the great majority has voted in favour of democratic parties, and anti-democratic groups have been marginalized politically. In France, Italy and Spain, where Communists initially organized as a *parti du combat*, ready to take to the streets in pursuit of their political aims, elections have given the masses a chance to reject such tactics. In consequence, Communist parties have developed a philosophy of Euro-Communism, seeking to work within the political system rather than against established authority.

Ordinary people can easily become blasé about the rights and duties of citizens, but in authoritarian regimes ordinary people appreciate the value of the vote because it is denied them. Without the right to vote ordinary people must accept what their rulers say, or else act in ways that the regime can treat as illegal. A person may lose a job or be threatened with arrest for expressing criticisms of the regime, and the private benefits of public policy can be confined to those who are active in the party. Bureaucrats can dismiss the wishes of ordinary individuals because they are not accountable to elected officials.

The governors of an authoritarian regime are deprived of indications of popular dissatisfaction that free elections provide. In many parts of the world regimes hold 'state-controlled' elections, in an attempt to increase the commitment of ordinary people to the regime without offering them a free choice of rulers (Hermet, 1978). In the Soviet Union ordinary people have not been able to express their views about their leaders at the ballot box, having to keep their views about what the state does to themselves. Thus, the seemingly all-powerful leaders of the Soviet Union do not know what most of their subjects are thinking. Under Mikhail Gorbachev the Russian government has sought to establish a dialogue with ordinary people, but, in the words of a Soviet political scientist, William Smirnov, 'Most of us simply do not understand how complex a society we have.' He adds: 'It is not easy to adapt to reality' (quoted in Peel, 1988).

Influencing the choice of governors. The paradox of universal suffrage is that the bigger the electorate, the less influence an ordinary individual has. Giving the franchise to tens of millions of people reduces the effect of one person's actions. If 12 million votes are needed to win an election, than one person can cast only 0.00008 per cent of the votes needed to elect the winner. In an era of mass politics, an ordinary person gains influence by being part of a mass.

The situation that an ordinary person faces in an election is structured by the laws of the electoral system. Laws and politics determine how votes are counted, which officers are elected, and how government is constituted. There are big differences between countries in the way in which votes determine the election of representatives.

Majority rule is neither necessary nor certain in Anglo-American elections, for the winner is determined by the winner-take-all rule of 'first past the post'; the candidate with the most votes is declared the winner, whether the leading candidate has a majority of the vote (that is, more than half) or a simple plurality (the greatest number). A candidate is certain of winning an absolute majority only if two candidates are nominated. In Britain, the majority of parliamentary seats have been contested by at least three candidates since 1964, and in the United States a third-party candidate can poll a significant number of votes for the Presidency if there is widespread popular disillusionment with the two major parties.

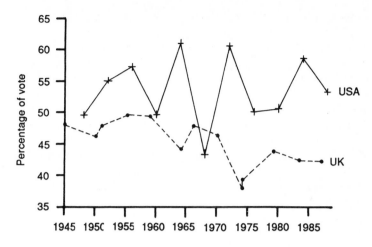

Figure 3.2 *Winning Party's Share of Popular Vote since 1945 (Mackie and Rose, 1990)*

In every general election in Britain since 1945 the victorious party has won with less than half the popular vote. Five out of every nine voters on average cast their ballot *against* the government of the day. Moreover, the proportion voting for the party winning control of government has fallen from almost half immediately after the Second World War to a low of 37 per cent in February 1974. While Margaret Thatcher has undoubtedly led her party to victory at the last three British general elections, the Conservative share of the vote has averaged less than 43 per cent of the total (Figure 3.2).

The vastness of the American population means that an ordinary person is only one among 150 million potential electors. and low turn-out enables a President to claim office with upwards of 40 million votes. For example, Ronald Reagan won a landslide victory in the 1984 Presidential election with the support of only 32 per cent of eligible voters. In three postwar Presidential elections the winning candidate has taken less than half the vote actually cast, and Jimmy Carter and Ronald Reagan first won office with just over 50.0 per cent of the vote (Figure 3.2). The striking feature of postwar American Presidential election is the variability in the vote gained by the winner. The average President can claim to be leader of little more than half the American people; 54 per cent vote for the winner and 46 per cent on average back the losers.

Proportional representation laws allow each individual's vote to influence the election of representatives by assigning seats in Parliament in proportion to the share of the vote that each party receives. If 55 per cent of the voters in a constituency favour one party, and 44 per cent another, then the former party will have five MPs and the latter four. If the vote divides three ways – 45, 44 and 11 per cent – then the first two parties will each have four MPs, and the third party will elect one MP. The only way in which one party can win all the seats in a constituency is if nearly every voter favours it.

From the underall position of the ordinary person, proportional representation immediately increases the influence of an individual's vote. A person's vote is not wasted if it is cast for a party with, say, 33 per cent of the vote, as in a winner-take-all ballot. Equally important, a vote is not wasted if a party takes more than half the vote. Since seats are awarded in proportion to a party's share of the vote, then a party with 67 per cent of the popular vote in a district will win more seats there than if it only gains 51 per cent of the vote (on electoral systems, see Bogdanor and Butler, 1983).

If the object of an election is viewed as the popular choice of government rather than as the mathematical representation of popular preferences in a national Parliament, then the important point is that ordinary people have the chance to choose between competing teams of governors (Schumpeter, 1952: chapters 21–3). What government does becomes the responsibility of the winners; it is not anything that ordinary people can direct. However, the prospect of having to run for re-election should make the government of the day keep in mind the interests of voters, adjusting policies in the light of their anticipated reactions at the next election. And the next election gives ordinary people the chance to re-affirm their approval of the government, or vote to 'turn the rascals out'.

If elections are viewed as a means to the end of letting ordinary people determine who governs, then the first-past-the-post electoral system can be defended *because* it manufactures a majority of seats in Parliament for a party with a minority of the popular vote. Elections give ordinary people the best chance to decide who governs (or who is refused office) if responsibility for governing is fixed upon a single party, or pair of candidates. For example, in the United States the Presidential election focuses the choice upon two politicians who have been exposed to intense public scrutiny in a year-long campaign marathon. In a parliamentary system a two-party contest gives voters a clearcut choice between the In and the Out parties. Satisfaction with the course of events will produce a vote for the In party, and dissatisfaction (or a belief that the Out party could do a better job) encourages a vote for the Out party.

If elections are about the choice of government, proportional representation both enriches and confuses the choice offered ordinary people. Proportional representation usually gives an individual a choice of half a dozen parties or more for which to vote. But the choice of government is confused, because no party wins a majority of seats. A coalition of parties is usually necessary to form a government; its composition is the outcome of bargaining between leaders of different parties and factions.

When government is a coalition, then an elector cannot fix responsibility on one party or be sure that a particular opposition party will enter office if there is some change in government. Confusion is a likely outcome of an election to confirm or reject a coalition government. In nearly two-thirds of all elections involving coalition governments, some members will lose votes while other coalition members gain votes. More than three-quarters of the net change in the vote for coalition parties is simply jostling; a gain in one coalition partner's vote is offset by a fall in the vote for another coalition partner (Rose and Mackie, 1983: Tables 5.2, 5.3).

The American Constitution is unique in the extent to which it is based on distrust of government. It requires concurrent agreement between a separately elected White House and Congress. Power is shared between two institutions in the belief that each can act as a check upon the other, and any measure agreeable to both is more likely to be agreeable to the populace as a whole. An ordinary American thus has two votes for national government, one for a representative in Congress and one for the White House. Until the 1950s most voters normally trusted a party, voting a straight ticket for candidates of the same party for both the White House and Congress. But split-ticket voting is now so common that the Republicans normally win the White House while the Democrats win Congress, because a substantial proportion of American voters split their ticket, voting for a Republican for the Presidency and a Democratic representative in Congress, or vice versa (Ferejohn and Fiorina, 1985).

Influencing policies. In a representative system of government, influencing who governs is much more likely than influencing what government does. Ordinary people are not supposed to determine the policies of government. Whereas government must make many decisions annually about the problems facing the country, an ordinary person can ignore the problems of government. From the underall position of an individual, the point of representative government is that other people can get on with the job of governing. Voters no more expect to make decisions about what government should do than sports fans expect to go out on the field and play for the football team that they support.

The infrequency with which referendums are held and their exclusion from definitions of democracy illustrates that ordinary people are not expected to decide most major policies of government. A referendum vote offers the electorate an opportunity to decide whether or not a bill or a constitutional proposal becomes a law. While this symbolically labelled instrument of 'direct democracy' can be traced back to classical Athens, the spread of democracy in the past century has not been matched by increased use of the referendum. Only once in the political lifetime of the ordinary English person has government asked people to declare their opinion about an issue, a nationwide referendum in 1975 about whether or not Britain should remain a member of the European Community.

In the United States an ordinary person may have a chance to vote in a referendum about one aspect of local taxes, and in states such as California to vote on statewide ballots. But there has never been a nationwide referendum to decide policies of the federal government.

Democratic government is not rule by the people but *for* the people. Elections are an integral part of the process of representative government, but they are not a substitute for government by elected representatives. The decisions of government are the responsibility of Parliament or of the President and Congress – and their decisions have the binding force of law. An individual cannot ignore or violate a law by pleading as an excuse that he or she did not vote for the government that enacted it. Everyone is expected to obey all the laws of a popularly elected government.

Americans prefer to rely upon organized interest groups rather than parties to represent their views on issues concerning business, unions, the environment or civil rights (Table 3.3). Organized groups are positively valued because they concentrate upon a narrow range of issues. Further-more, it is easier for an ordinary individual to be confident of what pressure group leaders will do than what elected politicians will do. The decline in confidence in parties is underscored by the fact that the more education an American has, the less trust is placed in parties and the more confidence placed in pressure groups.

In Europe organized interests representing labour, farmers and business are often strong, and pre-democratic traditions of collective representa-tion give legitimacy to the representation of ordinary people through corporatist institutions that are expected to defend their interests. Inter-ests are given status in corporatist bargaining groups even though they may represent a small number of voters (for example, farmers or owners of business) or even though they misrepresent a large number of their members (for example, while all British trade unions officially affiliate

Table 3.3   *American Reliance upon Groups for Political Representation (percentages)*

Question: Which group best represents the political interests of people like you?

Response by education	Organized interest groups, e.g. unions, business, civil rights	Parties	Other, don't know
College graduate	57	32	11
Some college	54	39	8
High school diploma	47	34	19
Minimum	34	34	29
Total	45	34	20

Source: ACIR, 1984: Table 14.

to the Labour Party, no more than half of trade union members now vote Labour).

Whatever the system of counting votes, the views of most ordinary people will be heeded insofar as there is an all-party consensus in favour of a measure. Invariably there is a consensus in favour of such generalized goals as peace and prosperity. When ordinary people vote on the basis of the current performance of parties in Parliament, often they are making a rough judgement about which party is most effective in achieving consensual goals. Politicians can thus compete for votes by encouraging popular confidence that they are best at achieving consensus goals.

Surveys consistently show that there is a substantial amount of consensus on specific policies among people who vote for different British parties (Table 3.4; see also, Rose, 1974: Table 11.1; Rose and McAllister, 1986: Table 8.3). It is particularly striking to find agreement when both Margaret Thatcher and Labour politicians have sought to polarize party politics, stressing the alleged ideological gulf between the parties. When

Table 3.4 *Similarity of Policy Preferences among Partisans*
(percentages endorsing policy)

	Total	Conservative	Alliance	Labour
Plurality in all three parties agree				
Spend more on health	90	81	96	98
Let council tenants buy their house	81	89	76	77
Government guide wage, price rises	78	81	80	76
Spend more against pollution	78	78	82	78
Promote equal opportunities for women	77	73	80	80
Spend to reduce unemployment	76	64	85	87
Bring back death penalty	64	68	61	64
Redistribute wealth to poor	61	43	67	68
Shift power to local government, regions	51	44	53	56
Reduce sex on TV and in magazines	50	53	52	48
Re-establish grammar schools	48	63	40	35
Allow abortion on National Health Service	46	44	45	51
Send back coloured immigrants	29	29	25	30
Give up nuclear weapons	22	8	35	27
Two of three parties agree				
Stricter laws on unions	57	79	58	36[a]
Cut spending to reduce inflation	53	64	37[a]	48
Withdraw troops from Northern Ireland	50	37[a]	52	64
Give more aid to Africa and Asia	44	39[a]	54	42[a]
Spend as needed to defend Falklands	39	58[a]	29	24
Take Britain out of Common Market	34	21	33	50[a]

[a] Party disagreeing with the majority.

Source: Author's analysis of Gallup Poll survey, 28 October 1983.

a sample of British voters are asked their views about a range of actions that government could take, a plurality of supporters for all three parties are in agreement on three-quarters of issues. Whichever party an individual supports, nearly everyone wants more money spent on the national health service, and more done to reduce environmental pollution and unemployment. The issues on which there are disagreements between groups of voters have political significance – for example, troops in Northern Ireland or nuclear weapons – but they are of limited scope. Interestingly, British voters are more likely to disagree about matters in the collective interest of the nation as a whole, such as defence policy or relations with foreign nations, than about matters that immediately relate to private benefits.

The substantial measure of cross-party agreement among voters sets limits upon the policies that politicians can endorse, and still compete successfully in elections. Since many divisions in the electorate cut across party lines, for example, on abortion or race relations, politicians have substantial leeway in electoral tactics and in government. For example, Ronald Reagan successfully appealed to what were called 'Reagan Democrats', people who normally voted Democratic but preferred Reagan's conservative views on many issues. Likewise, Margaret Thatcher has been able to appeal to the desire of working-class voters to better themselves materially while losing support among the educated middle class to the centre parties.

While an election casts a long shadow, it is an infrequent occurrence in the life of a government. During a Parliament, the governing party often falls behind the Opposition in popular favour in opinion polls, and it can lose safe seats in parliamentary by-elections. The popularity of a President can dip well below the 50 per cent level too (Rose, 1988a: chapter 13). An elected politician does not need to be popular all the time with all the electorate, but to be popular when it counts, that is, on election day. Measures unpopular midway through the life of a government, for example, a tax increase or a budget cut deemed necessary to make the economy work better, can even be in the self-interest of officeholders if their effects produce a positive response at the next general election.

The government is expected to worry about what the government should do each day. The most and the least that an ordinary person can do is to judge a government by its results. While most people have a limited interest in politics, the growth of government has brought government much closer to the lives of ordinary people by publicly providing many private benefits. An ordinary person has no difficulty in noticing when something goes wrong with the benefits that government is expected to provide, for it is much easier to evaluate social security payments or price changes at the supermarket than to follow abstruse arguments about new weapons systems or international monetary policy.

An election is a blunt instrument; it gives a rough verdict about who governs or, at least, which group of politicians should negotiate for office. An election outcome aggregates the views of millions in ways that leave politicians with lots of leeway to interpret what is in what might be called the 'stew pot' of public opinion. An election is not the occasion for negotiating a contract in which the mass of people delegate to elected officeholders responsibility for specified policies. The winning party has the authority to decide what the people ought to have wanted – and what people will get from the government that they have got. However, the authority of an elected government is limited by the prospect that it must put its claim to continue in office to the test of a future general election, in which its fate is decided by the votes of millions of ordinary people at the base of representative government.

Notes

1. This section draws heavily upon Richard Rose and Ian McAllister, *Voters Begin to Choose* (1986), especially chapter 7, which provides more detailed survey evidence.

2. For a discussion of Liberal and Alliance voting, see Rose and McAllister (1986: Table 7.4).

3. This is particularly true in Europe, where people are not accustomed to distinguish between the party they vote for and the party they identify with, and the ballot form usually prevents split-ticket voting. In America, with a widespread practice of split-ticket voting, it is possible to see a distinction between the two (cf. Budge et al., 1976; Dalton, 1988: 180ff).

4

Sending Signals to Governors

Power in this narrow sense is the priority of output over intake, the ability to talk instead of listen. In a sense, it is the ability to afford not to learn.

Karl W. Deutsch

The ship of state requires direction, if government is not to be perpetually adrift. Policymakers must monitor a vast flow of information about the environment of public policy; otherwise, they will not know what is going on. In a democracy ordinary people are meant to send the signals that direct how the ship of state ought to be steered. While information is a necessity in maintaining the large bureaucratic institutions of government, power is the ability to ignore directions that others are trying to give (Deutsch, 1963: 111). If government is to be about what ordinary people want, there must be signals that governors cannot ignore and to which they must respond.

When ordinary people want to claim the benefits of public policy or to express dissatisfaction, they must voice concerns in a form that policymakers understand. Ordinary people can send signals to governors in many different forms. Voting is the most obvious way to express a judgement about the overall performance of policymakers, but a ballot paper allows no scope to express views about particular public programmes. If a charge is made for the use of a public facility, then people can vote with their pocketbook, for example, paying a bus fare if they favour public transport or paying the cost of motoring to work. When laws specify clearly the criteria that entitle people to receive public services or claim a pension, it is sufficient to show a statutory entitlement. Sometimes ordinary people need help but do not know what should be done; they can then signal a demand for help by experts, for example, by going to see a doctor, who prescribes treatment.

Within government attention to signals differs according to office and responsibilities. Elected politicians are more concerned with indications about how the voting behaviour of ordinary people may change, whereas expert officials in public health concentrate attention upon statistics that could give warning of an epidemic or other public health difficulty. Low-level employees responsible for delivering services on a routine basis, such as clerks at the post office, look to rules and regulations to tell them what can and cannot be done. High-ranking bureaucrats and policymakers watch their budgets in order to know how much money they have in hand in a given fiscal year to finance the services that they provide.

Ordinary people can show their independence by withholding information too. The right of individuals to privacy is a constraint upon the desire of policymakers to monitor conditions in society. Ordinary people are free to move about a city or a nation, making census data less accurate, without regard for the impact of their movements upon urban or regional planners. Couples make decisions about having or not having children without informing education officials whose plans for primary schools are sensitive to fluctuations in birth rates. When policymakers ignore signals from ordinary people this is usually not intentional; it is because what goes on within the confined world of Westminster or the Washington Beltway is of more immediate concern than what happens in everyday life. The flow of information within public agencies consumes much of the attention of most public employees.

The pages that follow consider the network of communication between ordinary people and governors: who speaks to whom, about what, and by what means? The first section concentrates upon the asymmetries of position and interest that affect communication between ordinary people and policymakers. Four different signals important in giving direction to government are examined in the second section. Ordinary people can signal views through votes and by spending money in the market. Laws and expert values are signals of primary importance to policymakers, and ordinary people can make use of them too. The concluding section identifies the most important signals in the delivery of public services: these are not votes or money but laws and the values of experts.

Asymmetry of information

There is a great asymmetry in the network of political communication; policymakers are much more interested in giving direction to government than are ordinary people. While communication is a pervasive feature of everyday life, most of the time ordinary people are *not* concerned with political communication. The primary communication networks of ordinary people concern family, friends, workmates and others met in the routines of daily life. The signals that ordinary people send to government are often an incidental byproduct of actions taken without political intent, for example, a decision not to pay more for goods when prices are rising and inflation worries policymakers.

There is also an asymmetry in the subjects that ordinary people want to discuss and the concerns of high-level policymakers. At the top of government policymakers are concerned with macro-level problems, such as the rate of growth in the economy, allocating hundreds of billions of public expenditure, or maintaining national security. By contrast, ordinary people look to government for specific private benefits: total public expenditure is less immediately important than expenditure on local schools or roads, or the particular benefit that an unemployed person claims. Specific programmes, and the delivery of particular benefits on the doorstep or in the local community, are most likely to stimulate ordinary people to respond.

The growth of government and of population has made it more difficult for ordinary people to communicate with elected officials; the number of elected officials has actually *decreased* in relation to the electorate. The number of voters per Congressman is 40 times greater in the United States today than in the early nineteenth century, and the ratio of voters to Members of Parliament has increased by 8 times in the British House of Commons in the past century. The number of local governments and councillors has simultaneously been reduced. In the name of efficiency and economies of scale, many countries, including Britain and the United States, have amalgamated local authorities to create fewer and larger local authorities. In consequence, local government is no longer local; elected councillors are not well known and readily accessible to many of their electors (Rose, 1984: Tables 6.2, 6.3).

The public officials that ordinary people meet and talk with regularly are front-line employees who deliver services locally, such as a teacher, policeman, refuse collector or nurse. A study of the organization of public employment in the United States found that the median public office was not a mammoth building such as the Defense Department's Pentagon headquarters; it had less than half a dozen employees, like a small-town post office (cf. Goodsell, 1985: 112). As the human face of organizations, public officials behind a counter or a desk must listen to and respond to whatever ordinary people ask of government. As the hands and bodies of government, ordinary public employees deliver the mail, staff the armed forces, and provide the health and education services that people want from government. Without ' sense of direction provided by formal or informal signals, public officials would be directionless, not knowing what they ought to do.

In most Western nations, the largest number of public employees are teachers in schools, or health and hospital workers. Jobs advising a Prime Minister or President or conducting diplomacy are few by comparison with the labour-intensive task of delivering the private benefits of public services. In Britain there is an army of teachers; the total number of employees in public education is nearly three times that in the armed services and related defence work. In the United States the big battalions of government are not in the Pentagon but in local government, which is responsible for primary and secondary education. One in every six persons in the American workforce is a public employee and in Britain, even after intensive privatization efforts by the Thatcher Administration, more than one in four workers is in the public sector (Table 4.1; see also Rose, 1985b).

While political leaders spend a lot of time talking with each other in the national capital, ordinary employees of government spend a lot of time talking with and living like ordinary people at a distance from the national capital. The distance of service-delivery officials from policymakers creates difficulties in sending signals *within* government between those who have daily involvement with the delivery of public services and those whose responsibility it is to answer for these services in Parliament or Congress.

Politics is about the articulation of conflicting views, but the routine delivery of public services requires masses of relatively non-controversial information. The information needed to deliver everyday public services does not fit the stereotype of news used by journalists and highranking policymakers. Ordinary public employees are expected to accept without argument directives laid down in public laws and directives of policymakers. A hospital manager, for example, is immediately concerned with maintaining a 24-hour rota of nurses, juggling patients with

Table 4.1   *Public Employees by Programme (thousands)*

	Britain	USA
Social		
Education	1,538	6,750
Health	1,281	1,663
Social security, services	600	745
	3,419	9,158
Economy, public utilities		
Transport	401	681
Post office	177	664
Electricity, water, gas	311	325
Other trading enterprises	410	184
Roads, agriculture, recreation	161	1,273
	1,460	3,127
Essential defining concerns		
Defence	521	3,135
Police, fire	187	1,031
Tax administration	95	418
General administration	1,198	1,669
	2,001	6,253
Total (as percentage of all employed)	(27.9)	(18.3)

Source: Britain, 1985: Parry, 1987: Table 3. United States, 1981: Peters, 1985: Table 7.3.

different illnesses between beds in different wards, and repairing facilities that are temporarily out of action. Decisions taken by policymakers affect the way in which a hospital is administered, but these decisions are over the heads of workers in the hospitals and of ordinary patients in the wards. Routine rather than controversy is meant to characterize the public provision of private benefits.

Carrying out policies routinely requires public officials to know what they are looking for and what to do in response to signals. Routine operations of public services are directed by four major types of signals. Laws identify the criteria that entitle individuals to receive such private benefits as health care or a free education. The values of experts influence the particular way in which doctors treat patients, or teachers instruct pupils. Money affects whether a person receives a service, and it forces officials to ration services by queuing when there are not enough places for everyone, as in traffic queues at inadequate road intersections. Votes are important, for elected politicians do not want to challenge programmes that appear popular with the mass of the electorate; rightwing politicians do not repeal social programmes that are popular with voters of all parties, and radical politicians tone down their radical aspirations when seeking an electoral majority.

When public programmes are operating routinely, then elderly people receive their pension payments on time, hospitals use their facilities to heal patients, and teachers do what they are expected to do, give children instruction in the basics of reading, writing and arithmetic. As long as a public agency can provide the services that ordinary people expect from government and there is no controversy about the direction and level of services, then there is a 'non-political' equilibrium. A programme is in equilibrium insofar as the services provided are sufficient in quantity and quality to meet the claims of ordinary people.

An equilibrium can be disrupted by signals of dissatisfaction from ordinary people, if services deteriorate or are inadequate to meet rising expectations. The signals do not need to come from an election campaign; they can be a byproduct of experience with a service in use. Ordinary people will notice if they have to wait longer than expected to receive publicly funded hospital care, or if their children are taught in overcrowded classrooms or are failing to learn to read and write. A deterioration in the collection of rubbish will leave a visible mark in the neighbourhood. Low-level public officials may share the dissatisfaction of ordinary citizens, but their warnings may be discounted insofar as politicians view their demands as self-interested pleading for more resources, status and pay for themselves.

Policymakers monitoring programmes can notice problems that do not appear at the service-delivery level. Whereas an ordinary person is only concerned with a single instance of a service, policymakers are concerned with totals. For example, an elderly person thinks of what his or her pension will buy, whereas a policymaker will think of the total cost to government of millions of pensions. A rise in spending on pensions can create a disequilibrium by increasing satisfaction of ordinary people while increasing dissatisfaction among policymakers about the total cost of benefits. Policymakers and would-be policymakers can generate dissatisfaction as part of a process of promoting new programmes or changes in programmes. An Opposition party will argue that the actions of government are not properly directed, or that government is not spending enough on a given programme. Officeholders are in the ambiguous position of wanting credit for providing the best service possible, yet knowing that there will never be enough resources at hand to provide everything that could be asked.

Re-directing routine activities of a public sector organization is difficult, because procedural requirements tend to make bureaucracies respond slowly, and size slows down response time too. A politician may announce a new policy initiative with great publicity, but turning good intentions into benefits delivered on the doorstep is a time-consuming task. Likewise, an ordinary person may recognize deficiencies in a public programme delivered locally, but changing the course of public programmes is even more difficult from the underall position of an ordinary individual.

Comparing signals

While signals are cues to action, the meaning of these cues depends upon the framework within which policymakers interpret them. The information produced by an event, say, an air crash, may be interpreted by a Minister of Transport as threatening loss of popular confidence; by a doctor as requiring specialized emergency services; by a lawyer as indicating violations of safety regulations; and a budget official can see it as costing public money and being used to justify requests for increased public spending on air safety in future. In order to understand how signals affect public programmes we must compare the different ways in which they are interpreted.

Signals from laws. Laws are in principle the most compelling signal giving direction to government. Laws have the full force of the institutions of the state behind them; they are meant to be binding upon public officials as well as upon ordinary people, and there are sanctions or penalties that can be invoked if laws are violated. By definition bureaucrats are meant to carry out the law; no public official can systematically engage in illegal activity.

An ordinary person is best able to get what he or she wants from government when claiming a benefit for which there is an entitlement authorized by law. An older person can be confident of receiving a pension in response to his or her claim, for a social security act states the conditions entitling a person to a pension, such as reaching a stated age, and paying contributions to the social security fund. Laws require government to keep a register of each person's date of birth, and require employers to pay social security contributions that government must record as entitling a person to a pension in old age. Hence, the request of an ordinary retiree for a pension should trigger a series of bureaucratic responses producing the pension to which an individual is entitled. When laws confer entitlements, then an individual does not have to voice a demand; it is only necessary to claim what a person is entitled to.

The character of legislation has been changed by the growth of government, for the statute books no longer consist of laws laying down rules about what people cannot do or imposing obligations of citizenship. Today, most laws affecting individuals confer entitlements, laying down the terms on which an individual can receive a contingent benefit, such as a pension or a university education. Many laws are designed to secure an individual's wellbeing or property; for example, laws that set out how an individual can purchase a valid title to a house, or write a will that leaves a legacy as a person wishes (Rose, 1986).

Ordinary people do not want to have to go to court to claim treatment by a doctor or education for their children; they expect public officials to respond to requests for services to which they are entitled without requiring a court order. Laws are signals that direct public officials to do the will of a collective assembly of elected representatives, as expressed in an Act of Parliament or an Act of Congress.

Public officials are most likely to act as bureaucrats, that is, to have their response determined by laws, when they occupy relatively lowly positions within the hierarchy of an organization. Laws set parameters within which both elected officials and civil servants act. Since laws cannot prescribe action in every contingency, then directives may be provided by the elected officials or higher civil servants to fill in gaps in the law. The minister's directives are not meant to contradict but to complete the law by interpreting interstitial gaps in legislation (cf. Page, 1985).

The extent to which individuals can rely upon the law to determine what they receive from government is problematic; it depends upon characteristics of programmes and their delivery. If an individual wants to post a parcel, then rules and regulations can be specified about the conditions and cost of the post office delivering the parcel. However, if a person is interviewed by a social worker substantial discretion is left to the social worker to decide what problems people have and what actions public agencies might take to help them cope better with their problems.

A social security official processing pension claims with a computer is far more rulebound than the official of a state-owned railway assigned to market holiday travel by rail. While entitlements to benefits are necessary, they are not sufficient to give direction to public programmes.

Signals from expertise. An ordinary person can claim to know a lot about how he or she wants to live, but no one can claim to be an expert about all the things that are necessary to enjoy a good life, or about all the services that government contributes to a person's wellbeing. We do not want a doctor to treat a patient the way a spouse might prescribe a home remedy, or an airline safety inspector to look at a plane with no more knowledge of air safety than the average passenger has. Most public officials have some sort of expertise in delivering a particular public service; they are an authority about teaching or surgery or public safety.

The relationship of ordinary people and experts is meant to be complementary. An ordinary person knows what he or she wants done, but not how a goal may be achieved. For example, by buying a car a motorist signals a desire for roads; it is the responsibility of expert highway engineers to deal with the problems of building roads that people want to use. The scope for expertise is greater in government than in the market, for when programmes are mandated by law and the people benefiting are not charged for what they receive, then expert views are not subject to market signals from consumers.

The signals that give direction to experts are usually defined by professional associations rather than by laws or by the electorate (Dahl, 1970; Day and Klein, 1987). There is often a symbiotic relationship between professional associations and government. In the case of teachers, the state normally defines by law the educational qualifications required for teaching, and these laws are greatly influenced by the recommendations of teachers' associations and unions. The qualifications of teachers are not so much determined by what parents and pupils want but by what professional educational associations deem appropriate.

When expertise is learned on the job, it will not be formally codified; it will be expressed in standard operating procedures learned as part of informal role-socialization. These routines are derived by experience in dealing with problems in a practical way; they are the informal norms of such street-level bureaucrats as policemen or social workers, who have substantial discretion about what to do when delivering services for which they are responsible (Lipsky, 1980). Street-level bureaucrats may use this discretion to respond sensitively to individuals who demand help specific to circumstances that are not spelled out in laws. But experts can become so attentive to the guidelines of their profession that they pay less attention to signals for help coming from ordinary people whose wellbeing they are meant to serve.

In trying to give direction to experts, elected officials are also handicapped. Ignorance is the first handicap; a legislator or Cabinet member does not know how medical surgery is conducted, or how a water authority provides healthy water. Secondly, elected politicians usually have low status by comparison with many experts, and public opinion is more likely to trust a consensus of experts about a matter within their professional competence. Thirdly, experts are often not employed in government departments headed by an elected official. Specialist qualifications often place experts in organizations that are remote and insulated from direction by elected politicians. For example, a teacher will look to the school head or to professional associations for guidance rather than to elected politicians, and doctors can remain self-employed professionals even when most of their fees are paid from the public purse.

Results provide the best signal that experts are doing what ordinary people want. When ordinary people look to public agencies to provide good health care, a good education for their children, safe streets to walk on and motorways to drive on, they can judge the actions of experts by whether or not these results are produced.

Market signals. A defining attribute of a market is that individuals signal their preference for goods and services by paying a charge for what they want. However, most of the goods and services provided by government are not sold in the market place but given free of charge.

Ordinary people can appreciate the advantage of receiving benefits without paying for them. While people know that the benefits are not free – tax revenues are needed to finance the services – the link between taxes and benefits is obscure and indirect. A person who makes more use of public education or social security benefits does not thereby push up his or her personal tax bill. Many proponents of social policy argue that services are intrinsically better if entitlement is determined by the badge of citizenship rather than ability to pay. A sick person does not have to worry about finding the money to pay for treatment, and a teacher does not have to worry about whether pupils can afford to pay for a good education. The burden of financing social benefits is borne by the fisc, not the individual directly.

Economists and politicians on the right regard the absence of charges as a deficiency of public policies. Margaret Thatcher has repeatedly urged the civil service to be more 'businesslike', on the assumption that large private sector bureaucracies run more efficiently than public sector bureaucracies because of the profit motive. Since civil servants are not paid cash rewards for making profits, the new right assumes that they are inferior to businessmen in motivation. The absence of market charges is assumed to distort the supply and demand for the private benefits of public policy. In the absence of paying customers who can take their business elsewhere, public officials are expected to bias the provision of benefits toward what they and their expertise prefer rather than toward what is wanted by ordinary people – defined by the right as customers (cf. Seldon, 1977; Judge, 1980). Socialists argue the opposite, that the absence of the profit motive makes public sector firms better run.

There is one substantial, albeit neglected, field of public policy in which individuals do send signals by paying charges, that of nationalized industries and public utilities. By definition, public enterprises produce goods and services for sale to consumers, such as electricity, coal, rail transport, or postal services. Selling output makes public enterprises similar to private enterprises relying upon signals from the market to gauge supply and demand. But inasmuch as these enterprises are subject to state ownership and can draw upon tax revenue as well as market revenue, public enterprises differ from private ones.

Like private sector counterparts, public enterprises receive signals from the market about the demand for products at a given price; signals take the familiar form of information about how many people are paying a given price for a given service. This information is collected as part of routine operations in which public enterprises monitor their revenue as well as their expenditure. Enterprises can measure demand for their services by noting what percentage of electricity generating capacity is in use under different conditions, and what percentage of seats are occupied on different types of rail journeys.

The signals that ordinary people provide in their role as consumers can be used by public enterprises to evaluate the efficiency of their operations: the higher the utilization of productive capacity, the more efficient an enterprise is. They can also be used to adapt the provision of services to meet consumer preferences and when decisions are required about investing in future capacity, to assess future demand. Notwithstanding difficulties in evaluation that have some private sector parallels (cf. Millward and Parker, 1983), public enterprises can make use of market signals.

Public enterprises must respond to more than the market; otherwise the rationale for public ownership is merely historical and accidental. The fact that enterprises are owned by the state makes elected officials as well as business managers answerable for enterprises, and elected officials can influence what a particular enterprise does and whether or not it does or should make a profit. If a public service does not raise revenue to match its expenditure, thus operating at a loss, as in the case of bus transport, politicians can argue that bus transport is a social service for poor people without cars, and that it reduces the pressure of private motorists on roads at rush hour. In public enterprises unions may bargain for higher wages or to maintain employment above market levels on the grounds that this provides a social benefit to workers. In the absence of a conventional profit constraint, public officials may rely upon professional values in developing innovative products without regard to cost, for example, investing money in supersonic Concord planes that cost so much to develop that they cannot operate at a profit.

In the 1980s privatization became the buzz-word for dealing with public enterprises. Because these enterprises sell their services, it is in principle possible for them to operate as a normal business, selling services at a profit. The Thatcher Administration has pioneered the privatization of nationalized industries, selling in the market place shares in state-owned telephone, gas, airways, electricity and other companies. The logic is simple and clear: if public officials do not know what direction they wish to give to public enterprises, the enterprises are better operated in the market than subject to interference from politicians. However, the Acts of Parliament privatizing enterprises have shown that even a Thatcher government continues to believe that there are more-than-the-market considerations that affect most of these enterprises. Acts of Parliament that authorize privatization also lay down regulations affecting the ownership, pricing and the conduct of business by newly privatized firms, requirements that emphasize a public interest dimension absent in legislation about conventional profit-making companies (cf. Kay et al., 1986; Heald, 1986; Vickers and Yarrow, 1988; Rose, 1989b).

Signals from the electorate. As chapter 3 made clear, when ordinary people vote, they cannot and do not send clear, precise signals to policymakers. Public opinion surveys find that voters tend to have some general views about the goals of public policy, for example peace and prosperity, rather than detailed interest in programmes. Therefore, opinion surveys tend to avoid asking voters about the complex and often difficult choices that face policymakers; questions are instead asked about matters of principle that tend to give an over-simplified view of the problems facing government. Even in a referendum, voters do not choose policies, for the question that is voted on (and whether or not a referendum is held) is usually determined by national political leaders. While any popularly elected government can assert that it is doing what the people want since it is popularly elected, the statement is certain to be true only insofar as it is tautological.

Politicians are sensitive to the views of ordinary people in electoral situations, but this has little to do with giving direction to public programmes. It has a great deal to do with their own political careers, since an election defeat can terminate a Cabinet minister's career. When politicians look to the electorate, they are concerned with signals about their support by voters, and indications of personal popularity. However, popular assessments of personalities and party sympathies are not precise enough to constitute signals shaping the typical choices facing policymakers.

Politicians are likely to be expert in campaigning, using the mass media to cultivate favourable personal publicity to advance their ideas and their personal career in government. A politician who asks an awkward question in Parliament or issues a statement that is taken up by the television networks may not be interested in understanding the substance of the policy issue addressed. The immediate goal can be publicity for a self-employed, and therefore self-publicizing, politician. Politicians use the media to communicate en masse to ordinary people; they do not use the media to secure reports of what ordinary people may be thinking.

In the contemporary world it is misleading to think of government by the people as if there could be an assembly of citizens meeting in a market place to debate and decide issues, as in ancient Greece. Nor is it practical to think in terms of straight-line responsibilities for policies, with ordinary people sending signals of the programmes they want to elected representatives who then see that they are put into effect by public employees.

The good news is that there is more than one way to signal demands to government; the bad news is that the signals are not always in harmony. A directive to obey the law can lead to complaints about bureaucratic fixation on procedures and inflexibility in the face of substantive problems. A politician who is always looking for signals from opinion polls or the media will be accused of being more concerned with winning instant popularity than supporting good long-term programmes. Market signals can be criticized as introducing crass commercialism into what is meant to be a public service providing priceless benefits. Experts can be criticized for being more concerned with professional standards than with the people whom they are meant to serve.

The multiplicity of signals directing civil servants raises issues of political power as well as about communication. At the top of government, policymaking involves continuous interaction between a small number of elected politicians and high-ranking civil servants experienced in designing practical programmes more or less consistent with politicians' values and goals. Far from the national capital, specific services are delivered to individuals entitled to benefits. At that level, low-ranking public employees must act in ways that are consistent with the law and within budget constraints, but also consistent with their own professional values, and judgement. Ordinary people are not so concerned with which public officials make decisions; their primary concern is with the services that they receive on the doorstep.

The most important signals

Ordinary people and public officials are each concerned with a diversity of programmes and signals. A person does not expect to register views about roads or health care in the same way as registering concerns about foreign policy or claims for a social security benefit. The analytic question is: Which signal is dominant for a particular programme of government? Are all signals equally important or do signals differ in their significance from programme to programme?

To address these questions we need to identify the attributes of public programmes that cause signals to vary. By definition, market signals cannot be important in the non-market provision of education or policing. Nor would we expect signals from laws to be particularly important in military defence, for major national security issues rarely turn on matters of international law. The views of experts are likely to be important for services provided by specially trained professionals, such as health care; and the views of voters important when collective concerns are at stake, such as inflation.

Different programmes, different signals. Two related distinctions are fundamental in influencing the signals that give direction to particular programmes of government. We can first distinguish between programmes that are collective goods for society as a whole, or private goods that directly benefit individuals (Olson, 1965; Hirschman, 1970). Secondly, we can distinguish between public programmes for which charges are made to users, thus introducing market signals, and those programmes that are provided without the test of the market.

Classic concerns of the state are normally described as *collective* goods, because everyone in society is affected, the cost of providing the service is not altered by the number benefiting, and no charges can be made because individuals cannot be excluded from the programme's effects. Military defence is the textbook example of a collective good. Armed forces defend the whole of a nation's population, the cost is related to the perceived military threat, and ordinary people cannot be given a bill for national security as one would be asked to pay an electricity bill or have the service shut off. By definition, the market cannot provide signals for the provision of goods for which no charge can be levied. Macro-economic measures are collective goods too, for inflation affects the value of the money in everyone's pocket, and a recession or a boom in the economy will affect most people regardless of their occupation.

The pervasive significance of collective goods such as national security and law and order make them of widespread popular concern, and therefore subject to the views of the electorate. Ordinary people may not know much about technicalities, but order is preferred to disorder, and national security to insecurity. Ordinary people identify goals that policymakers are meant to pursue abroad through diplomacy, military action or a combination of the two, and at home by policing and encouraging voluntary compliance with laws. Within government, elected officials are much involved in classic concerns of diplomacy, defence, law and order and macro-economic issues. Politicians see these issues as important in themselves, and important electorally.

Experts also influence programmes concerned with collective goods, for elected officials want their actions to be effective. Diplomats maintain a stock of knowledge about countries and events in farflung parts of the globe, and career military officials are experts in mobilizing force to meet threats to security. In the face of crime or disorder at home, elected officials will turn to the police and the courts for advice about measures to stop a crime wave. When inflation threatens to erode the purchasing power of a nation's currency, economists are asked for their view about the most effective way of preventing inflation from destabilizing the economy. Because these policy areas are important, the final responsibility rests with elected officials not technocrats, but elected politicians risk failure if they ignore advice from experts (cf. Rose, 1987a).

Most of the programme outputs of government today are *private* goods and services, because they are provided to identifiable individuals and organizations. In the technical language of economics, even though education, health care and an old-age pension are produced by public agencies they are private benefits for particular individuals, just like food or clothes or sporting goods sold in shops. The cost of private goods tends to be proportionate to the number receiving the benefit; for example, the cost of pensions for the elderly is a function of the number of elderly people in society. Private goods can be financed by tax revenues and provided free of charge, as is normally the case with education, or charges can be made and those who do not pay a charge denied use, as is normally the case with public transport. While ordinary people are in a good position to evaluate the public provision of private benefits relevant to everyday life, the ability to signal satisfaction depends upon whether services are marketed or given free of charge.

Government can provide private benefits on market or non-market terms. By definition, private goods and services are marketable, for such services as education or health care can be sold, and individuals who do not pay would not receive these benefits. However, most private benefits produced by public programmes are, in fact, not marketed. There is no consistent rule about whether services are subject to market charges. For example, public libraries can normally be used without charge, whereas municipal swimming pools normally impose a charge for their use. In Italy a toll charge is levied for the use of inter-city motorways, whereas in Britain no charge is made and in the United States some motorways carry tolls and others are free of charge.

When charges are levied on the use of private goods, then market signals can indicate preferences. If people buying fuel for heating their homes prefer to heat with electricity or gas rather than coal or oil, this is signalled by changing patterns of consumption of products of public and private enterprises. If people prefer to travel by car rather than public transport, this will be signalled by a fall in the number of passengers paying for the use of buses. If people prefer to take holidays at distant places, then demand for charter flights from state-owned airlines will rise. If museum officials wonder what pictures visitors like most, they can examine the sale of postcard reproductions in the museum shop.

Laws cannot guarantee a profit in the balance sheets of public enterprises. Even if Parliament lays down that an enterprise should not run at a loss or make a profit on the money invested in it, there are some nationalized industries, such as coal and the railways, that chronically run at a loss. Elected officials provide the signals that justify lossmaking public enterprises. Elected officials decide what payments are made from general tax revenue to maintain services that cannot pay their way in conventional market terms. For example, maintaining rail or bus services in rural areas may be justified as a way of preventing social isolation of people living there or as a benefit maintained for fear of otherwise alienating voters in rural constituencies.

Many major social benefits produced by government are given away without charge, even though they could be sold in the market place. They are described as *merit* goods, and are deemed so desirable or meritorious that everyone should be legally entitled to receive them free of charge (Musgrave and Musgrave, 1980: 84f; cf. Walsh, 1987). It is a political decision whether private goods and services are merit goods. The fact that merit goods may be deemed necessities of modern life is not of itself an argument for their provision without charge. Housing, food and clothing are just as much necessities as education and health care; the former are sold in the market whereas the latter are not (cf. chapter 8).

Laws are of primary importance in directing the provision of merit goods. The benefits that individuals receive are not what an individual asks for but what he or she is entitled to under the law. Laws lay down the conditions in which individuals are (or are not) entitled to claim a benefit without payment. Laws also stipulate what individuals are entitled to receive (Weaver, 1988). Social security acts stipulate the formula for calculating income-maintenance grants, and education acts stipulate how many years of education a young person must have. Signals from laws are different from preferences of elected politicians and ordinary voters. Laws are public, fixed and binding commitments upon organizations. By contrast, the preferences of politicians and ordinary people can change momentarily, or alter with circumstances. An election result may change who governs but it does not change the laws that public officials are sworn to uphold. Laws are the rules that bureaucrats must follow, and elected officials must either repeal laws that they do not like, or see bureaucrats uphold laws inherited from previous administrations.

The values of experts do not affect merit goods that are calculated according to legal formulae for entitlements, such as the income-maintenance cash payments laid down in social security laws. Because there is little discretion in the payment of most of the money spent for social security benefits, very large sums are routinely paid out by low-status officials, or calculated by computer, without the intervention of judgements by expert professionals.

When merit goods involve experts providing education, health care or related social services, then their values are invariably important. While experts must follow laws defining who is entitled to receive services, the actual content of the service will be determined by judgements made according to their professional standards. This is most evident in the health service, where many decisions are taken by doctors with years of specialized training. Education is provided by teachers who must have professional training, and roads and bridges are built by engineers who must be qualified in civil engineering. The more remote those skills are from everyday knowledge, the greater the importance of expert values in determining the specific content of merit goods. As Day and Klein (1987: 56) note, an expert is not only someone trained by practice and skill; an expert is also an authority.

A fourfold classification of programmes according to whether they are collective or private and market or non-market identifies a seemingly deviant category, programmes concerned with goods that are both collective and marketed. Logically, this category appears an impossibility. However, debt interest payments may be considered as an example of this deviant category, for no one can exclude himself or herself from the obligation of paying taxes to fund the national deficit. Laws and markets direct the sums spent on debt interest. Laws obligate the government to pay interest on past debts. Although a newly elected government may think it has a free hand, it will be obligated to pay interest on borrowings by its predecessors. Markets signal the interest rate that the government must pay when it borrows money, and the fluctuation of interest rates up and down reflects market pressures.

Laws and expertise most important. Which signals are most important in giving direction to public programmes? To answer this question, we can turn to complementary sets of data about public employment and public expenditure. Public employment data are particularly relevant for service delivery, since they indicate how many officials are guided by particular types of signals. Public expenditure figures show how much money is affected by each type of signal. The measures are not identical, since two big-spending programmes, social security and debt interest, are not labour-intensive, and one labour-intensive group, public enterprises, does not make big claims on tax revenues because it relies primarily upon market revenues.

Health, education, and social services are principally influenced by signals from laws and expertise. Public enterprises respond primarily to markets and electoral opinion about subsidies. Electoral opinion and expert values are important in military defence, maintaining law and order and other collective goods. Debt interest reflects signals from the markets and involves a legal obligation for government to make public payments for private benefit. Since two types of signals influence most programmes, the total figures in Table 4.2 add up to more than 100 per cent. Although the total figures are rough-and-ready, the difference between signals is sufficiently great to show that the conventional idea of government by elected officials is inadequate, and attempts to apply market measures are even more deficient, for few employees and little money is directed by market signals.

Signals from laws and expertise tend to dominate the allocation of public resources; this is true whether public employment or expenditure is the measure. Laws are central because they specify conditions of entitlement for social security payments, education, and health care, defining groups entitled to receive social benefits from public employees, and the cash value of social security payments. Laws are more important in directing money than personnel, since laws and regulations routinize the payment of social security benefits, making it money-intensive without also being labour-intensive. Laws also bind government, most notably, in the commitment to pay interest on debts accumulated to finance public spending in the past. When budget officials classify more than five-sixths of public expenditure as 'uncontrollable' this does not mean that they do not understand what is happening to public funds. In fact, the expenditure

Table 4.2   *Relative Importance of Signals for Public Programmes (percentages)* [a]

	Important for	
Signals[b]	Public employees	Public expenditure
Laws	49	87
Expert values	85	68
Electoral opinion	46	13
Market charges	14	12

[a] Columns total to more than 100 per cent, since more than one signal can affect public employees or public expenditure.

[b]*Laws*: entitlements to private benefits; debt interest. *Expert values*: all private goods except social security; defence and other collective goods. *Electoral opinion*: defence, other collective goods, employees in public enterprises. *Market charges*: debt interest payments, employees in public enterprises.

Sources: Calculated from public employment data for Britain and USA reported in Table 4.1, and calculated from public expenditure data in Table 1.2.

is controlled; it is spent to finance entitlements that are laid down in statutes obligating public officials to provide private benefits for citizens (cf. Rose, 1986).

The values of experts also influence uncontrollable entitlement programmes. More than five-sixths of all public employees are directed at least in part by expert values. As public officials they are expected to be trained and skilled in a particular programme area. Teachers must be qualified teachers, nurses trained as nurses, and the armed forces train personnel to become expert in the use of force. Expertise is not quite so important in public expenditure, for social security payments are usually made with little scope for discretion by officials. The values of experts are impersonal, in the sense that there are published professional standards; there is substantial agreement about procedures among professional associations; and more or less routinized ways of training individuals to develop expert skills. Experiments with computerized expert systems are exploring the extent to which the 'rules of thumb' of experts, such as tax inspectors, can be codified for computerized administration and, incidentally, public inspection and approval of procedures in use (cf. Rose, 1987b: 167ff).

The significance of electoral opinion is often exaggerated in accounts of public policy. Preferences expressed by ordinary people in an opinion poll do not override laws controlling what government does, and the choice of governors at a general election has less immediate influence on the delivery of most public programmes than do the values of experts. The mass public can exert influence in areas of public policy where there is some scope for elected officials to make strategic decisions. Where collective goods are concerned, such as national security issues, elected officials can make decisions about defence and diplomacy, bearing in mind the views of the public whom they represent. The judgements that elected officials make about non-market subsidies for public enterprises reflect signals from ordinary people in their role as consumers of services of nationalized industries, and as taxpayers who must finance subsidies.

Market charges are important within the narrow field of public enterprises, signalling information about the demand for these atypical outputs of public policy. When demand grows, as in the case of state-owned telephone systems or electricity supply, then output will increase. When demand falls, as in state-owned railways and coal mines, production will contract. While money is an important signal for public enterprises they make a claim on public expenditure only when a subsidy is required to offset a shortfall of revenue as against expenditure. Market signals also affect the cost of interest payments on the public debt, which fluctuate in accord with international as well as national money markets. The very limited significance of markets in public policy follows from the fact that contemporary governments give priority to providing collective and private goods by *non*-market standards.

Consistent with popular preferences? Given the primary importance of signals from the law and from expertise, the crucial question is: To what extent is this consistent with popular choice?

Laws are established commitments of elected governments. Laws are only enacted if elected officeholders are prepared to propose them and they are endorsed by a popularly elected legislature. Laws are thus as much a reflection of the opinion of ordinary people as any other actions of representative political institutions. Laws are a protection against government by party patronage or clientelism, assuring equitable treatment by public officials, whether or not one has voted for the governing party or is a personal friend of an elected official. The ability of laws to regulate market conditions by marshalling political power against economic and institutional power collectively enables ordinary people to influence what is done by heads of major social institutions and sources of capital.

Because laws remain indefinitely in effect, they are an anchor against hasty or abrupt changes in public programmes. The inertia of the statute book gives great weight to the choices of past Parliaments and politicians. The fact that a law is not repealed can be regarded as evidence that old laws continue to have a broad base of public support. This is undoubtedly true of measures that direct the biggest programmes of government, such as social security, health care and education. Laws that today control programmes are not those that cause controversy in legislatures and courts. They are the old, widely understood and widely accepted laws that entitle ordinary people to many benefits of public policy. The statute book is not so much a catalogue of commands and prohibitions as it is a catalogue of benefits that public officials *must* provide ordinary people.

Expert values are more difficult to accommodate within conventional theories of representative government. When major political issues were posed in simple moral terms, then ordinary people could claim that their judgement of right and wrong was just as valid as that of anyone else. However, the growth of government and the growing complexity of life has made the role of experts very important in government. Many things that we take for granted, for example, an eye surgeon's ability to restore sight to a person with cataracts or a pilot's ability to fly a plane, require skills that the ordinary person does not possess. When a government sets up committees of elected officials to supervise the work of experts delivering health care or water supplies, elected officials find it difficult to know what to say (Day and Klein, 1987).

An ordinary person does not need to know how to do a job in order to judge whether it is properly done. A home-owner does not need to be a carpenter to tell whether a roof leaks, and a patient does not need to be a doctor to know if an operation has restored health. Ordinary people are not concerned with holding experts accountable as an auditor does, inspecting accounts to see that public money is spent honestly. Ordinary people are concerned with the public services that they receive; the more that expertise can be evaluated in terms of results at the point of delivery – for example, in education, health care or policing – the easier it is for an individual to judge its use. People will trust experts – as long as their activities help children to learn, promote the health of adults, and prevent crime in a neighbourhood.

For all their limitations, opinion surveys indicate that ordinary people tend to be satisfied with the way in which public employees provide their services. In both Britain and America ordinary people have the most confidence in what is closest to them, local government (see above, Table 1.3). When interviewers ask people about their encounters with public officials who provide services in local settings, the great majority believe that they are treated fairly, and with a reasonable degree of courtesy, efficiency and effectiveness (Katz et al., 1975).

If ordinary people do not like the way in which they are treated by public officials, or if laws are believed to be in need of change, then people can signal dissatisfaction to government in several ways. Votes can be used to express dissatisfaction with what elected officials are responsible for. Elected representatives then have to find ways of satisfying voters who can turn them out of office. The rise in incomes in the postwar era has also given ordinary people another means of signalling dissatisfaction with public services: people can vote with their pocketbook, buying a car to replace public with private transport, or buying a home rather than living in a publicly owned council house. As long as ordinary people are not wholly dependent upon public programmes, then they do not need to rely exclusively upon directing signals to government; they can look too to the market, or to their immediate family and friends, to secure what they want.

5

Economic Policies as Political Problems

Economy. From the Greek: house management.

Oxford English Dictionary

No President can have an economic policy; all his policies must be political.

Richard E. Neustadt

In the small world of ordinary people, the economy that matters most is the micro-economy. This view returns to the original Greek meaning of the word economy, which then referred to the management of household expenditure. This meaning still exists in the use of the term 'home economics' in some American schools and colleges to describe the teaching of the domestic skills needed to run a household, such as buying, preparing and cooking food, and running a household efficiently and with care.

Margaret Thatcher is fond of talking about economics in household metaphors drawn from childhood, when her father ran a family grocer's shop in the small town of Grantham. There everything was paid for in cash and you could easily see the connection between what happened in the shop and the wellbeing of her family, who lived above the shop. But those days are gone, for Margaret Thatcher has not lived in Grantham for more than forty years, and that corner shop is no longer in business. The people of Grantham and everywhere else in England have voted with their money against the low-volume high-price operation of the corner shop. Nowadays people prefer buying groceries from a large, impersonal cut-price supermarket chain.

Policymakers live in a world of macro-events, involving the nation as a whole and relations between countries and continents. From this perspective, the economy that counts most is the macro-economy. Instead of putting a hand in a jam jar used for household savings or consulting a credit card limit to see how much money there is to spend before the next pay day, policymakers consult forecasts of growth in the gross national product, for the total national product greatly affects the amount of tax revenue that government can collect. As international trade and monetary flows increase in scale, policymakers must also consider the state of the international economy when planning what the national government can spend.

The micro- and macro-economy are integrally linked, for the nation's macro-economic conditions reflect the sum total of decisions made at the household level and at equivalent decisions within firms; these decisions, in turn, are influenced by government's macro-economic policies on taxing, spending, the budget deficit and the money supply. Ordinary people who proclaim that government should not interfere with their business nonetheless are ready to prescribe how government ought to spend money to help their business and cut taxes without reducing the private benefits financed by the public purse.

The first responsibility of policymakers is not to manage the economy but to manage the political system, that is, to reconcile the many competing claims upon the resources of government advanced in the name of ordinary people by parties and pressure groups. Competing claims are meant to be reconciled in the budget process, in which money is assigned to competing programmes, for even though government now spends hundreds of billions, there is never enough money to go around. Another set of problems involves competing claims between the government's share of the national product and the share of the private sector. In principle, many disputes about the sharing out of resources could be resolved by a faster rate of economic growth that produced more resources for everyone. But the economy never grows fast enough to provide everything for everyone.

Policymakers must view economic problems through political lenses because economic problems raise questions of political goals and priorities. How much should government spend for collective benefits, such as military defence, and how much for private benefits, such as health care and education? How much should be raised in taxes to finance private benefits, and how much should be left in the hands of ordinary people to spend as they wish? In a modern mixed economy, in which the public and private sectors are interdependent, policymakers must also address macro-economic questions about economic growth, inflation and unemployment. While the abstractions of macro-economics may be unfamiliar or incomprehensible to ordinary people, the results are visible in the household in terms of a secure income (or not), increased prosperity (or not), and stable prices (or inflation).

So closely integrated are micro- and macro-economic activities that we must understand the top-down view that policymakers have in order to understand the framework within which ordinary people make micro-level choices about managing household finances. The first part of this chapter describes the politics of appraising economic policies in an effort to approach simultaneously all four goals in the magic square of the economy. Since politics is about conflicting opinions, the second section considers the importance of consensus or dissensus among economists and among policymakers. Given the pervasiveness of disagreements about economic policies, the concluding section concentrates upon reconciling competing views without consensus. Subsequent chapters then focus upon the ordinary person's underall view of the economy.

Circling the magic square; the political appraisal of economic policies

Ordinary people find it easier to identify the ends of economic policy than the means, and this is consistent with the idea of representative government. Ordinary people can identify the goals of the economy and leave policymakers to find the programmes appropriate to secure these ends. In Germany a law formally obligates the government to direct its economic measures toward four goals: stable prices, full employment, economic growth, and a stable currency in international trade. The four goals are said to constitute a magic square (*magisches Viereck*). But logically, it is impossible to move in four directions at once.

While policymakers may agree about the desirability of the four goals, they lack the magic necessary to achieve all of them simultaneously. One of the responsibilities of policymakers is to select priorities. To make economic growth the first goal does not mean that policymakers are indifferent to inflation, but that price stability has a lower priority. To give stable prices the first priority does not mean that unemployment is regarded as unimportant; it is simply given a lower priority. We can thus speak of policymakers trading off goals, that is, preparing to accept a shortfall in pursuit of one goal, e.g. a rising rate of inflation, as the price of success in another, e.g. a falling rate of unemployment. The art of giving political direction to the economy is to know when to switch priorities between four sometimes conflicting ends. Instead of pursuing all four goals with equal commitment at the same time, policymakers are continuously circling the magic square.

Ordinary people shift economic priorities too, in the light of the performance of the economy. Events have belied the assumption of some social scientists that ordinary people always expect government to provide more of everything (cf. Brittan, 1975). Ordinary people learn from experience that government can fail to do what they want, and what policymakers want. When the world went into recession in the mid-1970s, people no longer expected the economy to continue growing at a rate that would promise continuously rising prosperity. When prices started rising rapidly, doing something about inflation became a major popular goal. When unemployment subsequently started rising, doing something about unemployment became a major priority. Ironically, the less success that government has in tackling a problem, the more ordinary people are likely to conclude that the difficulty is beyond the power of government to correct. For example, Margaret Thatcher has been able to win re-election in

Britain with unemployment above 10 per cent, whereas two decades ago social scientists and policymakers alike assumed that an unemployment rate of 5 per cent would doom the governing party to electoral defeat (cf. Alt, 1979).

Priorities of economists. To define economics simply as 'what economists do' says nothing about the way in which economists view the economy. It also implies that the activity of economists is different from that of politicians, as it is certainly different from that of ordinary people trying to manage a household.

The evolution of economics in the past two centuries has led it away from a concern with political economy and moral science, interests of Adam Smith, who helped found the subject in the eighteenth century. It has also led away from the concerns of Karl Marx, who generalized a theory of the pervasive power of economic capital in the nineteenth century. While government has become more and more involved in giving direction to the economy, economists have tended to abandon their traditional concern with the actual workings of political economy in favour of mathematical economics. In the words of a leading Swedish economist, Assar Lindbeck (1976), economists now treat politicians as 'exogenous' variables, that is, influences beyond the horizon of their concern. The Dutch Nobel laureate Jan Tinbergen argued for separating the work of economists as 'information animals' specializing in knowledge of how the economy works from that of politicians as 'decision animals', specializing in the choice of societal priorities and goals (Kaysen, 1969: 137ff). Formal theories of the economy are now developed on the basis of very great simplifications of the world as it actually is; abstract economic models tend to exclude social and political phenomena. In the words of the distinguished Cambridge theorist Frank Hahn (1985), economic theories now provide 'too spare a description of the constraints under which agents act in society'.

Leaving politics out makes it much easier to achieve the solution of theoretical problems by analysing alternative policies in the closed world of a computer model, in which the most important feature is the *ceteris paribus* clause, that is, the assumption that everything omitted from the model remains the same. Given the assumptions of a particular economic theory, a computerized model can then calculate what would happen if policymakers followed a given course of action – if economic outcomes were determined exactly as in the world of theory. The divorce between the practice of economic theory and the concerns of policymakers responsible for the economy produces a great mismatch in the supply and demand for economic policies.

Policymakers want programmes that can be implemented by government and achieve a predictable positive impact upon national and household economies. Implementation involves political institutions that are normally excluded from economic theories. For example, in the 1970s a number of British economists recommended fighting inflation by measures that required agreement between unions and businessmen on wage and price increases. As the corporatist institutions required to secure such agreement did not exist, the policy collapsed. In the 1980s a number of international economists recommended resolving the unstable relationship between the dollar and other major currencies by co-ordinating American, Japanese, German, British and French monetary and fiscal policies. However, the political institutions to secure co-ordinated international action are lacking, especially in Washington, which has been a prime cause of international monetary instability (cf. Tanzi, 1988).

A predictable impact is usually uncertain, because the world in which policymakers and ordinary people live is far more complex than an abstract economic model. There are many more potential influences upon economic conditions than even a complex computerized model allows for, and there is no assurance that conditions will stand still in reality just because they are held constant in the computer. Insofar as economics is a policy science, it is a science like medicine rather than electrical engineering. Whereas an electrical engineer thinks in terms of certainties, a doctor thinks in terms of probabilities. A doctor's prescription, like the policy recommendation of an economist, is intended to make conditions better, and there is certainly no intent to make them worse. But if asked to forecast the effectiveness of a prescription, a doctor will speak in terms of more or less vague probabilities rather than make a certain prediction. Economists do the same.

Priorities of policymakers. Political desirability is the first concern of politicians, for elected officials want to do what will be popular with ordinary people. Because the goals of the magic square all appear desirable, collectively they are in competition, and political disagreements arise about which goal should have first priority. Once priorities are settled, policymakers can also disagree about which programmes are most likely to achieve an agreed goal, and ordinary people can disagree about which group of policymakers is most likely to be effective in achieving a generally desired economic goal.

Politicians evaluate economic policies not by economic analysis but by a political calculus which imposes constraints upon the acceptability of economic proposals. In the words of an experienced Washington economist (Sawhill, 1986: 109), 'Politics is what an administration puts off limits because of its perception about what the electorate will support, and ideology is what it considers non-negotiable because of its own philosophical predilections.'

Within government, economists are expert advisers, on tap but not on top. Knowledge is an asset, but it confers neither legitimacy nor power. Policymakers want *relevant* information and advice, not knowledge for its own sake. The first task of economic advisers in the corridors of power is to learn how to apply theoretical knowledge to concrete problems of government, where many factors that are treated as of no concern in theory become very important in practice, such as the votes of Congressmen or actions by trade union officials. The second task is to market economic analysis to policymakers. In order to be effective as an adviser, an economist must communicate with policymakers in language that they can understand. An inability to communicate will mean that economic advice is ignored; hence, skill in economic journalism is a positive asset in a world in which policymakers want advice quickly and clearly (cf. Nelson, 1987; Hargrove and Morley, 1984).

A description of the relation between politicians and economists as an arms-length relation between customer and contractor, with politicians setting goals and economists supplying the policies necessary to achieve them, is naive. The goals of government reflect political will, but they cannot be realized independently of the expertise of non-elected officials. The formulation of policies, and particularly of economic policies, requires the integration of political and expert skills (Rose, 1987a).

From the viewpoint of the ordinary individual, the good news is that responsibility for the direction of the economy remains in the hands of politicians who can be made to pay at the polls for their mistakes, rather than being in the hands of technocratic economists who may 'play' with an economy without being politically accountable. The bad news is that economists lack theories robust enough to produce effective policy prescriptions, whenever policymakers turn to them for help in achieving effective means to such generally desired economic goals as full employment, stable prices and economic growth. Nor can policymakers be confident that their own common sense or corner shop reasoning is sufficient to keep the magic square in equilibrium.

Consensus or dissensus in the political economy?

The term political economy implies appraising public policies by the standards of both politics and economics. When government becomes involved in the economy, decisionmakers must make a political appraisal, in which competing ideas are evaluated in the light of the values and goals of the elected government. But politicians cannot simply make decisions on grounds of popularity or political will; their actions must also be effective. Joint appraisal poses two different but complementary questions about a programme: Is it politically desirable? Is it likely to be effective in the economy?

Ordinary people want government to follow policies that are both desirable and effective. So do policymakers. But this is much easier to do when there is a consensus among policymakers about the goals and priorities of economic policy. It also assumes that there is a consensus among economists about effective measures to achieve these priorities. Not least, it assumes that a consensus of policymakers will be in harmony with a consensus of economists.

But consensus about economic problems cannot be taken for granted. We should not be surprised to find politicians disagreeing, for differences about political values and beliefs can lead to conflicts about priorities, such as the guns vs. butter debate that perennially crops up in America. Disagreements can also arise about the relative priority of different economic objectives, such as debates between British politicians about the priority to be given to fighting inflation or unemployment. Economists too can collectively register dissensus. While each model may be internally logical, the assumptions of different models may contradict each other. Models can differ in what they include, and what is left out for others to worry about. Within the field of macro-economic policy, different priorities may be given to particular objectives in the magic square, and there are major differences between Keynesian and monetarist models about how the economy works and policies that will make the economy work better.

When economic problems arise, policymakers can face any of four possible situations, depending upon whether there is consensus or dissensus among economists or among politicians.

1　*Choice with internal consensus.* When there is consensus about a programme of action among politicians and among economists – and both appraisals are in agreement – then a policy is doubly desirable, being attractive to politicians and effective according to economists (Figure 5.1). In a complementary manner, if politicians agree that a measure is undesirable and economists agree that it is ineffective, it will be rejected. Doubly desirable policies are handled by routines, far from the political spotlight, since there is no controversy and no need for continuous monitoring, since effectiveness is taken for granted. Policies regarded as doubly undesirable disappear from the political agenda, for no one considers them worth thinking about.

When politicians and economists agree among themselves but disagree with each other, then there is a test of which values prevail. A policy agreed as politically desirable but regarded as ineffective by nearly all economists can be described as economically dubious. Alternatively, a policy may be politically awkward, being considered effective by economists but undesirable by politicians (Figure 5.1). In such circumstances, whose judgement will prevail?

Endorsement of an economic policy by politicians is a necessary condition of government action. The choice of public policies rests with those who hold the highest offices of state. In addition to having the legal

Economic consensus

Political consensus	Effective	Ineffective
Desirable	DOUBLY DESIRABLE	ECONOMICALLY DUBIOUS
Undesirable	POLITICALLY AWKWARD	DOUBLY UNDESIRABLE

Figure 5.1   *Choice with Complete Consensus*

authority to commit the government, election gives politicians popular legitimacy, an important consideration when the co-operation of many different groups within society is needed to implement an economic policy effectively. Endorsement by economists is neither a necessary nor a sufficient condition for action. The expert opinions expressed by economists are no more and no less than advice.

Public choice economists have a theory to predict why a government ought to endorse economically dubious policies and reject policies that are politically awkward. If politicians are conceived as 'egoistic, rational utility maximizers' (Mueller, 1979: 1), then the stronger their egoistic interest in doing what is politically desirable, the less attention will be paid to economists' doubts. A politically awkward policy will almost certainly be vetoed by politicians, notwithstanding its economic potential, for the cost of adopting the policy is certain and immediate to politicians, whereas benefits are hypothetical and diffuse.

2   *Choice without political consensus.* If politics is defined as the articulation and reconciliation of conflicting views about the activities of government, then consensus is lacking by definition. Politicians will be expected to contest what should be done about every economic issue; differences of opinion can arise about priorities between goals, or about means to achieve a desired objective. If economics is conceived as a science, then economists may register a scientific consensus about the effectiveness of programmes disputed between politicians (Figure 5.2).

When politicians disagree, the influence of a consensus of economists will depend upon lines of political division. In an ideal-type parliamentary system, division can be expected between a disciplined

Economic consensus

Political appraisal	Effective	Ineffective
Contested desirability	ECONOMICALLY EFFECTIVE	ECONOMICALLY INEFFECTIVE

Figure 5.2   *Choice without Political Consensus*

and united governing party, and a disciplined and united opposition. In such circumstances, disagreement in Parliament is consistent with consensus among decisionmakers in Cabinet. In such circumstances, we would expect the government of the day to proceed as in Figure 5.1, endorsing a consensus view of economists when it is in harmony with consensus in the governing party, and rejecting it when it is not.

But many governments are coalitions of parties and factions. In the American system of checks and balances, the President is authorized to appoint a Council of Economic Advisers to proffer expert advice; simultaneously, Congress has a head of the Congressional Budget Office to offer alternative, and sometimes conflicting, judgements. For work on pure theory the Dutch economist Jan Tinbergen could become a Nobel laureate for his contribution to central economic planning. However, his country, the Netherlands, is a textbook example of a political system in which there are chronic disagreements in coalition governments. Even in the British system of single-party government, economic expertise cannot resolve intense political divisions within a governing party.

When major disagreements occur within government, they may be sufficiently strong to prevent any action being taken because of a political judgement that action would split the party or parties in power. In Washington, divisions within government are likely to threaten defeat in Congress, thus dooming a proposal that carries the consensus endorsement of economists. In a disciplined parliamentary system, divisions within government can be overridden by party whips, and if disagreements are not strong or there are strong pressures for action, then a consensus about economic effectiveness may even be decisive.

3   *Choice without economic consensus.* Is it reasonable to expect consensus among economists about an issue of public policy? The answer is often no (Figure 5.3). Dissensus at the theoretical level is often evident in the assumptions, the focus, and the outputs of abstract economic models. The extent of disagreement rises as attention is shifted

Economic assessment

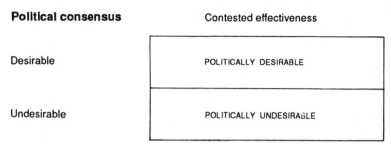

Figure 5.3 *Choice without Economic Consensus*

to prescribing public programmes that are affected by many conditions that are excluded from logically coherent but narrowly defined economic models. Public policy requires accepting the inherent messiness of the political process. Economists disagree about the desirability or necessity of moving from the world of models to the world of muddles (contrast Hahn, 1985 with Leontief, 1985).

The production of economic advice for policymakers is likely to reflect dissensus in at least four significant ways. First of all, there is likely to be disagreement about whether economics has definite guidance to offer for a given issue of concern to ordinary people. The cautious pace of the academy and the desire to hedge any conclusion with qualifications and pleas for more research is unsuited to the world of government, where busy policymakers want conclusions. Demand is sure to call forth supply. When an academic economist working in Washington told the Chairman of the President's Council of Economic Advisers that he couldn't supply a memorandum about a large, complex topic to meet an immediate White House deadline, the experienced policy adviser replied: 'If we don't, someone else will' (quoted in Allen, 1977: 52).

A second source of controversy is the appropriate economic context in which to analyse a problem. A monetary economist is likely to see a recession as a problem on the supply side, whereas a Keynesian is likely to see it as a problem of inadequate demand. Unemployment may be perceived as a micro-economic problem requiring special labour market policies, or as evidence of macro-economic shortcomings. A middle-of-the-road economist may complicate a policymaker's life further by suggesting that a variety of apparently conflicting theories are each correct in part.

Thirdly, economists can disagree about policies for dealing with a given problem. Theories of interest groups and of the sociology of knowledge predict that an economist is likely to prescribe a solution that is consistent with his own specialized training and personal experience and values. The Nobel Prize Committee in Economics often faces political problems when deciding to whom to award its valued prize, for leading figures in different schools disagree on lines that an ordinary policymaker would see as left vs. right political differences. With characteristic Swedish neutrality, the committee has awarded the laurels to such pro-government economists as Gunnar Myrdal, James Meade and James Tobin, and such anti-government economists as Friedrich von Hayek, Milton Friedman and James M. Buchanan.

Last and not least, economists differ in the extent to which they wish to become public advocates for particular programmes and politicians. Carl Kaysen (1969: 151), an economist with experience in the Kennedy and Johnson White House, notes: 'A political decision-maker finds the ability of a technical adviser to assist in the tasks of advocacy, which are indispensable to effect changes, an important element of his usefulness.' Once an economic adviser publicly commits himself to a party and to a policy, it is difficult for an individual to change his or her mind without losing face, resigning office, or both. Hence, economists with access to politicians can be forced to advocate policies on party grounds that are contested by other economists outside government, who are free to change their minds as often as they wish.

A plethora of conflicting views can be an advantage to politicians, for disagreements between economists neutralize their advice. As long as politicians in government agree about the policy that they regard as desirable, the political choice is easy: policies (and economists) that are politically undesirable can be rejected, and measures that are politically desirable can be chosen.

4   *Pervasive dissensus.* When both politicians and economists disagree among themselves, the result is pervasive dissensus (Figure 5.4). If sophisticated Keynesian and monetarist economists disagree with each other, then each group may find themselves with strange bedfellows, the Keynesians linked with politicians in favour of big-spending programmes without constraint, and monetarists aligned with politicians who see themselves as practical men of affairs, not economic theorists. Alliances between politicians and economists are forged by agreement about what is to be done rather than about why an action should be taken. Politics thus unites what professions divide.

Given the uncertainty generated by pervasive dissensus, there are good reasons for a politician to proceed by making serial, disjointed, and incremental decisions. The serial nature of economic policymaking is an advantage, enabling a politician facing conflicting advice to proceed by trial and error methods, altering policies in response to changes in political pressure, intellectual fashions or economic conditions (cf. Braybrooke and Lindblom, 1963). If a given policy does not appear to produce desired results, it can be replaced by another. However desirable disjointed policymaking may be on political grounds, its economic

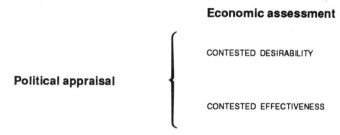

Figure 5.4　*Choice with Complete Dissensus*

effects may be negative, insofar as many serial choices cumulatively cancel out, if one day a policy is chosen to boost employment, and the next day anti-inflationary measures are endorsed that incidentally boost unemployment.

Elected politicians have little difficulty in accepting disagreements among economists about the course of public policy. Politicians are accustomed to controversy, and may even be suspicious of a consensus of economists, fearing that agreement exists only because significant political concerns have been omitted from their calculations. For example, economists may agree that it would be desirable for government to stop allowing home-owners to reduce their taxes by deducting mortgage interest payments from their income prior to calculating tax. But politicians are likely to agree that this proposal makes no political sense, for it would mean taking an established private benefit away from millions of ordinary people. When big issues stir up pervasive controversy economists can be sure to become involved in the policy process, not as neutral experts but as participants in a political controversy.

Combining perspectives?

The predisposition of any professional is to appraise problems by the standards of his or her profession – and to ignore others. Politicians ignore important issues of economic theory, and many uncomfortable results of applied economic research. Whatever a politician's will or rhetorical skill, in order to become a successful policymaker he or she must also learn to identify effective policies. Given criteria about what is and is not politically desirable, a politician needs the advice of expert economists who have sympathy with these goals, and are also expert in developing effective programmes.

An economist developing a theoretically elegant model is unconcerned with the mere intervening variables of politics and institutions. It is far easier to solve a set of equations than to worry about issues of political desirability or institutional implementation. An economist may enter public service with the belief that he or she is a neutral expert, but quickly learn that this is not enough to be effective in the policy process. Some economists become partisan advocates of efficiency, asking questions about costs and benefits and suggesting ways of using public resources to achieve goals more easily and effectively. But recommendations to make government more efficient as economists see the world may reveal that politicians do not define efficiency as they do. Public policies that distort the market, for example, agricultural subsidies, impose costs upon the nation as a whole, but they can also be a politically efficient way of providing private benefits for a particular interest group.

In the micro-polity and micro-economy of the household, ordinary people frequently face the need to make decisions that combine economic and political concerns. While members of a family are not joined together like a Cabinet or party leaders, their relationships have a political dimension. Decisions must be made about spending a limited amount of household income in ways that are regarded as fair and acceptable to all the members of the family. The object of the family budget is not to maximize efficiency or profit, but to maintain consensus as well as material satisfactions.

Maintaining consensus is a primary political goal of policymakers too, and in a democracy this requires governors to satisfy a large number of ordinary people. Moreover, ordinary people can judge satisfaction in the light of the private benefits that they receive from public agencies. The taxes needed to finance these benefits are also of concern to ordinary people. Although the advice of economists can be helpful in assessing the complexities of the national and international economy, when decisions have to be made about priorities, policymakers need to consider the impact of actions upon the household economy. If policies that appear attractive in theory fail in practice, then ordinary people can use their votes to eject from office politicians who become so enmeshed in technical macro-economic calculations that they forget the micro-political impact of their actions in the lives of ordinary people.

6

Paying Taxes Vicariously

Question to Willie Sutton: Why do you rob banks?
Answer: Because that's where the money is.

Ordinary people need money, but government needs money too. Politicians do not impose taxes because they like doing so; taxes are levied for the same reason that a bank robber such as Willie Sutton stole from banks: because that is where the money is. Taxation is necessary so that government can provide the beneficial goods and services that people expect from government. It is a means to an end, a cost necessary to finance public benefits. The object of politicians is to maximize tax revenue while minimizing political costs; the object of ordinary people is to maximize benefits while minimizing the costs of taxation (Rose, 1985c). Although taxes are the dues of citizenship, these dues are not paid voluntarily; that is why government relies upon tax handles that make ordinary people pay their taxes vicariously.

To finance the benefits of public policy, government must annually collect hundreds of billions in tax revenue without killing the goose that is meant to lay the golden egg, a growing economy, or stimulating a tax revolt that costs the governing party office. In an era of big government, the fisc must raise more than a trillion dollars in America, and more than £160 billion in Britain. In Britain taxation is equivalent to two-fifths of the national product and in the United States, more than 30 per cent of the national product. The average European nation claims more than 43 per cent of the national product in taxation.

Because of inflation, taxes have risen by thousands of per cent in the postwar era. In 1946 taxation in Britain was equivalent to less than £70 per person; by 1988 taxation averaged more than £3,000 for every man, woman and child in the country. In the United States in 1946 all levels of government collected taxes equivalent to an average of about $350 per person. By 1986 the total tax take was more than $7,000. While economists can deflate money values to control for the effect of inflation, reducing current taxes to 1946 price levels for purposes of comparing real or constant value sums, ordinary people cannot make such sophisticated adjustments. Most people have a degree of money illusion, that is, a belief that a £5 note or a $10 bill ought to have a stable value. Politicians who try to explain that taxes are higher because of inflation may simply prompt complaints about inflation too!

Collecting the dues of citizenship is a political and an administrative challenge. It is a political test of the willingness of ordinary people to accept the obligations of citizenship as a corollary of accepting the benefits of public policy. Rejection of these obligations does not require a person to take to the streets or to the mountains. In order to stage a so-called tax revolt an ordinary person can vote against the government, or vote with his or her pocketbook, turning to the unofficial shadow economy to evade taxes (see chapter 7).

For most of the era since 1945 government could finance 'policy without pain' (Heclo, 1981: 397); a high rate of economic growth led to a bigger and bigger national product. If taxation remained a constant percentage of the national product, government was sure to get more money, and the take-home pay of ordinary workers was sure to rise too. In fact, government usually took a disproportionate amount of the fiscal dividend of economic growth, while take-home pay rose steadily too. Economics was considered a joyful not a dismal science, promoting treble affluence – for ordinary people, for public policies, and for society as a whole.

Since the oil price shock of 1973 and the subsequent world recession, elected politicians and ordinary people have become conscious of the painful side of public finance, expressed in the motto: There is no such thing as a free lunch. Ironically, Americans have reacted most strongly against taxation, even though taxation in the United States is very low by comparison with most advanced industrial societies (Rose, 1989). Although nominally a conservative, President Ronald Reagan preferred tax cuts and budget deficits to maintaining a balanced budget or resolving international monetary problems by raising taxes, and George Bush won election in 1988 by promising: No tax increases. In Britain high taxes cut the take-home pay of workers whose earnings were already being squeezed by anti-inflationary wages policies. The Thatcher government elected in 1979 first cut the public deficit; and after the economy had grown sufficiently, introduced major tax cuts.

To understand how government collects the dues of citizenship effectively we must understand the tax handles that government turns in order to raise revenue. The first section of this chapter explains how tax laws and administration are designed so that most taxes are paid vicariously. A person does not normally pay the tax collector directly; instead, an employer or business firm is legally responsible for turning over income and sales taxes to revenue collectors. When taxes are collected vicariously, people pay them involuntarily. The second section draws a balance sheet showing what the average family pays in taxes, and what it receives back in benefits. While the sums paid in and paid out are large, the net effect is small, because of the churning of revenue between public and private purses. The concluding section asks: What do ordinary people think about the combination of taxes and benefits of public policy? Popular attitudes toward taxes are not determined by the level of taxes; highly taxed Swedes are far readier to accept their taxes than are Americans, because Swedes also receive more benefits from public policies.

Multiple dues of citizenship

Nobody likes to pay taxes but taxes are a necessity of big government. Government first resolves the problem by collecting taxes in a multiplicity of different ways; the total tax payments of a household are not presented in a single bill. Secondly, organizations rather than individuals are responsible for paying most tax revenue into the fisc, a handy Greek and Latin word referring to the jars in which tax revenues were once kept. It is far easier and certain to collect income tax and social security contributions from a large organization than to do so from their individual employees. While economists assume that ultimately the cost of taxation rests upon individual members of society, public officials prefer a system in which ordinary people pay taxes vicariously.

The principal determinants of tax revenue are few but diverse: laws, public administration and the economy. Tax revenue is not determined by just one of these three elements; it results from the interaction of all of them (Rose and Karran, 1987: chapter 3). The basic logic can be stated algebraically: tax revenue is a function of Laws (L), Administration (A), and Economic Activity (E).

$$\text{Tax revenue} = f(L, A, E)$$

The amount of tax collected is first a function of laws defining the tax rate (e.g. a 15 per cent rate of Value Added Tax) and the tax base (the sales subject to or exempt from VAT). Secondly, revenue depends upon the administrative effectiveness with which a tax is administered, that is, the percentage of money legally due that is actually paid into the fisc. The state of the economy is also important, for the larger the national product that is the ultimate base of taxes, the more revenue a given rate will yield to the fisc.

Many forms of taxation. A description of taxation in aggregate masks the dozens of different ways in which government collects taxes. There are taxes on income and taxes on wealth; taxes on spending and taxes on savings; the living are taxed on what they earn and spend, and the dead on what they leave behind; impersonal corporations are taxed as well as individual people; and buildings and intangible services are taxed as well as family earnings.

Britain levies more than 40 different taxes on things ranging from dogs to corporate profits. In the United States there are more than 80 different taxes, including state and local government as well as the federal government. In France, more than 137 different taxes are recorded. The greater the number of taxes, the smaller the bite that any one tax can take. A suspicious person might think that the greater the number of taxes, the higher the level of taxation, as many small bites can add up to a big meal. In fact, there is no significant correlation between the number of taxes in use in a country and the relative size of the total tax bill (Rose, 1985c: 296).

Three taxes – income tax, social security and sales taxes – together account for more than four-fifths of total tax revenue in the average advanced industrial nation. In Britain personal income tax accounts for more than one-quarter of tax revenue, and in the United States, personal income taxes account for 36 per cent. Continental European countries that have difficulty in collecting income tax compensate by imposing very high social security taxes. Social security taxes are atypical; employees want this tax to be paid to qualify them for benefits, and most of the cost is borne by employers. In most European countries a Value Added Tax on the sale of goods and services raises at least a quarter of public revenue. The United States is unusual in not having a national sales tax, and the sales taxes levied by state and local government raise proportionately less money than sales taxes levied by leftwing and rightwing governments throughout Europe.

The average British adult pays at least four different taxes, vicariously or directly (Table 6.1). Value Added Tax is the most comprehensive tax, for it affects everyone who spends money. More than nine-tenths of persons in paid employment are subject to income tax; in addition, workers must pay national insurance contributions for social security benefits. The 70 per cent of households owning a car must pay an annual tax to license it for road use, and pay tax every time the petrol tank is filled. Anyone who drinks beer, wine or spirits also pays a tax, the amount depending upon what is drunk, for the tax varies with alcoholic content. Taxes on tobacco and on capital gains from stocks and shares are minority levies, affecting only a limited proportion of the adult population.

The taxes that yield the most revenue to the fisc are those distributed most widely throughout the population: income tax, national insurance contributions and VAT. Nor is this an accident. A tax that affected only the wealthy few, no matter how high its rate, could only yield a limited amount of public revenue. But a tax paid by the majority of people can yield substantial revenue because it has a much broader base. For example, a pound a week paid as an individual worker's national insurance contribution totals more than £1.2 billion in a year. A 1 per cent change in income tax alters revenue by more than £1.6 billion in a year.

The growth in the public provision of private benefits has also expanded the number of people liable for taxes to finance these benefits. Income tax demonstrates how rising living standards and growing demands of government for revenue have vastly increased the number of people subject to it. In 1938 less than one-fifth of people in work paid income tax, because it was due only if a person earned much more than the average industrial worker's wage. The need for revenue in wartime led to a gradual lowering of the threshold at which income tax was levied. Increased real wages in the postwar era has further broadened the tax base for income tax. Today, 93 per cent of people in work pay income tax, including the great majority earning below-average wages.

Making tax handles that turn easily. To speak of ordinary people as taxpayers is a half-truth. People do not pay taxes like a bill at a supermarket cash register, or a monthly credit card bill. Political friction is greatly reduced because tax officials normally do *not* put their hands in the taxpayer's pocket to collect bills due. Tax laws are written so that revenue can be collected from organizations that can be compelled to pay large sums into the fisc on behalf of ordinary people. The crucial administrative feature of any tax is its *tax handle*, that is, the means by which money legally due from the taxpayer is turned into money in the hands of the fisc. A good tax handle assures both ease and effectiveness of revenue collection. Important properties of tax handles include whether or not transactions are: monetized (a money wage or payments in kind);

Table 6.1   *Number of Taxpayers and Taxes Paid*

Tax	Amount paid (£bn)	Payers	
		Number	%
VAT	21.0	43,000,000	100
Income tax	35.4	23,800,000	93
National insurance	21.4	23,400,000	92
Beer, wines, spirits	4.1	31,800,000	74
Motor vehicles	2.4	13,600,000	70
Hydrocarbon oils	6.3	13,600,000	70
Rates	13.6	12,800,000	60
Tobacco	4.3	14,600,000	34
Capital gains	1.2	100,000	0.4
Death duties, etc.	0.8	28,000	0.1

The base of potential taxpayers differs from tax to tax: all adults (VAT, beer, wines, spirits, tobacco); adults in work (income tax, national insurance, capital gains); households (motor vehicles, hydrocarbon oils, rates, death duties).

Source: Rose and Karran, 1987: Table 4.4.

recorded (payment by cheque or payment in cash); and readily accessible to tax collectors and inspectors (a transaction by a large firm, or by a housewife).

The importance of designing a good tax handle can be illustrated by alternatives for taxing gambling. To tax the proceeds of winners would be difficult administratively and limited in effectiveness. The crowd of people frequenting a bookmaker's shop or bingo parlour is transient, and money changes hands quickly over the counter. To enforce such a tax, government officials would have to be present in each shop and claim the money due every time a successful gambler collected his or her winnings. It would be difficult to trace winners at the end of the tax year, and proceeds could be lost in subsequent wagers. By contrast, a tax on the gross proceeds of bookmakers or bingo operators is easy to enforce, for tax officials need only inspect periodic returns from bookmakers to ensure that the tax paid is reasonable. If a return is not filed, a tax inspector can visit the bookmaker's premises to demand payment, and a bookmaker who refuses to comply with tax laws will lose his licence.

It is easier and more effective to collect money from organizations *before* it is disbursed among tens of millions of ordinary people. An organization offers a better tax handle than an individual. An organization is readily accessible at a registered address; its size and its legal form compel it to keep easily inspected written records; and it normally has assets that can be attached if taxes due are not paid. Organizations are better able than individuals to deal routinely with tax officials, and the total number of organizations obligated to pay taxes to the fisc is small by comparison with the number of people on whose behalf taxes are vicariously paid.

In a modern economy there are many tax handles, for economic transactions involve money rather than barter, and most transactions leave a paper trail, in records of the payer, the recipient and/or a third party, such as a bank or credit agency. Tax officials in modern economies thus have a much wider choice of tax handles than in a poor third world nation in which barter is a normal means of exchange, and few records are kept in a form readily accessible to a tax inspector.

Upwards of nine-tenths of tax revenue in Britain is collected from organizations not individuals (Rose and Karran, 1987: 54ff). Income tax is deducted by employers from gross earnings, before wages are paid to an employee. The same is true of an individual's national insurance contribution. Even when Value Added Tax is charged to customers in a shop, the legal liability for paying the money to the fisc rests with the shopkeeper. Collection can start with the producer, for example, petrol is taxed at a refinery, and whisky or beer where the alcohol is produced. The cost of the tax is then incorporated in bills sent to wholesalers and carried over to retailers, who incorporate these taxes as part of the over-the-counter price of a product.

An organization with a large number of employees is a surrogate tax-collector, vicariously paying taxes notionally charged against individuals. It pays income taxes withheld from the wages of thousands of employees; employer and employee social security taxes; sales and excise taxes levied on the goods and services that it supplies; and property taxes on its buildings. Profits tax is only a small proportion of the total tax revenue that an organization must pay to the fisc. Thus, a non-profit organization or public agency must pay most of the taxes paid by a profit-making firm. For example, a university must withhold income tax and social security contributions from its employees, make a contribution too from its own funds for national insurance, and pay sales taxes on what it buys to run the university, and collect sales taxes or Value Added Tax on some services that it sells.

It is the exception for an individual to reach into his or her pocket to pay a tax directly. In Britain the arrangements for withholding income tax make it unnecessary for most people to file a tax return; employers communicate directly with the Inland Revenue about the tax obligations of their employees. In the United States, federal tax collectors collect income tax and social security on a pay as you earn basis so that the return an ordinary person files at the end of the year need not require a big payment and may even produce a tax refund. When sales taxes are levied, ordinary people may not be aware of the element of tax in the price of goods; for example, the price of a gallon of petrol or a packet of cigarettes is usually quoted inclusive of tax, and the tax on the purchase of a new car is noticed only if a customer reads the fine print in the bill.

There are only three occasions when ordinary people are likely to pay taxes themselves. A car-owner is responsible for paying an annual licence tax on an automobile, but this sum represents a very small percentage of total taxes paid each year. Self-employed people must file their own tax returns and pay income and social security taxes appropriate to their earnings. Home-owners are obligated to pay taxes on their property. Since tenants normally do not pay property taxes, the Thatcher Administration is replacing rates on domestic property with a community charge or poll tax that each adult resident must pay. The theory of the poll tax is that it should reduce taxes by making more people aware of local authority taxation. Altogether, the taxes that individuals pay on their own behalf account for less than one-sixth of the total tax revenue of the British government.

Collecting taxes from organizations effectively insulates most people from personal involvement in paying large sums of money to the fisc. An individual who reads the fine print on his or her pay slip would know how much was deducted in income tax and national insurance before net wages are in hand. But it would require an unwarranted amount of paperwork to calculate how much a household paid in VAT and excise taxes on its purchases during a year, and arguable assumptions to estimate how much of the taxes levied upon corporations were passed on to ordinary individuals.

The acceptance of taxation is so widespread that government can routinely collect billions of pounds each week in taxes. After surveying many countries and cultures distant in time and space, Webber and Wildavsky (1986: 33) conclude: 'Tax revolts are rare. Either the alternative, if one exists, is regarded as worse, or members of polities do accept the right of others to rule over them.'

What you get is not what you pay for

Ordinary people combine two contrasting roles. As consumers, people are accustomed to getting what they pay for. But as citizens, people are accustomed to receiving many benefits without payment, and paying taxes without getting anything specific in return. Taxes are properly conceived as dues, because they are payments that individuals are obligated to make as citizens. They are not purchases of particular goods and services. The great bulk of taxes go into the general revenue fund of the fisc; they are not earmarked to finance a specific benefit and economists argue that this is correct because earmarking taxes restricts government's ability to allocate funds as it thinks best. Even national insurance contributions, nominally earmarked for social security benefits, cannot finance the whole of these payments; general tax revenues are also drawn upon. Moreover, individuals who have not made sufficient social security payments can still receive cash benefits by virtue of the badge of citizenship.

The extent to which particular taxes are linked to public programmes depends upon the degree of political centralization. Britain is an extreme example of a unitary state for tax purposes, since nine-tenths of tax payments are made to central government agencies, and what is paid to local authorities is subject to central directives. In a system such as the United States, federal, state and local governments each have particular responsibilities and taxes, and there are also special-purpose districts to levy a tax for a particular service, such as schools or sewers. The specific functions of different tiers of government in America make it easier in principle for ordinary Americans to relate taxes to particular programmes, but the transfer of funds between federal, state and local authorities confuses which taxes pay for what services. The fragmentation of taxing powers in federalism makes it harder to see the overall picture.

In broad political terms, ordinary people can see that taxes are about getting something for something. Politicians could never win re-election if the large sums collected in taxation were hoarded rather than being spent on programmes that provide private benefits for millions of citizens. In a mixed economy welfare state, government is about taxing *and* spending. In this process, ordinary people receive big benefits as well as having big taxes. But since public services are usually not bought and sold in the market, there is no direct and certain link between what an ordinary person pays and receives. What you get is *not* what you pay for.

A citizen's balance sheet. If an ordinary person sat down to draw up a balance sheet of the costs and benefits of citizenship, it would not be possible to include every tax paid, and every programme supported by public expenditure for while many benefits are private (that is, specific to individuals or families) others are collective (that is, they cannot be specifically allocated to individuals or families).

The taxes paid on behalf of individuals are not the only taxes levied by government. Profits taxes are paid by corporations, and employers must make national insurance contributions from their own funds as well as making deductions from the gross wages of employees. When corporations buy many goods and services, these are often subject to tax. Whatever the theoretical arguments for saying that all taxes are ultimately borne by individuals, these taxes do not enter directly into a citizen's balance sheet. Government also spends a lot of money on collective benefits directed at society as a whole, such as police and fire services and national defence. Collective goods and services are funded by taxes, but their value cannot be included in a balance sheet that concentrates upon what individuals pay and receive from government.

The complex exchange of payments and benefits can be illustrated by examining the way in which they visibly affect the household budget of the median British family. The starting point is the original total income of the median household; in 1985 it was £7,780. From gross earnings one must subtract £1,460 for income tax and national insurance contributions. This reduces take-home pay by 19 per cent (Table 6.2). However, the family's cash in hand is substantially greater once we take into account the cash benefits from the welfare state, such as pension payments or child benefit; these average £1,190. The net effect of government taking with one hand and giving with another is that the net disposable after-tax cash income of the median family is within 3 per cent of its initial gross earnings.

When a family spends money it not only pays for what it wants; it also pays a host of expenditure taxes. VAT, tobacco, alcohol, and other consumption taxes claim £2,050 in a year from the expenditure of the median family, reducing the effective purchasing power of household income to 30 per cent below original gross income.

The cycle of exchanges is not yet complete, for the average household also receives free of charge major benefits financed by taxation. If health

care, education and income security in old age were not financed by public programmes, a family would have to spend thousands in the private
sector instead. Official statistics estimate the value of social benefits in
kind to the median family as £1,430 a year, a sum equivalent to nearly
one-fifth of its initial income.

The median family receives less in benefits than it pays in taxes – but
the difference is not large. The result of all the transactions described
above is that 11 per cent of the original gross income of the median family
is retained by government to finance collective benefits for society as a
whole. The problem of evaluation remains: Are we to say that 'only' 11
per cent of income is kept by the fisc or 'as much as' £890 is taken from
the original income of the average household to finance the public goods
and services collectively provided to society?

Although the net impact of government upon the household budget is
limited, the bottom-line in Table 6.2 conceals much churning, that is, the
circulation of money between the family and the fisc. Between original
gross income and final income there are many intermediate steps. In the
course of a year government collects £3,510 in taxes from the income of
the median family, and spends £2,620 for its benefits in cash and kind.
The total gross exchange of £6,130 between the fisc, public employees
delivering services and the median family is equivalent to more than
three-quarters of its original income, yet it produces a net change of only
11 per cent in the household's total package of income and benefits.

Evaluation is further complicated because the median family is a
statistical construct, falling between well-to-do and poor families. Since

Table 6.2   *Impact of Public Policies on the Family Budget*

Median household	Public policies		Balance	
	Tax (£)	Benefit (£)	Net (£)	% of original
1 Original income	–	–	7,780	100
2 Less income tax and				
National Insurance contribution	1,460	–	6,320	81
3 Plus cash benefits	–	1,190	7,510	97
4 Less indirect taxes on expenditure	2,050	–	5,460	70
5 Plus benefits in kind:				
Health 710				
Education 580				
Housing, other 140	–	1,430		
Total income, cash and kind			6,890	89

Source: 1985 data for median household, as reported by Central Statistical Office, *Social
Trends*, 1988: Table 5.15.

high-income families today are usually those with two or more members working, and low-income families are retired elderly persons, the median family is at a very distinctive stage of the life cycle. This greatly affects its claims on public policy and the taxes it pays. A family with two children will consume more education services, and an elderly couple will claim a pension and make more use of the health service. A high-income family will pay more taxes than a low-income family, but it is also likely to consume more than a low-income family; for example, its children are likely to stay in school to a later age and make more use of the health service.

The importance of the life cycle for a calculation of the dues of citizenship is clear. The bottom fifth of the population, principally pensioners, normally receive far more in social security benefits than they pay in taxes. Among families in work but earning below average incomes, the flow of taxes and benefits results in their effective final income being greater than initial gross earnings. Less than three-fifths of families actually have their final income in cash and benefits reduced by paying taxes. Even those in the top fifth of income received benefits in cash and kind valued at £2,280 in 1985 (Central Statistical Office, 1988: Table 5.15).

Free-market critics of government can argue that the total amount collected in direct and indirect taxes from the median family is not only large, but too large. It is equivalent to 45 per cent of the family's original gross income. The value attributed to benefits in kind can also be disputed. The government calculates their value on the basis of what it spends. Free-market advocates argue that the value ought to be reduced, assuming that government is invariably an inefficient producer of goods and services. By contrast, proponents of the social programmes of the welfare state argue that the value is actually greater than is shown in public accounts, for the fact that public services are not sold should enhance their intangible value to recipients.

An ordinary citizen is not continuously recalculating the costs and benefits of citizenship. No one wants to maximize the ratio of benefits to taxes by becoming unemployed and seriously ill, thus reducing taxes and collecting a cash benefit. Nor does an ordinary family consider it a misfortune when children are born. Taxes as well as income rise when a wife returns to work, and they rise further when a youth leaves school and brings a third income into the family. Ordinary people expect to pay more taxes when their income rises, and to claim more benefits when family circumstances or retirement entitle people to do so. An ordinary individual does not engage in the long-term calculations assumed in theories of rational expectations, comparing current costs of social security benefits with pension payments in the year 2030. The government's reliance upon effective tax handles means that most taxes are paid vicariously and, equally important, the private benefits essential to ordinary people are provided routinely.

What ordinary people think about taxes and spending

To understand the outlook of ordinary people toward taxing and spending we must consider both what people say, and what people do. Public opinion surveys report what people think about what they pay and get from government. We also need to understand how people can lawfully arrange their tax liabilities to avoid paying the fisc all that would otherwise be due.

Passive acceptance. Because the great bulk of the revenue collected by the fisc is vicariously paid by organizations, ordinary people have no choice about the payment of most taxes. Yet expectations that people have about taxation are important. Popular expectations condition politicians' views about what must be done to maintain electoral popularity. If there is a widespread expectation of tax cuts, politicians will be more anxious than usual to avoid raising taxes. Failure to produce expected tax cuts could lead voters to turn the governing party out of office, and frustration could even lead to 'tax revolt' at the ballot box. However, if ordinary people usually expect taxes to rise, this makes it easy to leave taxes as they are, and to expect passive acceptance of marginal tax increases.

Annually the Gallup Poll asks Britons what they expect will happen to taxes in the year ahead: Will taxes rise, fall, or stay much the same? If people consistently vote for tax to be reduced, then they would normally expect taxes to fall. But insofar as ordinary people are passively resigned or pessimistic, the public would normally expect taxes to rise or remain high. Ordinary people are realistic in expectations about taxation. In three decades of polls since 1957 an average of 52 per cent expect higher taxes in the year ahead. The second largest group, averaging 30 per cent, believe that taxes will stay the same in the year ahead, or have no opinion. In the average year only 18 per cent expect taxes to fall (Rose and Karran, 1987: Figure 8.1). Since ordinary people usually expect taxes to rise, there is little surprise or frustration when the expected happens, and taxes do rise.

Voters expect taxes to rise whether there is a Conservative or Labour government. The percentage expecting a tax increase appears to fluctuate more in accord with the state of the economy than with the party in office. The low proportion of people expecting tax cuts means that few voters are surprised if tax cuts do not occur. In an era of big government, four-fifths of voters accept that taxes are substantial, and likely to remain so or to increase. Even in the United States, where the rhetoric of tax cutting is widespread, the implicit assumption of many attacks is that vested interests in public spending are so powerful that taxes will not come down.

Informed avoidance. People are more likely to accept high nominal rates of taxation if they do not have to pay high rates because they can invoke legal means of avoiding tax liabilities. Taxation is contingent, in that economic activities are subject to a tax only if they meet conditions stipulated in legislation. Economic activity is contingent too. Given a choice between receiving money in a form subject to higher or lower taxes, most people would arrange their affairs in ways that attract less tax. Tax avoidance occurs when individuals or organizations arrange their affairs so that the tax base and/or tax rate are reduced.

Politicians and economists tend to disagree about how tax laws should be written. Economists prefer a minimum of exemptions in order to maintain a broad base of economic activities subject to tax, so that a given amount of revenue can be raised with a lower tax rate. By contrast, many politicians like to endorse symbolically high levels of taxation to 'soak the rich'. Yet these rates are rarely paid in full by rich people who take advantage of loopholes in the tax laws, thus reducing the amount of income subject to a high rate. The exemption of economic activities from tax is often described as a 'tax expenditure'; the assumption is that the money left in the hands of citizens by tax collectors is a public benefit just as much as if it were a benefit paid from the fisc. But Aaron Wildavsky notes, 'Speaking of taxes as expenditures prejudges the question of exactly who owns the money' (cf. Wildavsky, 1985: 414; Surrey and McDaniel, 1985).

By definition, tax avoidance is within the law. The basic guideline was laid down by English courts in the 1936 case of the Inland Revenue Commissioners vs. the Duke of Westminster:

> Every man is entitled if he can to arrange his affairs so that the tax attaching under the appropriate Acts is less than it otherwise would be. If he succeeds in ordering them so as to secure that result, then, however unappreciative the Commissioners of Inland Revenue or his fellow taxpayers may be of his ingenuity, he cannot be compelled to pay an increased tax.

The Inland Revenue has since succeeded in having the courts narrow the scope for tax avoidance. But as long as tax rates are high, the incentives for pursuing tax avoidance remain. Persons and corporations subject to high rates search ingeniously for legal loopholes to eliminate or reduce liability to taxation.

Borrowing money to purchase a house is the common way in which an ordinary person practises tax avoidance, for a portion of what a person pays in interest on a mortgage can be deducted from gross income, thus reducing liability to income tax. Whereas a tenant must pay rent from after-tax earnings, a person buying a house can deduct monthly interest payments on a mortgage from gross earnings, the equivalent of a discount of one-quarter or more on interest paid.

A person can also reduce liability to taxation by transforming income into payments in kind. This occurs when an employer provides fringe benefits at work, such as free or subsidized meals or a company car. British employers have been more likely than employers elsewhere to offer company cars, because they are taxed at a much lower rate than income. Becoming self-employed extends opportunities for tax avoidance, for most self-employed people can deduct from gross earnings such expenses as using part of their home as an office. Earning less money is another way to reduce taxation but this does not attract people who want to increase their spending power, for it cuts post-tax income.

Turning income into savings for retirement is another way in which an ordinary person can reduce tax. Money deducted from gross salary as a pension contribution is not counted as part of taxable income in Britain. Nor is the sum contributed by an employer to a pension counted as part of an individual's taxable income. Since this can equal 10 or 15 per cent of gross earnings, the tax advantage is substantial. When money in a pension fund is invested without paying standard rates of tax, savings grow much faster because re-invested income compounds gross, rather than net of taxes. In the course of 20 years, such tax advantages can increase the value of a pension by 50 per cent or more.

While tax avoidance can be done legally, it cannot be done casually. Planning is required *before* money changes hands, in order that a transaction takes a form that minimizes tax liabilities. Planning is particularly important in reducing liability to death duties. An elderly person may reduce or avoid tax on an estate by carefully planned steps, such as making gifts to relatives or establishing trusts prior to death. Given the capacity to reduce so greatly the liability for estate taxes, it is often described as a 'voluntary' tax, paid only by those who refuse to contemplate their death and take steps to minimize tax on what they leave as their legacy.

The capacity of an individual to practise tax avoidance is contingent upon circumstances. An individual must have an income sufficient to justify the additional effort required to reduce or avoid taxation. Hence, wealthy people are more likely to practise tax avoidance than people with below-average incomes. The higher the rate of taxation, the greater the incentive to avoid taxation. If the marginal rate of tax is 50 per cent, then successfully avoiding tax will double the amount of money that a person has in hand. However, if the rate of tax is 25 per cent, then a person will keep 75 per cent after paying this tax; elaborate procedures for tax avoidance would at most increase income by one-third.

A taxpayer must be organized to manage money in ways that minimize taxation. A large corporation is well organized to make use of professional advice, and has staff concerned solely with tax and accounting matters. The sums of money involved in corporate cash flows are large enough to make small percentage savings worthwhile in absolute terms. A multi-national company can organize the flow of transactions within the corporation so that liability to tax is reduced in countries where rates are highest.

Ordinary people usually lack the income and the professional advice to practise tax avoidance consistently. In order to practise tax avoidance, an individual will need a substantial income, professional advice from an accountant, and enough control of earnings so that payments are made in ways that avoid high rates of tax. Hence, policymakers have been able to mobilize support for tax reforms that simultaneously lower tax rates that affect many people and remove tax expenditures that benefit relatively few. The net effect of such changes can leave the total revenue of the fisc unaffected, but it redistributes the burden of taxation by reducing tax avoidance. This is what happened in the much heralded 1986 US tax reform act.

How much is enough? For generations experts in politics and public finance have speculated without agreement about the limits of taxation and public expenditure. The argument continues, because questions about the correct size of government are political, not technical. In a democracy, the underall views of ordinary people are meant to be the ultimate arbiter of how much is enough taxation.

If a public opinion survey asks whether taxes are too high or too low, the results are predictable: people are much more likely to say that taxes are too high than too low. Everything else being equal, people would rather have more cash in hand than not. However, everything else is not equal. Economic conservatives assume that tax cuts will be popular even if they cause spending cuts, whereas liberals assume that spending cuts are less popular than tax cuts.

British experience provides a good opportunity to test the electoral impact of tax cuts and increases, for each year the Chancellor of the Exchequer presents to Parliament a budget statement of changes in the tax law, and Parliament invariably endorses these proposals. We can thus test the extent to which tax cuts increase support for the government of the day, and the announcement of tax increases reduces support. A systematic analysis of the effect of tax cuts upon voting in Britain since the 1950s shows that changes in taxes make very little difference to popular support for the government of the day (Rose and Karran, 1987: 167ff). The correlation between tax cuts and popular support (r: 0.28) is not statistically significant; it explains only 8 per cent of the change in party support before and after the budget. For every 1 per cent net cut or increase in taxation, the popularity of the governing party is estimated to go up or down by only one-quarter of 1 per cent. The governing party would need to cut taxes by more than £5bn in order to achieve a 1 per cent boost in its standing in post-budget opinion polls.

The reason why tax changes do not immediately influence popular support for the government is that the economic conditions that cause taxes to go up or down have already affected the public's views. A government is only able to introduce tax cuts when economic conditions have been favourable for six months or more. Before a tax cut is introduced, the economy must have registered sufficient growth to increase revenue. In such circumstances, a cut in tax rates will simply transfer benefits of economic growth from the fisc to the pockets of ordinary people. When the economy has been booming for six months or more, the governing party's standing in the opinion polls is likely to have risen already. A Chancellor forced to introduce tax increases will be in charge of an economy that has already experienced sufficient troubles to cause the government to be losing popular support. Tax cuts are normally the climax of a period of sustained economic growth.

The average voter, like the average politician, has little difficulty in stating a preference about the political economy: more of everything, that is, more economic growth, more publicly financed private benefits and more take-home pay. But if government is forced to choose between two alternatives, each involving something deemed desirable and something deemed undesirable – more benefits of public policy and higher taxes, or lower taxes and fewer benefits – which do ordinary people prefer?

We would expect the preferences of ordinary people to reflect the conditions of their country. Most dissatisfaction with taxation would be expected in Sweden, where more than three-fifths of the national product is collected and disbursed through the fisc. In such circumstances, a tax cut would increase take-home pay by more than it would reduce public spending. Reciprocally, we would expect the marginal benefit of taxation to be highest in the United States, where the fisc claims less than one-third of the national product. Higher American taxation would increase the benefits of public policy by more than twice the proportion that it would reduce take-home pay.

In Sweden, where taxes are the highest in the OECD world, ordinary Swedes do criticize the level of taxation: 83 per cent say that taxes are too high, and 65 per cent say that taxes are so high that it is difficult to make ends meet. But ordinary Swedes also like very high spending on social benefits. When offered a list of 15 different objects of public expenditure, ranging from health care to theatres and museums, a majority think that spending should be increased or remain unaltered for nearly every programme. The only budget heading that Swedes would like to see reduced is the cost of state and local government administration (Hadenius, 1986: 85, 135).

Given high taxes and high levels of publicly financed private benefits, it is particularly significant to ask Swedes the 64 billion kronor question: Do you think that the tax you yourself pay is reasonable with reference to the benefits you derive from the community? The results are clearcut: 62 per cent think their taxes are reasonable, as against 35 per cent thinking that they are not. Moreover, the proportion of Swedes thinking their taxes are a fair exchange for public services is actually increasing. In 1968, when taxes were much less than today, less than one-third of ordinary Swedes thought taxes were then reasonable in relation to benefits. Increased benefits have increased satisfaction with the government's combination of taxing and spending (Table 6.3).

In Britain Margaret Thatcher's success in winning three successive general elections since 1979 is often interpreted as a rejection of the welfare state, since Mrs Thatcher is an outspoken critic of taxation and

Table 6.3   *Popular Attitudes towards Taxes and Spending in Britain, America and Sweden*

Sweden (percentages)

	1968	1981
Taxes are reasonable	32	62
Too high	43	35
Don't know	25	3
Balance, pro-taxing, spending	−11	+27

Britain (percentages)

	May 1979	March 1983	June 1987	October 1988
Cut both taxes, spending	34	23	12	10
Keep things as they are	25	22	21	15
Increase both spending, taxes	34	49	61	71
Balance, pro-taxing, spending	0	+26	+49	+61

America (percentages)

	1975	1977	1980	1982
Decrease services and taxes	38	31	38	36
Keep taxes and services about where they are	45	52	45	42
Increase services and raise taxes	5	4	6	8
Balance, pro-taxing, spending	−33	−27	−32	−28

Columns do not add to 100 per cent because of the exclusion of don't-knows.

Sources: Sweden: Hadenius, 1985: Table 6. Britain: Gallup Polls *Political Index* for month indicated. America: ACIR, 1984: 29, 46.

many policies financed by the fisc. Moreover, since the Prime Minister is the centre of political attention, long tenure of office has given her the opportunity to propagandize in favour of lower taxes and lower public spending.

Since 1979 the Gallup Poll has monitored this issue by asking voters to choose which of three alternatives comes closest to their own views: (1) taxes being cut, even if it means some reduction in government services, such as health, education and welfare; (2) things should be left as they are; or (3) government services such as health, education and welfare should be extended, even if it means some increases in taxes? When the question was asked after five years of a Labour government, the electorate divided fairly equally; a third favoured cutting taxes and services, and a third favoured raising both (Table 6.3). Changes have occurred since – but not in the direction that the Prime Minister would like. In 1983 nearly half the electorate declared a preference for higher taxes and spending, and less than one-quarter supported the inclination of the Prime Minister. By the time of the 1987 general election, more than three-fifths of the electorate was in favour of *increasing* taxes in order to spend more on public services. By autumn, 1988 the proportion in favour of higher taxation and public spending had risen to 71 per cent (see also Rose and McAllister, 1986: chapter 8). The ordinary English person retains more sympathy for a Swedish-style welfare state than does the Conservative government of Britain.

A tax expert examining American government would be struck by how *low* taxes are in the United States; the proportion of the national product collected in taxation places the United States in the bottom quarter among OECD nations for tax effort (Rose, 1989). President Ronald Reagan and President George Bush believe that keeping taxes down is desirable. Ordinary Americans are more inclined to agree with the views of the President they elect than Britons are to agree with their Prime Minister. The median American is in favour of keeping taxes and services about where they are, whereas Europeans tend to favour increasing taxes in order to finance increased public spending. Moreover, the pressure to change comes from the right, not the left: more Americans endorse cutting services in order to cut taxes (Table 6.3).

Popular support for taxing and spending is high in Europe, where taxes and spending are relatively high, and there is popular support for keeping taxing and spending down where it is relatively low. Americans are much less inclined to trust government to spend money for their benefit than they are to trust themselves whereas Britons and Swedes have much more positive expectations of the state. Even though Americans are much more vocally patriotic than Britons and Swedes, Americans are much less willing to pay the dues of citizenship, as they are measured in dollars-and-cents taxes and benefits.

7

Getting by in Three Economies

The increase of the black economy shows that people do not, once
they are free of their companies, their unions and to a certain extent
their government, shirk the idea of work.

Prince Charles

The black economy can be large enough to yield a rich vein of
anecdotes without necessarily being a phenomenon of quantitative
significance.

Andrew Dilnot and Nicholas Morris

Ordinary people and policymakers are both under pressure when the
economy gets into trouble, but they have different concerns and ways
of responding. Ordinary people want to get by, that is, to maintain the
consumption of their household. In seeking to do so, ordinary people
can turn to the Do It Yourself resources of the household as well as to
the official economy; they can also turn to the unofficial economy where
everything is paid for in cash to avoid tax.

By contrast, when the national economy is growing more slowly
than spending for public policy, policymakers can only levy taxes on
the resources of the official economy recorded in the national income
accounts. If tax revenue falls short of expectations, then government can
seek more revenue by borrowing or printing money, thus making inflation a problem. Alternatively, policymakers can cut spending on public
programmes. But insofar as programmes that are cut provide private
benefits important in the consumption of ordinary households, then cuts
in expenditure lead to cuts in the economic wellbeing of ordinary people
(cf. Rose, 1980).

In the 1970s the conflict between the priorities of government for public consumption and those of ordinary people for household consumption
was interpreted by Marxists and many non-Marxists as heralding an era
of political instability. It was assumed that political authority could not be
maintained if government could not continue providing private benefits
without imposing taxes that cut household consumption.

Yet troubles did not come. Ordinary people today appear far more
satisfied than was often predicted. Prince Charles, a person with a great
stake in the stability of established institutions, has offered an explanation

that is good news for individuals but bad news for government. Prince Charles (1981) has suggested that when a household is under financial pressure ordinary people can transfer their efforts to the untaxed unofficial economy. In this way people can continue to get by, maintaining consumption on the basis of earnings in the shadow economy. But insofar as this happens, government loses its effectiveness as a tax collector. The loss in revenue reflects a decline in political authority, the growth of a state of mind that the French call *incivisme*. Moreover, if people believe that they will not have to pay more tax because of working in the shadow economy, then they may be readier to endorse increased government spending, leaving politicians with the problem of finding money elsewhere.

Sceptical economists such as Dilnot and Morris (1981) have concluded that the black economy is much over-rated. Its novelty accounts for an upsurge of anecdotes. Yet the fact that it is news when a taxpayer evades taxes implies that tax officials can still routinely subtract large sums from the gross earnings of ordinary people. As chapter 6 has shown, substantial sums of tax can be collected vicariously, whether ordinary people like it or not. Effective tax handles can enable government to finance rising costs, even if the sums collected threaten to reduce household consumption by cutting take-home pay.

To answer the question – how do individuals get by in times of fiscal stress? – we must broaden the discussion from the official economy, as recorded in the national accounts. In addition to the significance of the unofficial (alias black, shadow or cash-only) economy operating outside the national income accounts, we must consider the domestic economy, whose products are neither recorded in the national income accounts nor exchanged for money, because they are produced and consumed within the household. As subsequent sections of this chapter demonstrate, the three economies are inter-related; each can produce some of the goods and services that individuals consume each week. When the official economy is in difficulty, the important question for ordinary people is: How can the unofficial and the domestic economy help us to get by?

Maintaining consumption: the underall view

When management of the economy is the issue, policymakers turn to very large aggregate figures about the gross national product, as reported in the national income accounts that measure the gross national product. Policymakers cannot repudiate the evidence of their own official data. But the view from the underall position of ordinary people is different. Ordinary people can get by through turning to the unofficial economy and the domestic economy, as well as the official economy.

The *official economy* (OE) is measured by the national income accounts, based upon reports compiled by government departments. Strictly speaking, the national income accounts are no more and no less than money sums tabulated according to procedures and conventions agreed by economists, some of which are debatable, such as the assumption that there is nil change through time in the productivity of the public sector. The development of national income accounts is very recent, dating from the need to mobilize national resources in the Second World War. Long before economists devised this means of officially summarizing the economy, there was a lot of unrecorded economic activity. The further back that economic historians seek to extend their knowledge, the greater the gap between the official economy and the economic activity of a society.

In the *unofficial economy* (UE) all goods and services can be measured in money terms, because they involve cash-only transactions. The problem is producing an accurate and official measure. The output of the unofficial economy can be related to the official economy, since both use the measuring rod of money. But transactions in the unofficial economy cannot be officially recorded in national income accounts because they involve tax evasion.

The *domestic economy* (DE) represents the many goods and services produced in an ordinary household each day, for example, meals and washing clothes, and services in which ordinary people substitute their own labour for that of others, for example, driving a car to work rather than being driven in a bus. From a sociologist's perspective, such commonplace activities as caring for children or washing dishes are easily observed even if no money value is put on them. Time-budget surveys have measured activities in the domestic economy across a wide range of societies (Szalai et al., 1972). But the domestic economy is difficult for an economist to measure because the goods and services produced do not have a money price, since they are not bought and sold like products of the official and unofficial economies. As cash transactions do not occur in the domestic economy, it is usually ignored in the formulation of public policy.

An ordinary person trying to get by is more concerned about food, shelter, transport, clothing and recreation than about confining consumption to what can be observed by the measuring rod of money. To maintain a given standard of consumption, an individual can add together goods and services produced in three different economies. Individual consumption is the sum of goods and services produced in three very different economies.

$$\text{Individual consumption} = OE + UE + DE$$

From an analytic point of view, the official and unofficial economies differ because transactions in the former are subject to taxation and the latter are not, but both economies use money as the basis of exchange. The domestic economy differs twice over, because its goods and services are produced without cash changing hands, and since production is not monetized there is no legal obligation to pay taxes. Yet in principle the size of all three economies can be estimated empirically since all involve the production and consumption of goods and services.

The relative importance of the three economies to ordinary people is influenced by position in the life-cycle. An infant is likely to be heavily dependent upon the goods and services produced by a mother in the domestic economy. A young person with a job and no family can concentrate upon work in the official economy. A husband and wife invest more time in the home, and having children can cause a radical shift if the wife moves from paid work in the official economy to non-monetized work in the domestic economy. When children leave the parental home to form their own household a family's production and consumption patterns again alter.

Changes in the political economy also influence the relative importance of the three economies. In the 1950s and 1960s there was a substantial mobilization of labour into the official economy, as farmers or their offspring moved to jobs in cities. In addition, many women shifted the focus of work from the household to part-time or full-time jobs. Many studies of the unofficial economy assume nil or very little activity in this period, when taxes were not so high and jobs were plentiful. The 1970s recession was regarded as the trigger for people to invest more and more effort in the unofficial economy. Yet continuing recession should reduce the demand for services in the unofficial economy, as people run out of cash to pay 'cash only' workers. In such circumstances people can turn to the domestic economy, where consumption can be maintained by producing non-monetized goods and services. The economic boom in the mid-1980s could encourage a return to work in the official or the unofficial economy, because people now have more cash in hand to spend.

Continuing strengths of the official economy

Reports of the death of the official economy are much exaggerated. The sustained growth of the official economy in the post-war era is a matter of record. National income accounts show that the gross national product of the average OECD nation has increased by several hundred per cent in value in the past quarter century. Even in the difficult 1970s the official economy grew in nine of ten years. Furthermore, national governments have been able to increase greatly the amount of taxes collected from citizens. From 1960 to 1986 OECD nations on average increased their share of tax revenue as a percentage of the gross domestic product by two-fifths. Since the national product has grown greatly in real terms as well as in inflated currency values, the sums of money collected in taxes have grown even more. In Britain, for example, government collected £7bn in tax revenue in 1960, £19bn in 1970, and today it collects more than £150bn in tax revenue.

Working in the official economy is the norm – both statistically and in terms of social values – in every Western nation today. The majority of the population of working age is in work, and expects to be in work. Women are no longer confined to the home; the majority of women are now in paid employment in the official economy. Social status is derived from an individual's occupation within the official economy rather than from activities in the domestic economy. Except in deviant sub-cultures, working in the unofficial economy lowers social status.

Structural changes in post-war society have strengthened institutions of the official economy. The capitalization of production has made large factories and offices the typical place of work, rather than an artisan's workshop. The peasant or family farm, producing for its own consumption in the domestic economy, has been replaced by farmers who depend upon government regulation of imports and public subsidies. Whereas a horse could be reared and fed in the domestic economy, a tractor can only be manufactured and powered within the official economy. The shift of population to cities and suburbs has given women opportunities to take paid employment in offices and factories. Mass marketing has encouraged consumers to buy goods that cannot be produced outside the official economy. Sliced bread and corn flakes are typical products of the official economy, substituting for goods formerly produced in the domestic economy.

The great majority of people participate in the official economy as an inescapable condition of their occupation and the circumstances of their employer. This is most obviously the case in occupations in which the government is the sole or primary employer, such as teaching, postal work, the police and the civil service. Public employment today can provide jobs for more than one-quarter of the labour force (Rose, 1985b). Occupations concentrated in large bureaucratized firms that must keep accurate records to function are invariably recorded in the official economy. Individuals do not have an equal choice between a full-time job in the official or the unofficial economies; today the great bulk of the labour force is mobilized into the official economy.

Government offers positive inducements to participate in the official economy. Work in the official economy is a condition of qualifying for social security benefits. Only by doing so can individuals be registered for a pension or unemployment benefit; in many countries employment also affects participation in health insurance programmes. The bulk of social security taxes are paid by the employer as an addition to gross wages, thus giving every employee a vested interest in enforcing tax payments by others. This is particularly important in countries such as France and Italy, where there is a political and social history of avoiding or evading income tax. The bureaucratization of production has made it harder for producers to avoid taxes, because large impersonal organizations are far more subject to official scrutiny by tax inspectors than are individual households.

The size of the official economy today is great, but it is not constant. Rising unemployment has made it difficult for some people to enter the official economy. Since 1974 unemployment rates have doubled or tripled. With rising unemployment, individuals at the margin may shift to working in the unofficial or domestic economies to maintain consumption. But ordinary people first want to obtain the cash and public policy benefits of working in the official economy.

Constraints upon demand and supply in the unofficial economy

The spotlight of publicity upon the unofficial economy makes it inappropriate to describe it as an unobserved or shadow economy. However, well-publicized anecdotes tell us nothing about magnitudes. To estimate the consumption it sustains we need to examine the attitudes of people to buying and selling services illegally, and the structural opportunities and incentives for people to act as buyers and sellers in the unofficial economy.

What surveys show. Whether or not people become involved in the unofficial economy in part is a function of attitudes toward tax evasion. Surveys of popular attitudes toward acceptance of illegal transactions in the unofficial economy consistently find that most people disapprove of tax evasion (for full details, see Rose, 1985d: 116ff)

1 *Tax evasion is not socially acceptable.* Most people do *not* tolerate tax evasion. Vogel's (1974: Table 6) pioneering Swedish study found that only 22 per cent in that highly taxed country excused tax fraud on the grounds of economic need. In the United Kingdom the median person consistently disagrees with a series of statements justifying different forms of tax evasion (Keenan and Dean, 1980: Table 1). In the United States 87 per cent disagree with the statement that tax evasion is not a serious crime. The overall pattern of replies is aptly summed up as: 'Most people feel that the tax laws should be respected, but do not feel that violations constitute so serious a crime as to warrant physical imprisonment' (Song and Yarborough, 1978: 433).

2 *There is a low predisposition to participate in tax evasion.* Since direct questioning is unlikely to produce the admission of involvement in evading taxes, people can be asked about condoning tax evasion in

principle. The assumption is that people who tolerate tax evasion are likely to take advantage of opportunities to participate in the unofficial economy, and those who condemn it will not. Vogel (1974: Tables 3 and 4) found that an average of 79 per cent of Swedes disagreed with a series of five statements justifying tax evasion. Similarly, in the United States an average of 83 per cent disagreed with such statements justifying tax evasion as 'the chances of getting caught are so low that it is worthwhile trying to cheat', as against 12 per cent endorsing justifications for tax evasion (CSR, 1980: Table 5.11). Most ordinary people are thus subject to group norms discouraging tax evasion.

3 *Actual involvement in tax evasion is lower still.* When a national sample of Swedes was asked whether they had received untaxed cash payments in the past year, 7 per cent replied that this had happened once or twice, and 5 per cent said they had been involved more often than that. A total of 11 per cent said that they sometimes paid for goods or services in the unofficial economy, and another 31 per cent that they had occasionally done this (Warneryd and Walerud, 1982: Table 1; Zetterberg and Frankel, 1981: 41). A nationwide American survey asked people to report tax evasion by completing forms anonymously; it found that 12 per cent admitted purposely failing to report some income on their tax forms. The average amount of money not reported was $529, only 5 per cent of average income. Only 1 per cent of the sample reported that they had failed to report more than $1,000 in any one year.

Surveys consistently show that the great majority of people in Sweden and America, countries with very different tax levels, are *against* participation in the unofficial economy. Tax evasion remains socially unacceptable in Anglo-Saxon countries, and the predisposition to evade taxes is low. Since every transaction in the unofficial economy involves both a buyer and a seller, the general aversion of ordinary people to cheating on taxes makes it harder for a willing seller of 'cash-only' services to find a buyer, or for a willing buyer to find a seller. To regard tax evasion in the unofficial economy as high only makes sense if one has the naive assumption that all laws are always obeyed and that national income accounts ought to measure all economic activity.

Structural opportunities low. What people say is not a certain guide to what they do; we also need to analyse the structure of the economy for opportunities and incentives to participate in the unofficial economy. Insofar as structural analysis shows that there are many obstacles to buying and selling in forms that evade taxes, this will confirm survey evidence of the relatively small size of the unofficial economy.

The basic economic assumptions of the unofficial economy are simple: both buyers and sellers are better off exchanging goods and services there than in the more or less heavily taxed official economy. The official price (OP) of goods and services in the official economy can be determined by four factors: wages (W), materials (M), capital goods (C), and taxes (T) on the first three factors.

$$OP = W + M + C + T$$

For transactions to be transferred from the official to the unofficial economy, two conditions must be met: (1) the unofficial price must be less than the official price for the would-be buyer, and (2) the unofficial wage must be more than the official wage for the producer. Unless *both* these conditions are met, there is insufficient incentive for a transaction to occur in the unofficial economy.

A price saving due to the absence of a tax on wages is the principal incentive offered customers in the unofficial economy. The saving to the customer is less than the tax unpaid, for a worker will usually need a wage higher than take-home pay in the official economy as an incentive to work 'off the books'. The price advantage of the unofficial economy is thus heavily dependent upon the proportion of the total cost determined by wages, and the marginal rate of tax upon a worker's wage.

The paradigm example of a product of the unofficial economy is one that can be produced with virtually no capital investment in materials or equipment, such as baby-sitting or window-cleaning. But the scope for such services is limited; a joiner or an electrician will need some tools and a van to get to and from work. Furthermore, anyone who tries to depend solely upon the unofficial economy for a living will have little or no opportunity to acquire materials or equipment cheaply. By contrast, a worker who supplements a primary job in the official economy with a second or 'moonlight' job in the unofficial economy may borrow equipment with the tacit consent of an employer, buy goods at wholesale prices or obtain them without payment as a perk or by pilfering.

The unofficial economy is ill-suited to the production of manufactured goods, for labour costs are typically a limited fraction of their total cost. The cost of capital for manufacturing requires the formation of a limited liability company, and the machinery is so complex that it cannot be borrowed for the weekend. Whereas a motor mechanic may do repair work in the unofficial economy, an employee of a car manufacturer cannot make cars at home or borrow the use of the factory's production line for the weekend. Industrial workers may pilfer goods after they have been manufactured and recorded in the official economy. However, pilfering does not increase the total national product; it only redistributes it.

The marginal rate of tax upon a worker's wage determines the saving available for division between the producer and buyer of products in the unofficial economy. If wages represent 80 per cent of the cost, but a worker's marginal rate of tax is 20 per cent, then the potential price discount is at the most only 6 per cent. By contrast, if the marginal rate of income and social security tax is 40 per cent, then the official price can be discounted by up to 32 per cent (that is, 40 per cent of 80 per cent). Moreover, if a VAT charge of 15 per cent is also waived, then the official price can be further discounted. In such circumstances, the unofficial price can be up to 47 per cent below the official price and still make the effort potentially attractive to a producer. If a worker demands a premium for working illegally in what is often regarded as overtime, then the discount in price to the purchaser is reduced.

Lower income tax rates discourage work in the unofficial economy by reducing the margin for both buyer and seller to benefit from untaxed cash-only transactions. In Britain the standard rate of income tax has been reduced from 33 per cent to 25 per cent since Margaret Thatcher took office, and in the United States the 1986 Tax Reform Act reduced income tax to a standard rate of no more than 28 per cent for the average taxpayer.

Given advantages in each economy, a worker may be involved in both, moonlighting in the unofficial economy to *supplement* a job in the official economy. In Italy the government recognizes this practice, setting working hours for many public officials from 8 am to 2 pm; this qualifies an individual for social security benefits, and still leaves time for working in the unofficial economy later in the day. Yet the number of second jobs in an economy is limited. Even studies intended to highlight moonlighting as 'a problem of our times' (e.g. de Grazia, 1980: 551ff) conclude that less than 10 per cent of the labour force has a second job. Moreover, the time available for work in the unofficial economy is limited by the fact that it is additional to a job in the official economy.

Since every economic transaction requires a buyer as well as a seller, we must also ask: When is the unofficial economy attractive to the buyer? Price advantages are variable and often small. There may be a few non-monetized advantages in dealing with a known and convenient person, e.g. a neighbour's son who cuts the grass. But to employ strangers to do a major house repair runs the risk of fly-by-night workmanship for a relatively small cash saving.

When the concept of a buyer is extended from the household to a firm, the advantages of the unofficial economy decline sharply. A firm that spends money buying goods and services will want to enter this in its books in order to offset expenditure against revenue, thus reducing its liability to profits tax. More than that, a firm will want to have an effective and reliable source of supply for the products on which it must rely in its business. A person providing services on an irregular, limited and under-capitalized basis in the unofficial economy cannot compete with a well-organized firm, even if the latter pays taxes. Insofar as many firms buy their products from other firms, there is even less opportunity for tax evasion.

Cutting wage costs by sub-contracting production to the unofficial economy can be done in a few low-skill labour-intensive activities, for example, some forms of garment making. But it is far easier to cut wage costs by importing goods from low-wage countries in the Third World. If the same goods can be supplied more cheaply and efficiently from Hong Kong, Taiwan or Brazil, there is no need for a firm to organize the purchase of goods in the unofficial economy. Government action to reduce trade and tariff barriers further encourages imports from low-wage countries whose workers can produce goods and services at lower cost, and in forms that enter the accounts of the official economy when they are imported.

Estimating the size. While anecdotes of the unofficial economy abound, the important analytic question is: How widespread are the products and occupations suited to the unofficial economy? To be produced in the unofficial economy, goods and services must be labour-intensive and not require a high degree of capital. Moreover, they must not require complex technologies, accounting systems or bureaucracies, or extend nationally or internationally, as do banking, insurance, and the telephone service. The cost of materials must be low relative to labour, e.g. paint as against the components used to make a motor car. Products must be capable of being produced 'invisibly' rather than in factories visible to tax collectors. The greater the limitations on the goods and services capable of being produced in the unofficial economy, the less its total size.

Statistics of the official economy can be used to estimate the size of the unofficial economy, for the demand and supply of products in the latter is related to the former. The employed population of the United Kingdom can be divided into three broad categories according to the potential for unofficial production in different industries and services. There is a high opportunity to enter the unofficial economy in services requiring a moderate amount of capital and materials and produced by small-scale enterprises or by the self-employed; there is a low opportunity in industries that involve substantial costs for capital equipment or materials, such as manufacturing and energy, or in public employment, which must follow the law.

When the labour force of Britain is classified according to opportunities to work in the unofficial economy, less than one-fifth has the opportunity of such work (Table 7.1). Construction workers, persons in hotels and catering, self-employed workers and farmers have significant opportunities to supplement taxed earnings by untaxed cash-only earnings. Because more than four million work in these fields, plumbers, waiters, farmers, and a variety of self-employed professionals can provide many anecdotes about activities in the unofficial economy.

A sense of proportion is introduced by comparing the millions who may work in the unofficial economy with the tens of millions with a relatively low, or no, opportunity to do so. The opportunity to work off the books is present but relatively low in shops that must pay taxes on some employees and buy many services in the official economy. In garment manufacturing there are some opportunities for employing people as home-workers, but textiles are made in large factories easily subject to visits by tax inspectors. More than two-thirds of the labour force has virtually no opportunity to evade taxes, for individuals can only manufacture chemicals, run railways or work in a bank by being part of a large organization that is a visible tax handle. This is also the case for people working in the public sector, whether civil servants, teachers or in the health services.

Given that work in the unofficial economy depends upon access to resources of the official economy, Table 7.1 can be used to estimate the total amount of labour involved in the unofficial economy. A high estimate of work in the unofficial economy is that three-quarters of those with a good opportunity will participate for about 16 hours a week; of

Table 7.1   *Opportunity to Work in the Unofficial Economy*

	Number (thousands)	% of total
A *Relatively high*		
Construction	1,709	7.3
Professionals, other self-employed	1,090	4.6
Hotels and catering	1,046	4.4
Agricultural, forestry, fishing	537	2.3
Total	4,382	18.7
B *Relatively low*		
Retail distribution	2,044	8.7
Textiles, leather and clothing	548	2.3
Total	2,592	11.0
C *Virtually none*		
Engineering and allied industries	3,285	13.9
Other manufacturing	2,464	10.5
Public administration	2,226	9.4
Banking, finance and insurance	2,166	9.2
Education	1,559	6.6
Transport and communication	1,414	6.0
Health services	1,262	5.4
Other institutionalized services	1,258	5.3
Electricity, energy supply, water	681	2.9
Coal, oil and gas extraction	271	1.1
Total	16,586	70.4

Source: Compiled from *Labour Force Survey 1985* (London: HMSO, 1987), Table 4.11 and *Employment Gazette* 96, 5 1988), Table 1.2.

those with a low opportunity, one-third will participate the equivalent of 8 hours a week; and among those with virtually nil opportunity, 10 per cent will participate 4 hours a week. A relatively generous estimate is that nearly one-quarter of the labour force participates in the unofficial economy in the course of the year; a lower estimate is that it involves upwards of one-fifth.

At most cash-only work adds an additional 7.0 per cent to labour in the official economy; a more realistic estimate is that it is equivalent to 3.4 per cent of the hours worked in the official economy (Table 7.2). Most of this work is in relatively low value-added sectors of the economy, by comparison with the high value-added goods produced in the official economy, for example, electricity, computers or motor cars. Moreover, there are structural obstacles to increasing productivity, for this would tend to price cash-only workers out of the market by requiring the purchase of expensive equipment and materials.

The money value of this labour is sufficient to justify press headlines – 'billions in tax evasion' – and anecdotes – 'He'll do it for £50 cash in hand' – but the unofficial economy remains small as a proportion of total monetized economic activity in Britain today. Other studies of the unofficial economy in America and European countries come to similar conclusions (cf. Tanzi, 1982; Smith, 1986; Thomas, 1988).

Table 7.2   *Hours Worked in the Unofficial Economy*

	Low estimate		High estimate	
	Number of persons (thousands)	Hours per week	Number of persons (thousands)	Hours per week
A *Nil opportunity* (16,586,000)				
(1) High realization (10% @ 4 hours)			1,658	6,632
(2) Low realization (10% @ 2 hours)	1,658	3,316		
B *Low opportunity* (2,592,000)				
(1) High realization (33% @ 8 hours)			855	6,840
(2) Low realization (25% @ 4 hours)	648	2,592		
C *High opportunity* (4,382,000)				
(1) High realization ((75% @ 16 hours)			3,286	52,576
(2) Low realization (50% @ 12 hours)	2,191	26,292		
Total	4,497	32,200	5,799	66,048
As percentage of official economy	19.1	3.8	24.6	7.8

Source: Calculated from data in Table 7.1, estimating working time in the official economy as 40 hours per week.

Resources of the domestic economy

If we want to understand how ordinary people get by, we also need to estimate the goods and services that can be produced without any use of cash. Time is the great resource that constrains all economic activity; everyone has 168 hours to 'invest' each week, and the ordinary person has a large amount of time potentially available for investment in the domestic economy. When t_T is total time, then discretionary time (t_D) is what is left over after subtracting from total time what is spent in sleeping (t_S); personal care (t_{PC}) that an individual must provide for himself or herself, such as taking a bath; and t_{OE} and t_{UE}, time in the official and unofficial economies.

$$t_D = t_T - (t_S + t_{PC} + t_{OE} + t_{UE})$$

A major study of the use of time by British adults, based upon hour-by-hour time-budget diaries of activities in a 168-hour week (Gershuny, 1981: Table 1), found that the average person spends 45 hours a week sleeping; another 31 hours a week in personal care such as eating and washing; and 29 hours a week in paid employment. An average of 105 hours a week is thus committed to what might be called non-discretionary uses of time. If one adds two hours a week for participation in the unofficial economy, an ordinary person has an average of 61 hours a week in discretionary time.

Any analysis of the use of discretionary time based on averages obscures very important differences between persons in paid work and those who are not, principally housewives. While the amount of time spent sleeping remains the same for both groups and that spent in personal care varies little (30 hours for people in paid work, as against 35 hours for persons not in work), people not in work have a total of 88 hours of discretionary time in a week, as against about 50 hours a week of discretionary time available to those in work (Gershuny, 1988).

Given so much discretionary time, under what circumstances would we expect individuals to engage in production in the domestic economy? In the abstract, the answer is simple: when the domestic economy price (DEP) is less than the unofficial economy price and the official economy price. By definition, money wages are 0 in the domestic economy. Therefore, the domestic economy price is determined very differently; its money value is a function of the cost of materials and capital, and taxes upon these resources.

$$DEP = 0 + M + C + T$$

The domestic economy has a big advantage for labour-intensive services, such as child care or preparing meals. By contrast, the price advantage is low when the cost of materials is high, for example, laying a carpet costs less than buying a carpet. The price advantage is also low when the capital cost is high, for example, developing colour film. Capital cost includes human capital; the skill required for cooking a gourmet meal is greater than that for frying eggs, and the skill needed to care for a deaf child greater than that to care for a child with full faculties. The larger the wage element in the production of services and goods, and the simpler the skill required, the greater the price advantage of the domestic economy.

The production of goods and services in the domestic economy cannot be analysed in terms of a simple trade-off between unpaid work and leisure, for many household services are necessities. In an era when there are few domestic servants, the alternative to cooking some food for oneself can be hunger and the alternative to providing some care for one's children can be child neglect or abandonment. Domestic production not only provides household goods and services; the producer may gain intangible benefits from pride in workmanship. Ordinary people often prefer home-cooked meals or home-made child care to buying goods and services in the market. There are also 'priceless' benefits from the affectionate exchange of services outside the money economy.

The domestic economy can often undercut any price advantage in the unofficial economy. For example, the cost of an ordinary couple painting their own house is only the cost of the paint and paintbrushes; labour is unpaid. In the unofficial economy a painter must be paid and in the official economy an allowance must also be made for income tax and social security, and Value Added Tax too. When the official economy gains an advantage because the wage component of a product is small, both the domestic and the unofficial economies lose out.

Since people do not want to spend all their discretionary time working, it should be divided into three different primary categories:

1 *Housework and productive leisure.* Activities in the household that produce marketable goods and services without money payment, e.g., making meals for a family or servicing the family car.
2 *Pastimes.* Activities that do not involve the consumption or production of monetized goods and services, e.g., talking with friends at home or going for a walk.
3 *Leisure consumption.* Activities that require spending money in the official or unofficial economy, e.g., talking to a friend over a restaurant meal, watching a rented video, or taking a drive in a car.

The three activities differ greatly in their significance for national income accounts. Pastimes have only a trivial effect upon the official economy; leisure consumption is a significant entry in the national income accounts because it involves money expenditure; and unpaid housework and productive leisure do not show up at all in national income accounts.

Given so much discretionary time, ordinary people can spend substantial time in pastimes and leisure consumption as well as in productive housework and leisure. Time-budget data collected by J.I. Gershuny can be re-analysed to give a reasonable estimate of how ordinary people allocate their discretionary time. Housework and productive leisure account for the largest proportion of discretionary time, 23 hours per week for the average adult (Table 7.3). In addition, 21 hours a week is devoted to costless pastimes, and 17 hours to leisure consumption.

The domestic economy is large in absolute and relative terms. One reason is the high adult participation rate. Whereas there are about 23 million people in work in Britain today, there are more than 40 million adults who can produce goods and services in the domestic economy. If we multiply the average time spent in productive leisure (23 hours a week) by this population, we have a total of 920 million hours a week devoted to productive leisure. The time spent in productive work in the home is thus equal to the efforts of 23 million people in paid employment in the official economy.

The total amount of discretionary time in a week has increased by 2 hours since 1961, because of the shortening of the working week. The

Table 7.3   *Allocation of Discretionary Time in the Week*

	1961		1975		Change 1975–61	
	Hours	%	Hours	%	Hours	%
1 *Unpaid housework and productive leisure* Cooking, housework, odd jobs, gardening, shopping, child care, study, knitting, sewing, etc.	26	44	23	38	-3	-6
2 *Pastimes* Walks, visiting friends, relaxing, conversation, etc. half of TV–radio–records time[a]	20	34	21	35	+1	+1
3 *Leisure consumption* Travel, cinema, dances, clubs, pubs, reading newspapers, half of TV–radio–records time[a]	12	21	17	28	+5	+7
Total hours	59		61		+2.5	

[a] Time spent watching television or listening to radio or records – 17.5 hours, 1961: 16.5 hours 1975 – is divided between leisure consumption and pastimes, since there is a capital cost in buying equipment or records, but the marginal cost of their use is very low.

Source: Calculated from Gershuny, 1981: Table 1.

distribution has altered only slightly because of a rise in the number of part-time women workers in the official economy, and productive housework and leisure has remained most important. The continuing large amount of time devoted to unpaid housework and productive leisure reflects the fact that preparing meals, cleaning the house, shopping, caring for children and looking after a car are continuing needs of a household. Moreover, postwar prosperity has even made it easier for ordinary people to produce more in the household. Developments in modern technology have made the home increasingly capital-intensive. Do-it-yourself tools are sold in the official economy, but their principal use is to substitute unpaid leisure work for that of paid workers in the official or unofficial economies.

Studies of the use of time have found much similarity across nations in the time that people spend in unpaid housework and productive leisure (Szalai et al., 1972: 114). Similarities between many different societies are not surprising, for the domestic economy is important in every society, because it produces necessities in every culture.

Comparing the three economies

To determine which of the three economies is most or least important we must be able to assess them by a common measuring rod. Time, like money, is easily measured, and it has the added advantage of being applicable to activities in the non-monetized domestic economy.

A sense of proportion. When the time worked in all three economies is compared, the domestic economy appears most important, accounting for more than 52 per cent of all productive labour. While the average employee works more hours on the job than at home, the number of employees is much less than the total adult population involved in the domestic economy. The official economy thus accounts for just below 45 per cent of productive labour each week (Table 7.4). The unofficial economy contributes little to production in society, accounting for 2.5 per cent of total economic activity. The unofficial economy is at a disadvantage compared to the official economy, which can mobilize masses of capital for high-tech goods and services that cannot be produced outside the law, such as air transport or life insurance. It is also at a disadvantage compared to the domestic economy, where the money cost of labour is zero.

Estimates of the official and domestic economies in Britain are consistent with figures produced by a variety of methods in other countries. For example in the United States the contribution of the domestic economy has been estimated as from two-thirds up to equal that of the official economy, depending upon circumstances and methods used (Eisner, 1981: Table 22; Nordhaus and Tobin, 1973: 509ff). Since these are

Table 7.4   *Total Labour in the Three Economies*

	Million hours per week	%
Official economy	848	44.9
Unofficial economy	48	2.5
Domestic economy	993	52.6
Total	1,889	100

Source: Calculated from Tables 7.2 and 7.3, assuming four-fifths of workers employed full-time at 40 hours, and others at half-time; and all persons over 18 (43,181,000) participate in the domestic economy.

estimates of dollar values not labour input they are similar in size to figures in Table 7.4.

Getting by through substitution between economies. In the past two decades ordinary people have faced difficulties in getting by, that is, maintaining individual consumption. Inflation has greatly increased prices and reduced the value of savings. Unemployment has risen greatly, and new jobs are harder to find. The growing internationalization of the economy means that national governments cannot influence national economic conditions as heretofore. Fiscal difficulties registered in the national income have led politicians to assume that ordinary people have been equally under stress.

When conditions appear difficult in official statistics, ordinary people can get by insofar as they can draw upon goods and services outside the official economy. Since the unofficial economy cannot compensate, to what extent can goods and services of the domestic economy substitute for goods and services produced in the official economy?

Household expenditure in the official economy can be grouped into three categories, depending upon: a relatively high potential for substitution from the domestic economy; a medium to low potential; or no capacity for substitution. When consumer expenditure is examined, more than half can be substituted by work in the domestic economy (Table 7.5). Overall, there is at least some potential to substitute domestic production for purchase of three-fifths of the goods and services used by an ordinary household.

The potential is high for substitution in more than one-fifth of consumer expenditure through making meals in the home rather than eating out or dispensing with various purchased services. Insofar as people value drinking for its alcoholic intake rather than sociability, they can brew beer or make wine at home rather than go to a pub. There is some potential to substitute for an additional two-fifths of expenditure in the monetized economy. Food is the largest entry in this category: a small amount of food can be grown, and more time can be invested in preparing food at home rather than buying frozen or prepared foods. The cost of clothing can be reduced by making and repairing some clothes at home. Expenditure on travel can be reduced through pooled use of travel facilities, bicycling, or walking, and costless pastimes can often be substituted for leisure consumption.

About two-fifths of expenditure in the official economy does not permit substitution. It is impossible to rely upon home-made electricity, gasoline, tobacco, telephone or insurance services. A car can be driven slowly to

Table 7.5 *Expenditure in the Official Economy by Opportunity to Substitute in the Domestic Economy*

	£bn	%
A *High substitutability*		
Alcoholic drink	16.4	
Catering and accommodation	13.2	
Household maintenance	5.8	
Miscellaneous recreational services	2.6	
Other services	6.9	
Domestic service	2.3	
Total	47.2	(21.2)
B *Medium to low substitutability*		
Food	32.3	
Clothing	15.5	
Travel	7.5	
Maintaining cars	6.0	
Entertainment services (TV purchase; cinema, etc.)	13.9	
Other goods	13.2	
Total	88.4	(39.6)
C *No substitutability*		
Owning, running car	20.5	
Housing rent, rates	15.5	
Household goods	13.1	
Fuel and light	11.1	
Tobacco	7.4	
Chemists' goods	5.5	
Post, telephone	4.4	
Insurance	4.4	
Books, newspapers	3.2	
Betting and gaming	2.2	
Total	87.3	(39.2)

Source: Compiled from Central Statistical Office, 1987: Table 4.7, consumer expenditure by function, 1986.

economize on petrol, but it cannot be driven without petrol, and petrol can only be bought in the official economy after government has turned a tax handle. A person may make fewer telephone calls or confine use of the phone to times when cheap rates apply, but individuals cannot communicate simply by shouting across a city or from one city to another. Nor is self-insurance the same as pooling risks across many households.

To get by, families need only substitute a few activities in the domestic economy for a limited amount of goods and services in the official economy. The difficulties that ordinary people face do not arise because of having no money but because of not having enough money to maintain their living standard. While there is a real pinch when expenses exceed income, the gap is marginal, that is, a small percentage of total consumption. Goods and services that must be purchased in the monetized economy can continue to be purchased by people whose real income falls. The fall can be compensated for by not buying in the official economy some things that can be produced at home.

Getting by and getting ahead. Ordinary people can cope with the swings of the official economy that so perturb policymakers, by relying upon the domestic economy too. In a booming economy, people can have more to spend on leisure services and buy durable goods such as freezers to shorten the time spent on laborious household tasks. When the economy slows down, individuals have more incentive to substitute products of the domestic economy for those formerly purchased in the official economy.

The ability to make good use of both the official and the domestic economy depends upon ordinary people having a money income, for domestic labour cannot buy all the essentials needed in a modern money economy. The object of social security is to provide just this, cash income-maintenance grants for millions of ordinary people. A social security benefit may be the sole source of income or it may be in addition to other resources, such as savings and a private pension. An unemployed benefit is usually the second or third income in the house, for in a household in which husband and wife both work the loss of a job by one does not imply the other being out of work. Benefit payments to young people are normally a net addition to a household's cash income. The unemployed person who is the sole breadwinner in a family of four is today the exception, not the rule. Relying upon multiple sources of income and production makes it that much easier for a family to get by.

When the Gallup Poll asks ordinary people to describe the present financial situation of their household, the great majority say that they can get by. At the end of 1988, a period of economic boom, 41 per cent said that they were managing to save something, 45 per cent said that their family was 'just managing to make ends meet on our income', and 13 per cent reported having to draw on savings or going into debt in order to get by. In sum, 86 per cent were able to get by or save money when times are good.

The ability of ordinary people to maintain consumption is tested when the economy turns bad, and the national income accounts record a recession or a contraction in the economy, as occurred in the early 1980s. At the end of 1981, after two years of economic contraction and unemployment rising toward 3 million, 83 per cent reported in the Gallup Poll that they were managing to get by on their income or save a little. At a time when policymakers perceived real economic hardship (and the successful launch of the Liberal–Social Democratic Party Alliance was creating real political difficulties too) only 13 per cent said that they were drawing on savings, and an additional 4 per cent reported running into debt.

The economic problems imposed upon households by the shortcomings of government economic policy are not so great as government's own statistics make them appear. In a buoyant economy the substitution of official for domestic production makes the height of the boom higher, just as the substitution of domestic for official production in recession makes the depth of the recession appear greater. From the viewpoint of the ordinary individual, however, moving between the official and the domestic economy has a positive advantage: it is a strategy for getting by in an economy that is full of ups and downs.

8

Individual Welfare in the Mixed Society

Is then the lesson to be learned that the proper policy for governments should be one of systematic abstention before the increasing horrors of the later 1980s? No. We need a recipe for the contemporary situation, on which our salvation depends.

Lady Wootton

If one wants salvation, one should go to a bishop and not to a politician.

Prime Minister Harold Macmillan

The welfare concerns of ordinary people are much the same in every advanced industrial society: adequate food and housing, health, income-security, education, and care in sickness and old age. No individual can meet welfare needs by relying solely upon his or her efforts; institutions are necessary to produce goods and services that individuals cannot provide for themselves.

The means to achieve these ends are multiple: food can be grown in a household garden or purchased in a market; health care may be paid for by the recipient, by an insurance company or by government; and in old age an individual may look after himself or herself, or be cared for by family, a profit-making residence or by a public agency. There is no logical necessity for the welfare concerns of individuals to be met solely by the state or by the market or by households on their own.

The welfare state is a familiar phrase, but it is also misleading. Although the state plays a major role in providing such services as security of income in old age, the term is misleading insofar as it reduces welfare solely to the actions of government. Welfare is the conjoint product of many different activities in society. The market also produces welfare; employers can provide pensions, health care and training for their workers. Defining welfare solely as products of the market and state is limiting too, for it assumes that it must be measured in money. The household is the third major source of welfare production. No money changes hands when parents look after children, spouses care for each other, or children help care for elderly parents.

To argue that there is no scope for the household or market to produce welfare is to endorse the implicitly totalitarian view that the state is responsible for everything that happens in society. The veteran Fabian and social policy expert, Lady Wootton, revealingly speaks of looking to government for salvation. In fact, the outputs of public programmes are only one among many inputs to the wellbeing of ordinary people (cf. Figures 1.1 and 1.2). To understand how ordinary people secure welfare we must think in terms of the *welfare mix*, which is produced by three very different social institutions – the household, the market and the state.

The state is not the chief institution to which most people turn for their welfare, let alone for salvation. Although the major family concerns identified by opinion surveys – employment, health, education and income – are the object of public policies, when people are asked who can most help with these problems, the great majority look to their own actions, to other members of their family, or to friends and neighbours, and not to the state (Rose, 1980a; Sniderman and Brody, 1977: 520). Ordinary people get by through reliance upon multiple sources of welfare.

Nor is welfare the primary concern of the state. Historically, the first concern of the state was the maintenance of public order and defence against foreign attack. Secondly came the provision of transport, communication and other services required as part of the infrastructure of a modern economy. Providing welfare was a later policy commitment of the modern state. Today, spending on such private benefits as health, education and income-maintenance involves big claims upon public resources, but not to the exclusion of other claims. Interest payments on the debt are increasing greatly too (cf. Table 1.2; Rose, 1976a).

From the underall view of ordinary people, the total amount of welfare is more important than its source. Total welfare in society is likely to be greater if there are a multiplicity of sources rather than a monopoly supplier. If government has difficulty in providing a high standard of services, then individuals with a sufficient income can substitute services purchased in the market. If individuals lack the income to buy welfare for themselves, they may turn to government or rely upon personal care in the household rather than upon bureaucratized public provision. Insofar as there are failures of services of the market, government or household, then, the strengths of each sector may compensate for limitations of others (cf. Wolf, 1987).

Understanding the multiple sources of welfare is particularly important in international comparisons. A primary characteristic of the Third World is that most production and consumption is *not* monetized; the household is of primary importance. In advanced industrial nations money is important but not all-important, as the role of the family in Japan demonstrates. Nor is the state all-important. To argue that Americans have less health care than Europeans simply because the United States does not maintain a comprehensive state health service is to ignore the role of the market in providing health care through private-sector insurance and individual payment. Whereas the welfare goals of individuals and families are much the same whatever their citizenship, the means to achieve these goals differ significantly from country to country.

The source of welfare affects its distribution. Insofar as the state is the primary source of welfare, then access depends primarily upon the badge of citizenship. But citizens are entitled to benefits only if they meet bureaucratic regulations, and such services may be heavily influenced by the expert values of producers. Insofar as the market is the primary source of welfare, access depends upon income as well as need. Insofar as the family is the primary source, then single persons, widows and divorced persons will be handicapped, given the importance in welfare production of the output of non-waged housewives.

Because ordinary people secure their welfare from a mixture of institutions, the first section of this chapter sets out a simple model of the roles of state, market and household in producing welfare in society. The second section uses evidence from Britain, often described as a typical welfare state, to show how the role of the state, the market and the household varies from one form of welfare to another. The concluding section shows how families rely upon a mixture of institutions, and difficulties that can arise in making use of each.

A bottom-up view of welfare in society

From the perspective of an ordinary family, primary welfare needs are defined by household concerns rather than public budgets. Income in old age was needed before social security laws were introduced, and health care before government began to finance health services. Primary welfare concerns are goods and services that necessarily affect everyone all the time, such as food and housing, or at a major stage in the life cycle, for example, education in youth or income in old age. We can identify at least seven major welfare concerns. Every individual has a continuing need for money, food, housing and transportation, and at some point in the life cycle for education, health and personal care by others.[1] It is an open empirical question *whether* a particular welfare need is met by the state, the market or the household, or by a combination of several sources.

Each welfare product can be identified empirically. Income, housing or health care are measured far more easily than such abstract welfare goals as community. In examining the welfare mix there is no need to invoke the empty definitions that have tended to turn pure welfare economics into 'an uninterpreted system of logical deductions which would not be about anything at all' (Little, 1950: 81f).

Welfare goods and services are private benefits but they are also social goods, being produced as part of a system of social exchange. For example, a meal can be bought in a restaurant, provided by a public institution without charge as a school lunch or a hospital dinner, or prepared in the household. Some services, such as a university education, can only be provided by large and sophisticated institutions, whether public or private. Other services, such as care for the elderly, can be provided by such informal institutions as the family or friends and neighbours. The focus here upon exchangeable goods and services excludes self services that everyone must provide for himself and herself, such as sleeping and eating. The approach also excludes such important intangible concerns as happiness and life-satisfaction, which reflect individual states of mind.

The production of welfare goods and services can be monetized *or* non-monetized. A farmer does not need to buy food to have a meal. Nor does a child need to buy a parent's affection to receive care. Conventional national income accounting includes only the cost of meals produced outside the home, and omits the labour involved in making meals within the home. Much of the large portion of time spent in unpaid work within the home is devoted to welfare production (cf. chapter 7).

The consumption of welfare can be monetized *or* non-monetized. Welfare produced within the home is not sold to the consumer; it is given freely. It is thus priceless from both a consumption and production point of view. Welfare produced and sold in the market, such as private education, is fully monetized, involving consumers paying producers. The private benefits of public policy are usually provided free, that is, without charge to the consumer, but at a cost to the fisc. While the British national health service is free to users because they are not charged, it claims 10 per cent of total public expenditure. Richard Titmuss's (1970) famous interpretation of blood donation as a gift relationship, in which altruism replaced economic calculus, was only *half* correct. While blood is usually given free by altruistic donors, the national health service staff whose labour is necessary to transfer the blood to patients are unionized employees working for money wages.

There are four different ways of providing a given welfare service (Figure 8.1), depending upon whether or not the service is monetized at the point of production or at the point of consumption: the *market* (production and consumption of services monetized, e.g. private education); the *state* (production monetized, but non-market provision of consumption, e.g. public education); the *household* (neither production nor consumption monetized, e.g. a father teaching his son how to use a saw) and *barter* (a market exchange without money, e.g. a teacher giving tuition to a plumber's child in return for household repairs). Given the limits of barter, which quickly leads to the need to re-invent money, if only in some form of scrip or labour tokens, it is not further explored here.

In the United States non-profit institutions are sometimes treated as a separate source of such welfare services as hospital care and university education. But American non-profit institutions are only a variant of

Monetized in production	Monetized to consumers	
	Yes	No
Yes	MARKET	STATE
No	BARTER	HOUSEHOLD

Figure 8.1   *Alternative Sources of Welfare in the Mixed Society (Rose, 1986b: Figure 1.1)*

market provision. Even though these organizations are not making a profit, professors, doctors and service workers in universities and hospitals expect to be paid for their labour. Since profit is a small portion of the total cost of producing a service, the cost per beneficiary is virtually the same in these organizations as elsewhere. An estimated 70 per cent of all revenue of non-profit organizations comes from the charges made for the provision of goods and services; philanthropic gifts account for a limited portion of income. Moreover, the operational definition of non-profit institutions in the United States is provided by the Internal Revenue Service, which defines the conditions under which an organization is exempt from paying taxes on its income and any surplus that it may accumulate (cf. Weisbrod, 1988; Dean and Ware, 1986).

Total welfare in society (TWS) can be described by a simple identity, in which H equals the household production of welfare; M equals welfare bought and sold in the market; and S equals welfare produced by the state.

$$TWS = H + M + S$$

While the total amount of welfare is determined by the sum of these three sources, the welfare mix is a distributional measure. The mix is independent of total welfare; it is the percentage of goods and services produced by each of the three sectors. The distribution of sources of welfare in society can take many different forms, ranging from monopoly provision to each institution providing one-third of a given welfare service.

Growth and substitution in the dynamics of welfare production. The growth of total welfare in society reflects a net increase. Insofar as one sector expands by substituting for another, then the growth of state provision does not thereby produce a net increase in welfare. For example, the provision of meals to children at school can substitute for meals that would otherwise be obtained at home. We cannot infer growth in total welfare simply by looking at public expenditure on private benefits. To understand changes in total welfare, we must consider the decline of the traditional role of the household; the monetization of welfare production by the Industrial Revolution; and the fiscalization of welfare production by the state.

The household was the original economy, *producing without money* virtually all the goods required by its members. The household economy has been the chief source of most welfare goods and services for most of the history of the world. Health care was provided at home. The needs of the elderly were looked after by younger members of a family. While children might not learn much reading, writing or arithmetic from parents, they learned how to do household chores, and an apprentice artisan lived as part of the extended household of a master craftsman. Until comparatively recently the domestic economy of a peasant emphasized household production and consumption outside the market.

The Industrial Revolution began to *monetize* welfare production. Paid employment became the norm rather than labour in exchange for shelter, food and other services. In rural communities family-oriented peasants gradually turned into market-oriented farmers. A millworker or miner rented a home, and bought food from a local shop. Welfare goods and services were now bought and sold in the market by those who could afford them. Because families in towns needed a weekly money income, mutual benefit societies developed to insure people against the risks of sickness, old age, and death. In the late nineteenth century a major role of many British unions was the provision of such private benefits to dues-paying members. Insurance companies expanded, selling sickness benefits and pensions to millions who now had money to save. Rising income enabled some families to pay for the education of their children and to hire domestic servants to produce services in the household.

Fiscalization followed, the development of the state's capacity to collect substantial money sums as tax revenue. In order for the state to provide social benefits two conditions were necessary: a national product had to be monetized and substantial, and government needed the political authority to collect a substantial portion of that product in taxation. In pre-industrial societies, where money was scarce, taxes were often levied in labour or kind, or not collected at all. Fiscal capacity is still very weak in many Third World countries today (Goode, 1984). As national wealth and fiscal capacity grew in the late nineteenth century, states began to develop programmes for the collective good of public health; individual care was left to the market. Elementary education was provided for citizens without charge by the state. In the twentieth century the state provision of welfare has grown slowly; it has also grown greatly (cf. Flora and Heidenheimer, 1981).

Monetization and its concomitants of industrialization and economic growth have led to an *expansion* in total welfare in society. By comparison with a half-century or a century ago, individuals today have far more education, health care, and security in old age, and these advantages are more widely distributed.

Insofar as fiscalization transfers to the state a welfare service of the market (e.g. health insurance) or the household (e.g. child day-care centres), then an increase in state provision in the first instances is only the *substitution* of one source of supply for another. Taxes raised to increase public spending on social benefits may subtract from private spending for these concerns. When peasants shift from growing their own food to buying food in the market, they do not necessarily eat more or better just because they buy what they eat. The creation of a national health service immediately alters the effective demand for health care, but initially it does not alter supply. Producers of health care are simply paid by the state rather than by the private sector.

In the medium term, the introduction of public programmes to provide benefits without charge to the recipient can be expected to increase demand, as ordinary people find that a valued service is available free of charge. Substitution and growth in welfare has the potential to alter radically the welfare mix. As more of society's activities become monetized, the household provision of welfare can be expected to decline in significance. As the fiscal capacity of the state grows, the state's share should increase, and state programmes provided without charge may reduce the market provision of welfare. The growth of welfare services provided free of charge implies the prospect of the *state as the monopoly source* of welfare production.

By contrast, a pluralistic *mixed society* model assumes that the growth in state provision of welfare does not completely substitute for the market and household. It is even possible that ordinary people will use rising incomes to purchase more welfare in the market, or the rising costs of welfare may lead to an increased reliance upon non-monetized household care. A mixed society accepts the importance of fiscalized welfare, but hypothesizes that the market and the household also have a comparative advantage, enabling each to make important contributions to total welfare in society. The household, the market and the state are not so much competing as complementary.

Differences in sources of welfare

Materialist conceptions of welfare, shared by market-oriented liberals and state-oriented Marxists, tend to be neutral as between market and state provision of welfare. If the money isn't there, then neither the market nor the fisc can finance it. It follows that total welfare in society should be greater in an advanced industrial nation than in a poor Third World country, but this says nothing about the source of the goods and services that constitute the welfare mix. Three propositions are explored here: (1) the welfare mix differs from one social concern to another; (2) the welfare mix changes across time as the fiscal resources of the state crowd out the household and market; (3) nations differ in the extent to which the state provides welfare.

1   *Sources of welfare differ with concerns.* The existence of a plurality of sources of welfare implies that each has a distinctive comparative advantage. The state can provide goods without charge, the market can use charges to adapt services to the taste of consumers, and the household can provide services flexibly and freely without the cash calculations of the market or the procedural constraints of a state bureaucracy.

Insofar as each welfare concern has distinctive characteristics these can confer a comparative advantage to one or another source. For example, the state can provide everyone with a secure inflation-proofed pension in old age because of its taxing powers; the market can sell food to individuals according to their varied tastes; and members of a family can provide personal social services with imagination and affection. While each welfare concern would tend to depend upon a single source of supply, in total there would be a mix of sources for total welfare.

Alternatively, differences in the sources of welfare could reflect contrasting characteristics of families. Poor people are more likely to depend upon publicly financed services because they cannot afford market prices, whereas well-to-do people can buy education, health care and pensions. Differences in family circumstances affect the use of the household. A family with several small children must provide much care for their offspring in the home; a young single person has neither need nor opportunity to do so; and a widow may live in a state-funded nursing home. Insofar as the circumstances of recipients rather than characteristics of products are of primary importance, then we would expect the welfare mix to be found within each concern.

The relative importance of the state, the market and the household in meeting the basic concerns of ordinary people can be tested for Britain, where state welfare services have been institutionalized for generations (see Rose, 1986a for details). If one is accustomed to thinking of welfare solely as a product of public expenditure, the results are surprising. Table 8.1 ranks programmes according to the importance of the contribution of the household. The household is pre-eminent in three areas, personal social services, preparing meals, and housing maintenance; the market is pre-eminent in providing food and in transportation; and the state ranks first in only three areas: health care, income-maintenance and education.

However, when welfare is viewed from the underall position of ordinary people, the analysis is not surprising.

The pre-eminence of the household is greatest in *personal social services*; caring for the young and the elderly occurs as a byproduct of everyday family life. More than five-sixths of child-care is provided in the home, and 96 per cent of care for the elderly. The market and the state can also provide child-care centres for working mothers and care for the elderly. However, the role of both remains small compared to parents looking after their children; elderly couples looking after each other; and widows or widowers looking after themselves rather than live in an institution. While the motive of family members in caring for one another is affection, the results are significant for the fisc. If families did not provide so much care, the state would have to finance comprehensive child care for the fifth of the population too young to look after itself, and residential care on a massive scale if everyone in retirement were unable to care for himself or herself. Upwards of one-third of the population would have to receive daily care from the state if the household did not look after all its members.

Although *nutrition* is a daily necessity, food is usually ignored in conventional discussions of the welfare state. Table 8.1 shows why: it is not a concern of the state. Nearly all the food that people consume is bought in the market. But food purchased in the market is only the raw material of a meal, which combines different grocery products according to taste. Most meals are prepared in the home; the market sells meals to people who find it convenient to eat out or at work, or who relax by paying others to prepare their food. Since restaurants calculate that the

Table 8.1   *Sources of Welfare in the Mixed Society in Britain (percentages)*

	Source		
	Household	Market	State
Personal social services			
Children	85	8	7
Elderly	96	2	2
Nutrition			
Food supplies	2	98	0
Preparation of meals	82	15	3
Housing maintenance	45	44	11
Health care	37	7	56
Income	32	30	38
Transportation	24	55	22
Education	0	6	94

Source: Adapted from Rose, 1986a: Table 4.9.

cost of food is less than half the cost of a meal, the notional value of meals prepared in the home is very large indeed.

The state's role in the provision of food is very limited. Public subsidies of agriculture raise the income of farm producers but not ordinary people, for food thus becomes more costly. Government seeks to ensure that everyone has adequate nutrition by guaranteeing an income. The American food stamp programme has been unpopular because it originated in a desire to help the Department of Agriculture dispose of surplus farm products, rather than giving people the food they want. Only in extreme circumstances, such as wartime, is government concerned with the nutrition of ordinary people. Even in wartime rationing did not dictate what people must eat; families were assigned ration books with tokens that could be spent as the family chose for different types of food in short supply.

Both the household and the market are important in *housing*. Much routine maintenance is undertaken by residents outside the market and without public assistance. This is true not only of routine daily and weekly cleaning chores, but increasingly of do-it-yourself repairs and home improvements. As the cost of labour has risen and the price of specialist tools has fallen, more and more families are prepared to look after painting, gardening and minor repairs. Major repairs must still be purchased in the market, whether from a supplier paying taxes or from an unofficial supplier. The state's role in housing maintenance is particularly large in Britain, because upwards of one-quarter of the population live in municipally owned council houses. But when tenants buy their homes from the council, they thereby assume responsibility for maintenance.

In buying and selling houses, the market is dominant, and the state indirectly subsidizes house-purchase through tax relief on mortgage interest payments. However, most families do not sell houses for profit. Instead of considering a house as an investment asset, most people think of a house as a home and a centre of non-market activities.

Health is best when an individual follows a healthy household routine, and therefore does not need to see a doctor or enter a hospital. Keeping fit is a personal responsibility that each person can meet by diet, exercise and daily routines. Health care is needed when something goes wrong with a person's body. When a person feels ill, he or she does not need to go to a hospital or a doctor. A person with a cold may stay home from work or school and be cared for by other members of the family, or buy a variety of self-medication drugs. Treatment within the home is common for many minor complaints. Among employees certified as too ill to be at work, 80 per cent remain at home because they are not sick enough to be hospitalized. If everyone who was too ill to work was treated in hospital rather than at home, the cash cost would be tens of billions greater than health spending today.

The state appears important in the provision of health care because the money cost of its activities is stated in public expenditure documents, whereas the 'in-kind' value of household care can only be estimated. The value attributed in Table 8.1, more than one-third of total health care, is a minimum figure for it is based principally upon family care for persons too ill to go to work. Only when health care is restricted to monetized care does the British national health service appear pre-eminent, accounting for nearly nine-tenths of what is spent on medical and hospital treatment.

In a money economy everyone needs an *income*, but differences in individual circumstances cause people to rely on three sources almost equal in size. The household accounts for nearly a third of incomes because there are major transfers within the family from parents to children, from husband to unwaged housewife, and sometimes from elderly parents to children or vice versa. The state accounts for just over a third of incomes because public employment covers a quarter of the labour force or more, and income-maintenance grants to the elderly, the unemployed and others affect even more people than public employment (Rose, 1985b: 42ff). The market provides less than one-third of incomes, since the majority of the population is not in employment. Many children benefit indirectly from the earnings of parents working in the private sector, many also benefit from earnings of parents in the public sector, and in two-income homes one person can work in the public sector and the other in the private sector.

Mobility is an important but often neglected feature of welfare in society. People need to get out and about to hold a job, to look after household needs and to relax. Confinement to the home because of a physical disability is bad for an individual's psychological and economic wellbeing. In the course of a month, an ordinary person will use a mixture of sources for transportation, walking to shops or to visit friends; driving a car or riding with others; and making use of public transport for a bus or train journey.

The market provides more than half of total *transportation*; the automobile is used for pleasure and for journeys to work, and long-distance aeroplane journeys must be paid for too. The household ranks second as walking is important for many journeys near home and within a city centre. The household is also important in running a car, for a person usually drives himself or herself and a housewife may be an unpaid chauffeur for children. The state is third in importance, as the use of a car has replaced public transport in the postwar world. Furthermore, the state pays for the roads that are necessary for the use of private automobiles as well as public buses, and it can regulate private-sector transportation.

Education has the unique distinction of being the only British welfare product that is almost exclusively produced by public institutions. When education was made compulsory in the late nineteenth century it was also necessary for the state to provide schools to which children could go. The home can provide support and encouragement to studies, but parents cannot teach the full range of subjects in a contemporary primary or secondary school, let alone a university. The market can and does sell education, but the cost is very high. Notwithstanding the attention given fee-paying (misleadingly called 'public') schools in England, those schools provide for only 6 per cent of all youths.

Overall, the first proposition is upheld: there are big differences in the source of welfare from one concern to another. The state, the market and the household each has a comparative advantage for at least one welfare product. The household is uniquely suited to provide personal social services and prepare meals; the market is best at selling people the food they want; and the state can provide education without charge.

Comparative advantages are not absolute, for three concerns – income, housing and transportation – very much rely upon a mix of sources. Ordinary people prefer to buy food, receive public education and be given care by their family; no one wants to depend for all their welfare solely upon the household, the market or the state.

2 *No crowding out by the fisc.* On theoretical grounds, the growth of welfare services provided free of charge by the state could be expected to crowd out services sold by the market and by the household, because of giving people what appears to be something for nothing. Yet this has not been the case.

From the perspective of more than a century, the greatest change has been the monetization of welfare, enabling both the market and the state to become major sources of welfare, thus breaking the dominance of the household in a pre-industrial society. Industrialization increased both cash income and products for sale in the market. It also increased the tax base for the fisc. From this followed the second great transformation: the vast expansion in the quantity and quality of welfare products available. Food, housing, health care, transportation, education, and income available to ordinary people today are of a far higher standard than what was available when Britain first became an urban, industrialized society in the mid-nineteenth century (Rose, 1965).

While the growth of the economy was a pre-condition for increasing welfare, it was neutral as between the role of the state or market. It took more than a half century after Britain became an urban industrial society for Acts of Parliament to begin laying the foundation for major public programmes that we recognize today. A century ago there was virtually no public provision for health care, income or transportation, and churches operated more than three-fifths of primary schools. In such circumstances, the only direction in which public policy could change was to grow. There was growth in the market sector too; for example, railways, trams and omnibuses began to supplement travel on foot.

Evolutionary changes in the first half of the twentieth century resulted in the growth of total welfare; the gross national product expanded, and so did real incomes and public spending. New programmes for council housing were introduced and education greatly expanded. The expansion of publicly financed health care resulted in the establishment of a national health service by the 1945 Labour government, which also extended social security legislation. In such fields as health care, there was substitution as state replaced market; substitution occurred also in transportation, as nationalized industries took over from private enterprise.

The state now shares but does not monopolize the provision of welfare in a mixed society. By any standard Britain today has all the programmes associated with a welfare state. Yet the state's provision of welfare has not crowded out the market or the household (Table 8.1). For example, even though Britain has an extremely wide-ranging national health service, it accounts for little more than half of all health care, when non-monetized household services are taken into account. In a fully developed system of welfare provision, the mix of state, market and household has remained relatively stable since 1950 because each retains a comparative advantage, whatever the government of the day (cf. Rose, 1986a). The growth in total welfare in society since 1950 has depended primarily upon growth in the economy.

Examining changes since 1851 in how people gain access to a money income can illustrate the way in which there has been a shift in sources of income without any crowding out. In 1851 Britain had a market system, for nearly half the total population was employed for a money wage, and the great majority in industrial jobs or service occupations, rather than more traditional agricultural jobs. Within the employed economy, nearly everyone relied upon the private sector; public employment involved only 1 per cent of the population. Because families tended to have more children, and most women were not in paid employment, half the population depended upon the transfer of money within the household, as male breadwinners provided money for their wives and children (Table 8.2). By 1911, just before the First World War, the population of Britain had more than doubled but the sources of income had altered little; household transfers accounted for more than half the incomes in society.

The state started to become a significant source of incomes between the First and Second World Wars. The principal reason was the growth of public income-maintenance grants for the elderly and the unemployed. Such programmes were unknown in mid-Victorian times. Income-maintenance grants were almost twice as numerous as paid posts in the public sector. The growth in publicly provided incomes was offset by a

Table 8.2   *Changing Sources of Individual Income in Britain,*
1851–1981 (percentages)

Provision by	1851	1911	1938	1951	1981
Market (private employment)					
Non-agriculture	39.2	37.1	37.1	32.0	28.8
Agriculture	9.9	3.7	2.0	2.5	1.1
Total market	49.1	40.8	39.1	34.5	29.9
State					
Public employment	1.2	3.0	4.7	12.5	13.7
Income maintenance	0	2.5	8.9	12.5	24.8
Total state	1.2	5.5	13.6	25.0	38.5
Household transfers	49.7	53.8	47.3	40.5	31.6

Source: Rose, 1986a: Table 4.1.

contraction in agriculture; otherwise, private sector employment remained unchanged in scale.

In the postwar era the total population of Britain has remained relatively constant, but sources of income have shifted in keeping with demographic as well as public policy changes. By 1951 public incomes had increased to one-quarter of all incomes, divided equally between an enlarged public employment sector and broadened provision of income-maintenance grants. By 1981, the state had become the largest single source of income, as demographic changes greatly increased the number of elderly people claiming a pension and other income-maintenance programmes also expanded. The household fell in importance as a source of income as the average number of children per family dropped and as more women entered paid employment. While the household has declined in significance it remains more important than the market, which now accounts for fewer incomes than state or household.

From an historical perspective the shift from two to three sources of income has greatly altered the welfare mix. The mix can be found within families, where children depend upon parents and one parent works in the public sector and the other in the private. For the foreseeable future changes in the mix will be marginal, not structural. Children will continue to depend upon care in the home, the state will continue to have a substantial number of employees and persons dependent upon income-maintenance grants, and the market will remain the principal source of earnings within the labour force, though not of total incomes in society.

3   *Common ends but different means.* While welfare concerns are common to ordinary people throughout the world, the means used can differ, in particular, the extent to which people in different societies rely upon

the state, the market, or the household to meet their needs. For this reason, comparing societies simply in terms of the state provision of welfare can be misleading. In Sweden public spending on social programmes is 33.4 per cent of the national product, more than double the level in Switzerland, where it is 14.9 per cent and almost double the level in Japan (cf. Rose, 1989; OECD, 1985: Table 1). The differences are particularly striking, given that all three nations are very prosperous in terms of gross national product per head.

From a top-down statist perspective, the ordinary Swede would appear to have more than twice as high a standard of health, income, food, housing, social services, and education and transportation as the average Swiss or Japanese. But such an inference is false, because it ignores the contribution that the market and the household make to the production of total welfare in society. Where the national product is high, then we would expect the provision of welfare to be high, whatever the source. Even though the means differ, the ends are likely to be the same.

From the underall position of the ordinary individual, the primary concern is not the amount of public spending but how much is spent by society overall. Health care illustrates the importance of viewing welfare services in terms of three sources, for governments of advanced industrial nations differ substantially in funding health programmes. In Britain the ideal is a publicly financed national health service that provides comprehensively for the needs of everyone. It is assumed that this will keep people in good health, and the government can invest in preventive medicine and avoid expensive frills. In the United States much responsibility for health care is left to the market; health services are sold by doctors, and hospitals will usually refuse to admit people who cannot guarantee the payment of hospital charges. Insurance financed by employer and employee contributions meets much but not all of the cost of health expenditure. Japan has the national wealth to spend on health care, but because it has only recently industrialized, most Japanese have matured relying a great deal upon household care.

When we compare public effort, there are contrasts in health care between Britain, Japan and the United States (Table 8.3). In both Britain and Japan national health systems cover the whole of the population for both hospital and medical services. By contrast, in the United States federal laws cover only one-quarter of the population for medical treatment. It is thus hardly surprising that in Britain and Japan public spending on health accounts for a higher share of the national product than in the United States.

However, when total societal spending on health care is examined, a very different picture emerges, for public spending accounts for less than half of societal spending on health in America, while accounting for three-quarters to nine-tenths in Japan and Britain. When all sources of

Table 8.3   *Comparing Health Care and Conditions across Continents*

	Japan	Britain	USA
Health expenditure			
Public spending (as % GDP)	5.0	5.5	4.5
Total spending in society (as % GDP)	6.7	6.2	10.8
Public as % of total health spending	75	89	42
Health conditions			
Life expectancy born 1980 (years)	76	73	73
Infant mortality (as % live births)	0.62	1.02	1.09

Source: OECD, 1985, 11f, 15, 69, 131, 145.

health care are taken into account, the United States spends 10.8 per cent of its national product on health services, more than half again as much as Britain or Japan. Given that America's per capita national product is higher too, the result is that American spending per person on health care is more than double that of Japan or Britain, and this difference remains when controls are introduced for differences in health care costs.

For the ordinary individual, the bottom line is not measured in money but in health conditions. On this count, Japan ranks first. The average Japanese born today can expect to live three years longer than the average Briton or American, and infant mortality is two-fifths less than in these two countries. Differences in the household appear important in explaining why the Japanese enjoy more health for less money. Japanese appear to follow a healthier household routine than do Americans, for example, having a very low consumption of butter and other foods likely to encourage disease. The relatively low level of health in the United States, notwithstanding a very high level of health expenditure, indicates that not only are medical costs in the United States inflated, but also that many people follow unhealthy routines in the home.

When we compare sources of welfare across nations, we should carefully distinguish between similarities in goals, and differences in means. National history and the creation of specific institutions can easily lead to noteworthy differences in the organization of welfare by the public sector, in the public–private sector mix, and in the role of the household. Only by examining welfare production in the whole of society can we determine whether or not the state is pre-eminent in a programme. In particular we should avoid the confusion of means and ends. Ordinary people, less concerned with the mechanics of welfare production and more concerned with maintaining individual wellbeing, concentrate upon such goals as good health, rather than treating institutions of the state or the market as ends in themselves.

Getting access and getting by

In the course of a day, each ordinary person is likely to make some use of the services of the household, the market, and the state. Although ideological contrasts can be drawn between state and market or between family and state, ordinary people do not organize their lives according to such distinctions. In order to maximize total welfare, an individual normally combines all three sources. Total welfare in the family (TWF) is thus the sum of goods and services obtained from the state, the market and the household.

$$TWF = H + M + S$$

In terms of total welfare in the family, a money income remains a sum of money, whatever the source. A house is a roof over one's head, whoever maintains it; and a meal can have the same amount of calories, whether prepared at home or bought in a restaurant. Multiple sources of welfare provide more than a sole source. An elderly person who depends solely upon a state pension has less than a person who has both a public and a private pension, or a family at hand to provide care when needed.

Multiple sources of welfare make it possible to maintain welfare by changing the mix of resources. For example, an individual in work may rely upon earnings in the private sector, while out of work relying upon unemployment benefit and others in a family. Because welfare products are only inputs to the lives of individuals, everyone can add value to welfare by their efforts. For example, if the pupil : teacher ratio in a school deteriorates, then a pupil can study harder to maintain a constant level of learning in an enlarged class.

Individual access to welfare, however, is much influenced by differences between institutional sources. Terms of access also affect the extent of costs and benefits. State provision of welfare makes access depend upon the political status of citizenship rather than purchasing power in the market. Any citizen who can meet an entitlement laid down in a public law can demand such services as education or health care. The rationale is political. Citizens are conceived of as members of a single national community, deserving benefits by virtue of belonging to the same nation. In a democracy, such benefits are considered an expression of mutual regard; in an authoritarian regime benefits are given by the state in order to extract more services from subjects.

The state provision of welfare benefits is also bureaucratic. Because state welfare services require authorization by public law, access is not simply on individual demand, but also by virtue of statutory entitlement. To receive a state benefit an individual must meet legal criteria for eligibility; those whose needs are not recognized in law cannot appeal for help on a personal basis, as can be done in the family. As welfare services are provided without charge, the values of experts such as doctors and teachers greatly influence the way in which particular services are produced. The conventional measure of the quantity and quality of publicly provided welfare services is money, but the cost of programme outputs cannot be automatically equated with the benefits that individuals receive in welfare outputs. For example, an extra pound or dollar paid to a teacher is not evidence of an equivalent improvement in the learning of a pupil (cf. Heller, 1981).

The distinctive characteristic of the market is that you get what you pay for. People can satisfy their tastes by spending more on housing and less on transportation, or vice versa. At a given level of expenditure, people can satisfy their tastes by buying very different types of food, or of cars. Laws do not dictate what people must eat, or whether they live in a new house, an old house or a flat. The state provides both public transport and roads for private cars; the choice of which to use is left up to the individual.

The limitation of the market is that you *only* get what you can pay for; income determines access. Choice is effective only insofar as a person has the income to pay for what he or she wants. Whereas all individuals share a common status as citizens, individuals are unequal in income. Each citizen can stand as tall as the next in claiming benefits; and those whose need is greatest, whether because of financial or physical handicaps, can claim most. A rationale for the state provision of welfare is that it compensates for income inequalities by providing benefits for those who could not afford to buy them. For example, even in a society in which most people have a car there remain some people who must rely upon subsidized public transport for their mobility.

Within the family access to help from others is not restricted by laws or the ability to pay; family members help each other because of emotional commitments. The claims that family members have upon each other are the unlimited claims of affection. The reciprocal services that parents and children provide each other and that are exchanged between spouses are not conceived in terms of political rhetoric or national income accounts. We do not think of people having (or being refused) access to a family; children enter a family by birth and marriages create families by choice. The resources of the family are substantial and relevant at all stages of the life-cycle.

For most ordinary people, major inequalities in welfare are a function of differences in family structure. A person can only have access to services from others if a family is there. A single-parent family cannot produce as much welfare in the home as a two-parent family, and a widow will not be able to draw upon the help that a husband can give, as well as not having a husband to help. A single person in ill health will have no one to care for him or her at home, whereas people living in a family can seek help from their spouse or other relatives.

As long as the ordinary family can secure welfare from a mixture of sources, then it can get by or get ahead in a mixed society; use of the state, the market and the household varies from one concern to another. But access depends also upon the character of individuals. Some people fail to meet the income test that the market imposes. Others may not meet bureaucratic standards for public benefits, be left waiting in a queue for scarce services or not like treatment provided by experts. People living alone, in broken homes or without long-term family ties have less access to welfare based on family affection. In any society there will be many people who cannot claim access to services on at least one count. The maintenance of total welfare thus depends upon the ability of ordinary people to have a portfolio of claims as family members, consumers and as citizens.

Note

1. While clothing is a necessity it is not examined here because of the large element of fashion and taste in clothing; its provision is similar to food, being bought in the market or made in the household rather than being provided free by the state. Leisure, which is also excluded, can be provided by the market or produced in the household; relatively few leisure facilities are provided by the state. Adding these two concerns would not alter conclusions.

9

Ordinary People in Out-of-the-Ordinary Economic Circumstances

> Liberal representative democracy suffers from internal contradictions, which are likely to increase in time and, on present indications, the system is likely to pass away within the lifetime of people now adult.
>
> Samuel Brittan

In a mixed society the provision of public programmes for private benefit requires large and growing tax revenues from a large and growing economy. From this it is sometimes inferred that what is good for the political economy must be good for individuals, But if a nation's political economy runs into economic difficulties, then this implies big trouble for ordinary people.

For a generation after the end of the Second World War, social democratic confidence in the benefits of government action was in the ascendancy, ideologically as well as electorally. Writers sympathetic to the growth of government set the tone of most discussions of public policy. Even when a nominal party of the right took office, such as the Heath Administration in Britain or the Nixon Administration in the United States, proposals to change policies were seen as reforms intended to improve rather than cut back government. Keynesian economists prescribed how government could sustain growth, sociologists prescribed ways to use public policies to promote income equality, and political scientists assumed that the natural party of government was the party that offered most benefits to most people, that is, Labour parties in Europe and the Democratic Party in the United States.

Ordinary people were not asked whether they believed in the unlimited capacity of government to do good. Nor was this necessary: ordinary people could simply enjoy the benefits produced by the knowledge and power embodied in the philosophy of the mixed economy welfare state. As long as this philosophy appeared to produce results, there was no reason for ordinary people to doubt that those in public office knew what they were doing.

The unexpected onset of economic difficulties in the mid-1970s brought about a crisis of political confidence. Politicians suddenly found that they could not rely indefinitely upon the fiscal dividend of economic growth to finance a never-ending expansion of publicly provided private benefits. Samuel Brittan (1975: 9) concluded that internal contradictions threatened the death of liberal representative government, because of the generation of excessive expectations of public benefits. Politicians who owed office to popular election did not trust ordinary people to respond sensibly to the very real economic difficulties confronting governments. There was anxiety that economic recession could lead to a collapse in popular confidence in political institutions. The elite motto appeared to be: 'Distrust the people' (see e.g. Huntington, 1974).

But ordinary people did not react as expected. Instead of investing more efforts in political activity to correct economic difficulties, most people seemed not to worry that their governors were unable to stop inflation, rising unemployment and a decline in economic growth. 'Distrust the governors' appeared to be the popular assumption. The experience of a decade and one-half since then has shown that ordinary people are able to cope with economic difficulties that cause politicians alarm, relying upon the market and household as well as the state to maintain their wellbeing.

In the 1980s the gloom of social democrats has been replaced by the optimism of politicians variously labelled as new right, conservative or (in the economic sense) liberal free-market. Ronald Reagan and Margaret Thatcher campaigned with the argument: 'Distrust government'. Public policies – and particularly programmes intended to influence the market – were said to cause economic difficulties. 'Trust the market' has been the motto of a new breed of politicians, who are radical in their rejection of the belief that public policy can guarantee the material wellbeing of all citizens. Yet there has been no massive cutback in the public provision of private benefits, which remain at a level well above that of the 1960s (see chapter 2).

Today, it is not easy to tell extraordinary from ordinary circumstances; it is all a matter of expectations. If we expect government to fail, as the new right argues, then inadequate public policies must be regarded as everyday occurrences. However, if we expect government to do what the people want, and people want government to make public provision for private benefits, then shortcomings will be much more serious. Popular expectations of government are therefore the subject of the first part of this chapter, which shows that most people have limited expectations of government. Thus, the inability of policymakers to increase prosperity continuously does not surprise people or produce frustration. The second section looks at what ordinary people think about how the economy does (and ought) to work. Limited expectations of government are not proof of unlimited trust in the market. There is widespread ambivalence: people are prepared to give two cheers for the market and two cheers for government too.

Limited expectations

Expectations are important, for the more that people expect government to do, the more frustrated they will be if government only achieves a limited amount of what is expected. Reciprocally, the less that is expected, the lower the standard of success. There are thus two opposite ways in which government can meet popular expectations. If expectations are high, meeting them means providing generous and expanding levels of private benefits. But if expectations of the political economy are low, then government meets these low expectations when it presides over a slow or no-growth economy, or imposes public spending cuts.

What should government do? In a mixed society, ordinary people expect government to look after some but not all of their material concerns. Public opinion surveys can help us identify how much or how little government is expected to do, and priorities for public action.

When British people are asked what government should definitely be responsible for, an overwhelming majority endorses two central programmes of the welfare state: health care, and maintaining a decent standard of living for the old. More than half also think that government should also keep prices under control and help industry to grow. However, the endorsement of social benefits does not reflect a philosophy consistently placing responsibility upon government for the market. Less than half think it is definitely government's responsibility to reduce income differences, ensure a decent standard of living for the unemployed, or provide a job for everyone who wants work (Table 9.1).

Table 9.1 *Popular Views of Government's Responsibilities*

	Percentage saying government definitely should be responsible	
	Britain	USA
Health care for the sick	86	35
Decent standard of living for the old	78	40
Keeping prices under control	60	29
Helping industry to grow	53	16
Reducing income differences, rich and poor	45	16
Decent standard of living for the unemployed	43	15
Job for everyone who wants one	37	13
Average	57	23

Source: Davis, 1986: 102.

By contrast, the American people usually do *not* expect government to be responsible for major concerns of society. When Americans are asked whether government should be responsible for the same socio-economic concerns, only 23 per cent on average say that these are definitely the responsibility of government (Table 9.1). Five-sixths or more of Americans do *not* think it is definitely the responsibility of government to help industry grow, reduce income differences, or provide a job or income for the unemployed. The extent of self-reliance – or at least, rejection of reliance upon Washington – is indicated by the fact that no concern is considered definitely a responsibility of government by a majority of Americans surveyed.

Given that the American people expect government to do less, it follows that these expectations can be met by it spending less on public policies than does the British government, and this is in fact the case. The American government in total spends nearly one-quarter less of the national product than does the British. While expectations of government are higher in Britain, this does not mean that there is a positive consensus across a range of responsibilities. To say that 57 per cent of Britons on average believe that government should definitely take a responsibility for socio-economic conditions means that 43 per cent do not have such a strong expectation.

In both countries, expectations for government action are highest for measures that are likely to affect everyone at some stage of the life-cycle. No one can expect to go through life without needing health care, and everyone who lives into old age wants a decent standard of living in retirement. Even if government is not the sole source of health care and income in retirement, it is expected to guarantee wellbeing in the British mixed economy welfare state. Americans are more likely to see government as important in ensuring living standards in old age and health care than in providing jobs for all, or reducing differences in income between rich and poor.

Some fundamental responsibilities of government are *not* big-spending items in the budget. The maintenance of law and order is by definition a responsibility of government. There is a broad consensus that crime cannot be solved simply by throwing money at the problem, for example, buying new computers or squad cars for police, or raising police salaries. Abortion is another issue that excites passions. The debate about abortion does not concern its cost, but its morality. The diplomatic activities of policymakers affect a country's position in the world, but they do not depend primarily upon the amount of money spent on diplomatic travel. The wisdom of a country's foreign policy is more important than the lavishness of the hospitality provided by its embassies.

Learning from experience. Ordinary people learn from experience when things go wrong as well as when government works. Changes in expectations are evidence of ordinary people learning from experience, altering their views in accord with the ups and downs of the economy. When the economy is booming it is reasonable to expect living conditions to improve, and when the economy goes into recession, it is reasonable to expect economic conditions to worsen.

Contrary to what the doom-mongers assumed, ordinary people did not invariably expect the state and market to provide steadily rising living standards, even at the height of the postwar economic boom. A survey of aspirations and affluence undertaken in 1968 in America, Britain, Germany and the Netherlands found that most people did not expect a continuing improvement in their material living standards. In Europe a majority said that they had not seen their living standards rise in the past few years. Expectations of the future were equally subdued; some people expected their position to deteriorate, while others looked forward to increased affluence. The perennial optimists, experiencing past prosperity and expecting prosperity to continue in the future, were less than a third of Americans, a quarter of Britons, a sixth of the Dutch, and one-eighth of the Germans (Katona et al., 1971: 44).

The roller-coaster progress of economies in the past two decades has reminded ordinary people that government cannot be expected to achieve every year a high rate of growth and a low rate of inflation and unemployment. In accord with the persistence hypothesis – people expect past trends to continue – we would expect people to expect things to get better when the economy is booming, and to get worse when it is in recession. Fluctuations in the economy can thus produce a surge of optimism, and then a surge of economic pessimism. As national economies have differed somewhat in their success in responding to the ups and downs of the international economy, in any one year we would expect to find differences between nations in expectations too.

At the end of each year the international Gallup Poll network asks people whether they think the coming year will be better or worse than the year just concluded, 'as far as you are concerned'. The question invites ordinary people to comment on their overall sense of wellbeing from a perspective that includes both economic and non-economic concerns. Four different answers are possible: people can expect their position to become better, worse, remain the same or may be unsure what will happen. Insofar as people have an unvarying belief that their lives ought to get better every year, then optimistic expectations should always dominate. Insofar as changing events and experiences influence expectations, then there should be fluctuations between optimism and pessimism, depending upon national and international, as well as personal, circumstances.

Since expectations can take any of three different forms, often no one view is held by half the electorate. Most of the time the median person makes the simplest forecast: as far as he or she is concerned, the year ahead is expected to be much the same as the previous year. At the beginning of 1989, for example, 46 per cent of Britons said that they expected the year ahead to be better, 33 per cent said that they expected it to be the same or didn't know what to expect, and 21 per cent expected it to be worse (Table 9.2). While optimists outnumbered pessimists by a margin of 25 per cent, the median Briton expected the year ahead to be the same as the year before. As long as personal circumstances do not get worse, then a majority of people will have their expectations met or exceeded.

When we review popular expectations during the major economic ups and downs of the past two decades there is ample evidence of people learning from experience, adjusting expectations in accord with changes in the world about them. At the start of 1972, when affluence had not yet been challenged, optimists outnumbered pessimists in most major Western nations (Table 9.2). After the first oil shock had registered its effects, those expecting 1975 to be worse than the year before outnumbered optimists. The pessimists were right; 1975 was a year in which the economies of most major Western nations actually contracted. In Sweden, where the economy had been unusual in continuing to grow, Swedes reacted in line with their national experience: optimists outnumbered pessimists.

The 1980s has seen an upturn in the international economy, even though recovery has been uneven. At the beginning of 1984 the median person in major Western nations expected economic conditions to remain much the same. By the beginning of 1988 optimism was once more in the ascendance in most nations. Just as the 1970s had taught ordinary people not to take continued economic growth for granted, so in the 1980s people learned that economic difficulties, while real, can also be temporary.

The ability of people to adapt expectations in the light of experience is shown by examining shifts in attitudes within a nation. In Britain, for

Table 9.2   *Expectations for the Year Ahead, 1972–89*

| | Percentage replying change for better minus percentage replying for worse | | | | |
	1972	1975	1980	1984	1989
America	35	n.a.	−25	55	40
Britain	14	−50	−50	−1	25
France	8	−48	−36	−27	13
Germany	−23	−42	−7	4	16
Italy	n.a.	−44	−26	−8	28
Sweden	25	25	8	−11	42
Average	12	−32	−23	2	27

Source: Gallup Poll, *Political Index* (normally January of the year cited).

example, optimists outnumbered pessimists in 1972, when the economy was expanding, but pessimists were an absolute majority in 1975 and 1980, before improvements in the economy brought about a return to a situation in which the two were almost evenly balanced. In the United States there have been major swings too. At the start of 1980, when the country was in the grips of a major recession, pessimists much outnumbered optimists, whereas by the start of 1984, a year in which Ronald Reagan won re-election, an absolute majority of Americans were optimistic about the year, and this also characterized America on the eve of President Bush's inauguration in 1989 (Table 9.2).

Two decades ago political scientists borrowed from social psychologists the theory of unmet expectations leading to frustration and then aggression. If people did not have their expectations met, they would become frustrated, and frustration was expected to lead to aggression, that is, an increase in popular protest or rebellion (Gurr, 1970). The theory encouraged forecasts of economic recession leading to political instability in the 1980s, if not before. The forecasts have been disproven. Because ordinary people adapt their expectations in keeping with changing circumstances, there was no cause for frustration and thus for aggression. Government continued to meet popular expectations in times of recession as in more affluent periods, because ordinary people reversed their expectations in accord with their changing experiences.

Politicians in office have an interest in encouraging people to expect bad news, in order to prevent an electoral backlash. Challenged to defend a disappointing economic record, governments can argue with some justification that the fault lies not in national policies but in international economic conditions. Asked to explain why problems persist, policymakers can respond that if they had not acted as they did, the results would have been even worse.

The worse economic conditions are made to appear, the more likely ordinary people are to feel a sense of reprieve (Rose, 1980: 224ff). If the headline news is about millions out of work, then the tens of millions still in work will feel better about their job, even if their pay has not been rising as expected. Headlines about recession can create anxiety, but ordinary people will feel relieved if they find that their standard of living has not been greatly reduced; it has only failed to rise. When people expect circumstances to get worse, this can lead to a sense of relief and reprieve when things turn out to be not so bad as the media make them appear.

Two cheers for the market and for the state

Party politicians have been quick to impose self-serving interpretations upon the views of ordinary people. Ideologues of the right claim that the difficulties of the 1970s are proof of the unwisdom of ordinary people relying upon government to provide many benefits, and claim that election results of the 1980s show that most ordinary people share their views. The left counterattacks by arguing that the needs of ordinary people can only be met by government and, after a decade or more of rule by parties of the right, the need will be even greater in the 1990s than it was in 1980.

Election victories enabled rightwing politicians to advocate their views from the vantage point of office in the 1980s. In Britain Margaret Thatcher's Administration has cut taxes and promoted privatization, selling off major nationalized industries such as telephones and gas (Rose, 1989b). The Reagan Administration concentrated upon cutting taxes and the deregulation of the economy to stimulate the supply side of the economy. Cuts in taxes have not only put more money in the hands of ordinary citizens; they have also meant that there is less money in the public purse to finance spending on private benefits. The Thatcher Administration has succeeded in keeping public spending from rising in order to eliminate the deficit that had long characterized the budget. By contrast, the Reagan Administration financed increased federal spending on health and social security as well as defence by increasing the budget deficit.

The shift to the market has affected politicians nominally on the left too. In France, for example, after briefly flirting with Keynesian-style expansion and Socialist-style nationalization following his 1981 election victory, President François Mitterrand's government soon shifted to a tight money policy and began promoting privatization. The Swedish Social Democratic Party returned to office in 1982 with a plan to promote economic recovery; it succeeded in doing so by a massive devaluation and wage freeze that cut the earnings of industrial workers and boosted exports and business profits. Communist bloc nations in Eastern Europe, such as Hungary, have begun to appreciate that the market can provide information that cannot be supplied by central planners.

The turn to the right was tested and confirmed when unemployment began to rise in the early 1980s and this was accepted, albeit regretfully, on both the left and right. While unemployment continues to be regarded as undesirable, it is no longer regarded as unexpected. The shock of rising unemployment can move public opinion and upset policymakers when it initially rises but it then tends to level off on a plateau that is much higher than two decades ago. Ordinary people learn to accommodate to a higher rate of unemployment, and greater difficulties for young people finding a first job. Since most people remain in work, and two-thirds or more have no direct fear of unemployment, its impact is low upon the voting behaviour of ordinary individuals. In the extreme case of Britain, Margaret Thatcher's Conservative Party has seen its vote remain constant while unemployment increased by two million.

The underall view. If election results are blunt instruments for representing the views of ordinary people, economic statistics are even less suitable as indicators of public opinion. Economic statistics may not even refer to people; for example, figures for the gross national product refer to money. Secondly, statistics may refer to aggregate totals, but an ordinary person may be more concerned with the standard of living of his or her family. Thirdly, many statistics concern only a limited portion of the population. For example, the number of unemployed is invariably less than 8 per cent of the electorate, and even the number in work is little more than half the electorate.

The literature of economic theory is short of empirical evidence about the behaviour of ordinary individuals, and full of assumptions and predictions about how people ought to behave. The empirical study of economic psychology provides an alternative to the a priori assumptions of economists (e.g. Lea et al., 1987; Furnham and Lewis, 1986). But it does not normally link psychological attitudes with political behaviour. The political science literature of economic attitudes invariably concentrates upon the link between economic attitudes and voting (cf. Alt, 1979; Kiewiet, 1983). However, this literature does not address larger questions about the relation of state and market pushed forward by events since the mid-1970s. Nor do politicians such as Margaret Thatcher provide evidence about what ordinary people think about state and market; they simply proclaim their own convictions.

Any examination of survey data about the views of ordinary people is likely to conclude that they are far less coherent and logical than is assumed in economic theories, or in debates between right and left. Preceding chapters have shown that ordinary people are prepared to give two (but not three) cheers for the public provision of private benefits, welcoming these benefits, but not to the exclusion of other sources. Likewise, ordinary people appear willing to give two (but not three) cheers for the market too (cf. Rose, 1983a; Collins, 1987).

For ordinary people, the market is a familiar and continuing presence in everyday life. An ordinary person spends more time in making calculations as a consumer of goods and services than as a voter. Problems of not enough money are much more immediate to an individual than those of backing a party that does not have enough votes to win an election. While one individual's vote can do little to influence the outcome of an election, a decision as a consumer about how to spend money has an immediate and personal impact upon the comfort and satisfactions of an ordinary person.

Work is regarded as socially desirable as well as a means of gaining an income. When British people are asked whether working is more than just earning a living, nearly three-quarters say that work is more than just a way to get money. This view is re-affirmed when people are asked whether or not they would continue to work even if they did not need the income. A further indication of positive attitudes toward work is that more than three in five say that they do the best work possible regardless of pay and only 7 per cent report that they are only willing to put out as much effort as they are paid for. While positive attitudes toward work are more likely to be found higher up the occupational class ladder, it is striking that a majority of Britons in all social classes, from the least skilled workers upwards, have positive attitudes toward work (Table 9.3).

The money that people earn at work supports a pattern of consumption and style of living that combines market, state and household resources. Earnings from work are no longer a matter of survival, for income-maintenance grants from public programmes are available under a wide variety of headings. Nor are people under pressure to raise their earnings because they are falling into debt. Yet this does not mean that everyone is satisfied with the current distribution of incomes, for differences in earnings are seen not only as market evaluations, but also in terms of political and social values about what is deemed fair or proper.

When Britons are asked whether they think the differences between high and low incomes are too large, about right or too small, three out of four reply that they think the gap is too big. The belief is found at all occupational levels of society. It is particularly striking that the government is seen to offend against standards of 'fair' pay more than the private sector, for 46 per cent complain about earnings differentials being too high in the public sector, compared to 30 per cent in the private non-manufacturing sector (Jowell and Witherspoon, 1985: 41).

However, it appears that much of the dislike of big differences between rich and poor is stimulated by media stories of the life-styles of rock stars and multi-millionaire tycoons, juxtaposed with the travail of the unemployed and single-parent mothers rather than by personal experience. When people are asked about the earnings that they know most about, namely, about pay at their own place of work, a very different

Table 9.3   *Popular Attitudes towards Work (percentages)*

British responses	Total	Middle-class		Working class	
		Professional/ managerial	Routine	Skilled	Semi-unskilled
Would work even if no financial need	72	73	72	73	70
Work is more than just earning a living	70	87	68	65	54
Do best work possible regardless of pay	61	66	58	59	57

Source: Mann, 1986: 24.

picture emerges. Half say that the differences in rewards are about right, as against 23 per cent saying they are too big, and 15 per cent saying that they are much too big (Jowell and Witherspoon, 1985: 41).

Cumulatively, differences in weekly earnings lead to major differences in wealth: a large and comfortable house versus a small abode, a comfortable, even luxurious life-style as against habits governed by financial stringency. Economists assume that differences in wealth reflect differences in achievement, whereas the conventional sociological view is that they reflect class differences that from birth give people very unequal chances in life. These contrasting evaluations have conflicting political implications. If inequalities in earnings reflect differences in achievement, the implication is that they should be accepted by government, but if they reflect class differences in life chances outside the control of the individual, then the case is boosted for promoting egalitarianism through public policies.

When British people are asked what they consider the cause of people getting ahead in life, two-thirds attribute success to personal ability and another fifth to education. Less than one in ten thinks that social background is the cause of getting ahead. By contrast with the conventional wisdom of academic sociologists, only 6 per cent believe that social class is a significant influence upon access to education. People usually see educational achievement as a reflection of individual ability and effort (Harrop, 1980: 93f).

The majority of ordinary people accept inequalities in earnings and think profits make possible higher public spending as well as greater private affluence (Rose, 1983a; Collins, 1987: 34). But most people do not see themselves as profit-seeking entrepreneurs, taking initiatives and risks in order to receive a profit in reward (Fogarty, 1985: 181). Self-employed entrepreneurs are the exception; nine-tenths of the labour force are employees of organizations, and one-quarter or more are in the public or voluntary sector, that is, employees of *non*-profit institutions. Most employees work in more or less routine tasks in offices or factories.

Reward is related to risk. An entrepreneur who starts a successful business can make millions, and even gain a seat in the House of Lords. But an entrepreneur can also lose his or her savings and end up an employee of a large risk-averse organization. Reward without risk is the ideal of most British people. As employees, ordinary people are ready to leave decisions about the finances of an organization to their employer. Very few workers have their earnings affected by profit-sharing schemes. When ordinary people invest in order to improve their earnings, this is typically done in risk-free ways. Working overtime requires the investment of extra effort, but it also promises the certainty of increased earnings. Studying for a degree or a vocational qualification involves the investment of effort but it also carries with it the promise of increased earnings without risk. When people buy special-offer discounted shares in privatized public utilities such as British Gas and British Telecom they do not see themselves as risking money but as buying a share of profits in a quasi-monopoly public utility.

Insurance against risk is as important as rewards. While reward without risk is impossible in a pure market system, it is the practical object of many programmes of mixed economy welfare states. Even in the United States, where unemployment insurance provides a much thinner cushion against the vicissitudes of the market, politicians accept that ordinary people without work are entitled to some form of public income-maintenance grant. Ordinary people can thus use the state to insure against risks of the market, and the market to provide rewards independent of laws and bureaucracy.

While the idea of giving two cheers for the market and two cheers for the state may sound confusing, politicians of many different colours seek ways to combine both, in recognition that ordinary people rely upon both state and market for their wellbeing. On the left, nominally Socialist politicians from Westminster to Moscow are promoting something that has been labelled market Socialism, seeking to combine consumer choice and incentives with the state provision of welfare. On the right, President Ronald Reagan showed that it was possible to campaign against government while underwriting its growth. When questioned about the specific commitments of government, Reagan made clear that government to him symbolized 'waste', and not the principal programmes of the federal government, defence, social security and health care, all of which grew greatly in expenditure during the Reagan Administration. In Europe, more sophisticated right-of-centre politicians have campaigned on behalf of what German Christian Democrats describe as the social market, which is meant to combine the rewards of the market with public policies for private benefits.

The Thatcher experience. The record of the Thatcher government since 1979 has been paradoxical. Public expenditure documents show the maintenance of the mixed economy welfare state. While priorities have shifted between programmes, the Thatcher government has been spending much the same proportion of the national product on public policy as did its Labour predecessors. Margaret Thatcher has found herself a prisoner of spending commitments inherited from previous governments, which granted entitlements to education, health care and pensions on terms often inconsistent with free-market logic. She is also a prisoner of the electorate, which favours a high or increasing level of spending on these popular private benefits (cf. Rose, 1984a).

At the ideological level Margaret Thatcher has crusaded for rolling back the state. Even when the government is bringing in another increase in public spending, the Prime Minister attacks the idea of reliance upon government by ordinary people, business or unions. In her ideal world, the market would play the primary role in providing welfare as well as wealth. It is her conviction that the market is better than government for meeting needs of ordinary people.

Three electoral victories can be cited in support of the claim that Margaret Thatcher has achieved a transformation in the outlook of ordinary English people. But the Conservative victories have each been won with less than half the vote, and votes reflect many influences besides political principles (see Figure 3.2 above). Three electoral victories for the Conservative Party under Margaret Thatcher's leadership are not proof of three cheers for the market.

Uniquely among postwar British politicians, Margaret Thatcher has given her name to an 'ism', Thatcherism (cf. Kavanagh, 1987; Jenkins, 1987). While there is not always agreement about the precise meaning of the term, there is no doubt that in her person the Prime Minister symbolizes a view of life in which the principles of the market are far more important than to any British Prime Minister of the twentieth century. Insofar as there has been a Thatcher Revolution in the lives of ordinary people (as distinct from the lives of ordinary Conservative MPs or Cabinet ministers) then we would expect most people to identify positively with it.

Yet when ordinary people are asked what they think of the Thatcher Revolution, the majority react unfavourably. While the Conservative leader has succeeded in winning parliamentary majorities, she has not won the hearts and minds of ordinary people. Only 28 per cent identify favourably with the idea of the Thatcher revolution. The rejection of the Thatcher revolution is found in all parties. Most who are prepared to vote Conservative react unfavourably to the idea of the Thatcher revolution; less than two in five endorse it. Among Labour and supporters of the Alliance parties, less than one in four react favourably (Table 9.4). While Margaret Thatcher has established a modern record for electoral success, and her name is now identified with a distinctive view of the role of government, she has not won the hearts and minds of a majority of

Table 9.4 *Popular Views of the Thatcher Revolution (percentages)*

Question: When you hear people talking about the Thatcher Revolution, do you think they are taking a favourable or an unfavourable view of how things are going in Britain?

	Total	Conservative	Alliance	Labour
Favourable	28	38	22	20
Unfavourable	49	42	55	57
Neutral, don't know	22	20	23	23

Source: Gallup Poll, *Political Index* 328 (December 1987), p.8.

ordinary people. Those against her efforts to change Britain outnumber the supporters of her cause (cf. Rose and McAllister, 1986: chapter 8).

Such is the logic of representative government that ordinary people are forced to vote for personalities, parties and programmes simultaneously. In such circumstances it is not possible to differentiate between giving one, two or three cheers for a party or a candidate. Nor is it possible to differentiate between voting for a leader in spite of her policies, or because of them. Upwards of a third who say that they like Margaret Thatcher add that they dislike her policies, and more than a quarter who say they like her policies tell the Gallup Poll that they dislike her personality.

In the United States a similar phenomenon is observed of people hedging their votes between the Republicans, a party identified with a businesslike approach to keeping government small, and the Democrats, identified with using public programmes to promote private wellbeing. The separation of powers gives ordinary people votes for candidates for Congress and for a President. Given two choices, a large proportion of Americans split their ticket. For a generation Republicans nominally in favour of low taxes and business have usually won control of the White House, and Democrats in favour of using tax money to provide more social benefits have won control of Congress. Washington thus combines the voices of representatives who cheer for the market, and those who favour the public provision of private benefits.

10

Consent as the First Priority

Ordinary voters are not fools.

V.O. Key Jr

If people do not look to the state to raise living standards in this world or produce salvation in the next, then what are the political priorities of ordinary people? As Key (1966: 7) says, ordinary people are not fools; their priorities concern those things that only the state can do. People value most priceless civil and political rights, such as freedom from arbitrary arrest, freedom of association, equality before the law and the right to vote in free and fair elections. Given these rights, ordinary people are prepared to consent even when they dispute the government's reasoning, its actions turn out to be mistaken, or the economy goes into recession. Without these priceless rights, a government may maintain authority, but it depends upon coercion not consent (Rose, 1969).

Consent is the first priority of government, because making authority legitimate comes before making people rich. Money means a lot, but it does not mean everything to ordinary people. Material goods can complement but cannot substitute for priceless political rights. In the Anglo-American world most people take basic civil and political rights for granted. The denial of civil and political rights to blacks in the American South for more than a century illustrates how a political system can be distorted when these rights are denied. Peoples of the Mediterranean lands from Portugal to Greece and Turkey appreciate their civil and political rights more because they have had recent experience of living under authoritarian regimes.

From the early nineteenth century onward Britain was admired throughout Europe as a paragon of political virtues, because ordinary people enjoyed liberty under the law and then the right to vote in free elections. The first faltering steps toward the welfare state were taken a half century after the expansion of the franchise, and completed generations after civil and political rights were taken for granted. Generalizing from English history, T.H. Marshall (1950: 8ff) propounded a three-stage model of the extension of the rights of citizens. First in point of time came civil rights, such as freedom from arbitrary arrest. Political rights, such as the right to vote, came second. Social rights were identified as a modern innovation, involving claims to an income, education, health care, and security in old age. Marshall's model is ambiguous about priorities; rights granted in the past may be considered first in importance as well as in point of time, or as *passé* because granted in the past.

Bismarck's Germany provides an alternative model, that of an authoritarian regime trying to buy the allegiance of its subjects by offering social benefits *in place of* political and civil rights. The state created in 1871 under a Prussian Kaiser proclaimed as a 'social monarch' was the pioneer in Europe of social security legislation to guarantee an income in old age and protection from industrial injury or hardship. But German workers in receipt of welfare benefits were denied the right to choose a government, or the right to strike. A wide-ranging study by Peter Flora and Jens Alber (1981: 72f) concludes: 'When allowance is made for different levels of economic development, non-parliamentary monarchies were found more apt to have initiated welfare programmes than liberal parliamentary democracies.'

Earlier European experience remains relevant today. The annual growth rates of Mediterranean dictatorships in the 1960s and early 1970s – 6.9 per cent in Portugal, 7.2 per cent in Spain and 7.7 per cent in Greece – were higher than in any other country in Europe. But higher material living standards did not slake the thirst of ordinary people for political rights. When the opportunity arose, each of these countries welcomed the introduction of democracy in place of authoritarian regimes. Notwithstanding lower growth rates since the introduction of free elections, these Mediterranean countries have remained committed to systems of government that grant long-denied civil and political rights.

The social benefits that ordinary people receive are not rights of citizenship. They are authorized by ordinary statute laws. This is very clear in the United States, where the written constitution contains a Bill of Rights and the courts are ready to enforce these rights. However, the American constitution does not contain any guarantees to social security benefits, health care or education. These benefits are authorized by ordinary Acts of Congress. The rhetoric of party controversy tends to blur the distinction between rights guaranteed citizens in a constitution and entitlements under ordinary legislation. Constitutional rights cannot be revoked without threatening consent, but statutory entitlements can be altered by the actions of the government of the day, at the risk of electoral defeat but not constitutional collapse.

Whereas the language of rights is the language of obligation, the language of benefits is the language of bargaining. Because government will never have enough money to meet every political demand, bargaining about public expenditure inevitably results in the rejection of some demands while meeting others. Although there may be disappointment if government does not increase spending on a popular programme, ordinary people cannot be surprised if some demands receive a low priority. By definition, political demands are claims that have *not* been met, and to which there is no statutory entitlement at the moment. To confuse rights with entitlements, to assume that every demand made must be granted by an Act of Parliament, and that every entitlement is an entrenched constitutional right necessary for popular consent, is to make the loyalty of citizens a byproduct of material benefits (or bribes) from government.

Consent is dynamic, not static. Ordinary people want government to respond to changes in the environment, and to adapt institutions and programmes. As the first section of this chapter emphasizes, there is widespread acceptance of the principle of gradual and peaceful demands for change – and rejection of extra-constitutional protest. The importance of consent is underscored in the second section, which illustrates what can happen when it is absent. This is done by contrasting the evolution of consent in the American Deep South in consequence of civil rights actions with the forceful absence of consent in Northern Ireland today. Since ordinary people view politics as a means to an end rather than as an end in itself, the final section considers the extent to which people find satisfaction in life beyond politics.

Agreeing to differ and to change

Free elections recognize the right of ordinary people to have a say in how a country should be governed. Competition between two or more parties guarantees every individual a choice. Because an election produces losers as well as winners, it means that some people will vote for parties that are in opposition, not office. While not everyone is expected to like the government of the day, everyone is expected to consent to its authority. Free elections commit losers as well as winners to accept what is done in the name of a duly elected government.

Change: gradually, and by degree. Popular election does not guarantee that a government will be effective in achieving what it wants. During its term of office, the governing party will take some actions that are widely unpopular, and will make some mistakes. At the end of its term of office, anyone who is dissatisfied can vote to turn the incumbents out of office, and even a relatively small shift in votes can be sufficient to make control of government change hands. Insofar as a party enters office by raising expectations of achievement among ordinary people, then its coalition of support is vulnerable to defections, as performance in office cannot match high expectations raised when campaigning for office. Insofar as ordinary people are disenchanted with government, then every election ought to see the governing party voted out of office.

In fact, one-third of governing parties have their vote go up and two-thirds of incumbents have their vote go down when seeking re-election. The tendency is general across Western nations, and there was no rise in unpopularity for incumbent parties during the 1970s, when some doom-mongers expected that the electoral process would reject every major party in turn as each failed to meet unrealistic expectations (cf. Rose and Mackie, 1983: Table 5.5).

While governing parties tend to lose some votes, the decline in popular support is on average so small that 65 per cent of incumbents are normally returned for another term of office. Given the choice, voters are more likely to return the governing party for another term of office than to 'turn the rascals out'. Since 1948 three-fifths of incumbent parties that have had their vote fall have not had it drop so much that they have been forced from office. In 53 per cent of postwar elections the governing party remains in office; in 24 per cent of cases there is a reshuffle among coalition partners; and in the remaining instances the governing party or coalition loses office. In sum, half of all elections introduce some change, and half maintain continuity in government (Rose and Mackie, 1983: Table 5.8).

Because some party must emerge victorious from an election, if only as the lesser of two evils, we must also examine the opinions of ordinary people about the political system as a whole, in order to see how content ordinary people are with the way they are governed, and how much change they would like in the system. Since 1973, just before the OPEC-induced oil crisis triggered a world recession, the European Community has commissioned semi-annual Eurobarometer surveys of public opinion, measuring trends in attitudes toward major political and economic issues. Equally important, the surveys ask ordinary people whether they are satisfied with their life overall.

When the Eurobarometer survey of the member nations of the European Community asks people – On the whole, are you very satisfied, fairly satisfied, not very satisfied, or not at all satisfied with the way democracy works? – there is a division of opinion. For every four people who say they are satisfied, more than three express a measure of dissatisfaction. This does not mean that there is widespread support for extremist anti-democratic parties, but that the workings of political institutions are judged as falling short of an ideal. Three-quarters of the replies are moderate: 46 per cent report that they are fairly satisfied with democracy, and 30 per cent that they are not very satisfied (Table 10.1).

Satisfaction with democracy tends to vary from nation to nation in ways consistent with historical experience. In Germany more than three-quarters of people are satisfied with democracy. This judgement not only reflects the performance of the government of the *Bundesrepublik*; it also reflects comparison with the previous regime, Hitler's Third Reich. At the

Table 10.1 *Satisfaction with the Way that Democracy Works (percentages)*

	Satisfied			Dissatisfied	
	Very	Fairly	Total	Not very	Not at all
Germany	13	64	77	18	2
Denmark	17	57	72	21	3
Luxembourg	14	56	70	15	4
Netherlands	8	53	61	28	6
Britain	10	47	57	27	11
Belgium	9	46	55	27	11
Ireland	9	46	55	23	15
Portugal	8	45	53	30	12
Greece	14	37	51	20	24
France	5	46	51	32	10
Spain	11	36	47	35	13
Italy	2	25	27	46	25
Total	8	45	53	30	12

Totals do not add to 100 per cent because of omission of don't knows.

Source: Eurobarometer 29 (June 1988), Table B 2.

other extreme, only 27 per cent of Italians say that they are satisfied with the way that government works in the Republic of Italy. This judgement does not reflect a desire for a return of Fascism or the introduction of a disciplined Stalinist regime, for extreme parties of left and right secure few votes at Italian elections. Instead, it reflects a realistic assessment of a system of government that is subject to severe criticism by both Italian and non-Italian commentators.

Criticism of the operation of democratic political systems should not be misinterpreted as a rejection of democracy. The right to criticize government is a basic civil right. Criticism reflects a widespread desire to see improvements in the working of democratic institutions. While ordinary people are prepared to consent to government as it is now, this is consistent with a desire to change things in future.

The Eurobarometer also assesses the extent to which people want to see society change, and believe it can be changed through established institutions of government. It asks a question in which everyone is offered three alternatives: radical change by revolutionary actions, gradual improvement by reforms, and defending the status quo against subversive forces. The alternatives offered are extreme, but they are also clearcut. Two-thirds of Europeans favour the gradual reform of society (Table 10.2). The proportion in favour of reform is highest in Portugal, where the reaction to a dictatorship of the right has been in favour of democracy rather than a dictatorship of the left. A similar endorsement of reform is found in Spain and Greece, which have also recently emerged from a lengthy experience of dictatorship. In every country of the Community, an absolute majority of public opinion is in favour of reform, and this has been the case since surveys commenced nearly two decades ago.

Rhetorical talk about revolution has little or no popular resonance in rich or poor countries of Europe. Overall, only 4 per cent endorse the idea of truly radical change. The proportion of people who believe that society must be defended against subversion is significantly larger, 22 per cent. Insofar as this reflects a strong commitment to the status quo it adds further weight to the view that while ordinary people may sometimes be unhappy with the way democracy works, it is preferred to any alternative.

Protest: conventional and unconventional. Student demonstrations in 1968 dramatically showed that voicing views through the ballot box or an opinion poll is not the only way in which people can express political dissatisfaction. While a small portion of the electorate, student protesters gave striking evidence of the capacity of unconventional measures to draw attention to political views, and to force those in authority to pay attention to the protesters. In the United States, civil rights demonstrations and protests against the Vietnam war also showed the significance of unconventional protest.

In an age of mass media, protests by a few hundred or a few thousand demonstrators can have their significance multiplied many thousand

Table 10.2   *Popular Attitudes toward Social Change (percentages)*

	Revolutionary action	Reform	Defend against subversion
Portugal	6	77	8
Italy	5	74	17
Luxembourg	2	71	20
Britain	4	71	20
Greece	11	69	14
Spain	4	66	13
France	5	66	25
Belgium	6	66	18
Ireland	5	61	25
Germany	2	59	34
Denmark	1	51	46
Netherlands	5	67	23
Community average	4	68	22
United States	5	66	20

Don't knows omitted.

Source: Eurobarometer 29 (June 1988), pp. B 25–36. USA: 1981 CARA Values Survey.

times by publicity. People who do not live where protests occur will see demonstrations on television, thus learning from the media about forms of political action that are not prescribed in conventional manuals of citizenship. The media also show who the demonstrators are and what the demonstrators are protesting about. Insofar as ordinary people sympathize with demonstrators then they may wish to emulate their unconventional methods. But there is another possibility: protesters may rely upon the multiplier effect of media publicity, because they are too few in number to be effective in elections.

To measure the extent to which protest movements reflect a widespread willingness to step outside the bounds of conventional political behaviour, multi-national surveys have been undertaken of popular attitudes to protest in the United States and Europe. A five-nation study in 1974 found that a majority of people approved of conventional forms of expressing political views, such as signing petitions and taking part in lawful demonstrations. A majority also disapproved of unconventional methods of protest, such as occupying buildings, unofficial strikes or damaging property.

When people are asked if they have ever engaged in a variety of forms of protest behaviour, more than half of Britons and Americans say that they have signed a petition to government, and almost half of French and Germans (Table 10.3). However, only a small fraction say they have ever taken part in a lawful demonstration, ranging from 10 per cent in Britain to 26 per cent in France. Unconventional forms of political protest attract

Table 10.3 *Conventional and Unconventional Political Protest*

	Percentage saying have protested			
	USA	Britain	Germany	France
Conventional				
Sign petition	61	63	46	44
Take part in lawful demonstration	12	10	14	26
Unconventional				
Join boycott	14	7	7	11
Take part in unofficial strike	2	7	2	10
Occupy building	2	2	1	7
Damage property	1	2	1	1
Commit violence against person	2	1	1	1

Percentages do not add to 100 since some individuals have not engaged in any form of protest.

Source: 1981 European Values Survey and CARA Survey, as cited by Dalton, 1988: Table 4.1.

media attention because they are novel; that is, they are not things that ordinary people are likely to do, nor do they occur frequently. Only 1 or 2 per cent of the population claim to have taken part in occupying a building, damaging property or engaging in actions that involve violence against a person. Boycotts, which can be peaceful even if contentious, have failed to mobilize about nine-tenths of the population.

Ordinary people expect the freedom to voice criticisms of government through conventional channels; but people also believe that it is wrong to protest in ways that break the law. The great majority of Americans and Britons disapprove of people engaging in a wide variety of unconventional forms of protest; as actions tend toward violence, disapproval rises toward 100 per cent. Even when people recognize that certain forms of unconventional protests may have some impact upon policymakers, they still voice disapproval (cf. Barnes, Kaase et al., 1979: especially 544ff).

Ironically, the outburst of protest demonstrations in the late 1960s and early 1970s demonstrated the isolation of the protesters. Protest groups did not become mass movements, attracting large-scale electoral support for radical means or radical ends. Moreover, their actions stimulated a counter-mobilization of popular support for defenders of law and order (cf. Table 10.2). In both Britain and America two-thirds of ordinary people say that they approve courts giving severe sentences to protesters who disregard the police, and approve the police use of force against demonstrators (Barnes, Kaase et al., 1979: 87ff, 556).

The commitment of ordinary people to democratic forms of government is not a blind loyalty. Many people see faults in the governing party, and in the system of democracy itself. There is a widespread desire to reform institutions. The desire for change is normal; only a very dogmatic person would believe that everything that government did was always for the best, or that institutions of governance were perfect.

In order to govern effectively and deserve the consent of ordinary people, a government must be prepared to change policies, personnel and ways of governing. Free elections give voters the right to change control of government. A change of governing party cannot make all the difference, given the commitments it inherits from its predecessors to maintain a great variety of public policies. A change of party is expected to make some difference, but not all the difference. Moreover, public policies can alter without a change of party in office, as policies that do not work are abandoned and events stimulate fresh responses. We can characterize this form of gradual change of policies as the dynamics of a moving consensus (Rose, 1984a: 152ff).

When consent is absent

An agreement to differ about changing control of government presupposes a basic agreement upon fundamental rules of the game. But such agreement is contingent, not certain. Conflicts can arise between those who have rights within a system and those who are excluded. Conflicts can also arise because groups differ about which rights should be recognized by government, or what the national boundaries of a political system should be. In most member-states of the United Nations such agreement is lacking or uncertain, and regimes in such countries do *not* trust the people to choose government.

Consent has been contingent within both the United Kingdom and the United States in the postwar era. In the American Deep South blacks were usually denied civil and political rights until the 1960s. The civil rights movement launched in the late 1950s by Martin Luther King was a demand for blacks to be granted equality of citizenship *within* the American constitution. The demands of the civil rights movement were for the enforcement of equal rights amendments to the constitution. By contrast, in Northern Ireland there is a fundamental conflict about the basis of the state: whether the six counties of Ulster should be part of an Irish or British political system. Predominantly Protestant Unionists pledge allegiance to the British Crown whereas predominantly Catholic nationalists and republicans have favoured being ruled by an independent Irish government based in Dublin.

The contingency of consent is highlighted by contrasting the evolution of the American Deep South and Northern Ireland in the past generation (cf. Rose, 1976b). In that period, American blacks have been incorporated as citizens with political and civil rights; the basis of consent has thus been broadened, and political disagreements are expressed through normal channels such as elections. By contrast, in Northern Ireland what started out as a civil rights protest turned into a confrontation between two armed and violent groups with mutually exclusive national identities, a conflict that cannot be resolved by bargaining through normal democratic processes. In the absence of consensus Northern Ireland is subject to the arbitrament of force (cf. Rose, 1971: especially chapter 14). This chapter is too brief to encompass a proper account of the dynamics of the Deep South and Northern Ireland. Yet recalling events there can show the importance of the absence of consent.

Incorporating blacks as citizens. The United States Constitution initially did not treat blacks as citizens and the amendments enacted after the end of the Civil War in 1865 were not effective in the Deep South. The doctrine of 'states rights' gave Alabama, Georgia, Louisiana, Mississippi, South Carolina and other states of the old Confederacy the power to write election laws as they chose, and to administer the courts and police as they chose. The majority of white voters consistently voted for candidates pledged to maintain white supremacy and racial segregation.

The crucial steps on the road to black citizenship in the Deep South were taken through the courts rather than the ballot box. Blacks entered United States federal courts to seek rights as citizens; the courts were asked to declare unconstitutional measures to which blacks could not consent because they had been denied the right to vote. In turning to the courts blacks were not defying authority but the reverse; they were invoking the superior authority of the federal government to enforce the equal rights clauses of the Constitution in all parts of the United States. Beginning in 1938, the Supreme Court consistently found in favour of black claims; the doctrine of segregation was finally declared unconstitutional in 1954.

At no point did blacks claiming civil rights argue that they represented majority opinion where they lived. The opposite was the case: they were seeking to overturn state segregation laws enacted with the support of the majority of residents, who were white. Because Southern states were slow to abandon segregation after it was declared unconstitutional in 1954, the civil rights demonstrations that followed were intended to secure the prompt acceptance and enforcement of anti-segregation decisions of the highest court in the land. The civil rights movement focused upon conditions in which popularly elected governors, school boards and sheriffs were still denying the constitutional rights of black citizens. The enactment of a strong federal voting rights act in 1964 gave Southern blacks a statutory guarantee of the right to vote, complementing the civil rights enforced by the courts.

In the period since the implementation of voting rights, Southern blacks have demonstrated their integration into the political system in two ways. In all Southern states blacks now elect representatives to the state legislature in districts where black voters are a majority, and a few Southern districts have also elected blacks to Congress. Yet in no Southern state have blacks been able to elect a Governor, for the gubernatorial election normally requires a statewide majority, and in every Southern state blacks are a minority of citizens. The experience of Rev. Jesse Jackson in Democratic Party primaries in 1988 illustrates the position of Southern blacks today, for while he won a large enough vote to finish second he had to give way to the candidate finishing first. Given equality before the law and the right to vote, blacks everywhere have the same basis for giving consent to government as white citizens – whether their votes are cast for a winner or a losing candidate for office.

Escalating conflict in Ulster. Northern Ireland has always been governed without consensus; divisions follow lines of nationality and religion, not race. The Protestant two-thirds of the population is committed to maintaining the territory as part of the United Kingdom. By contrast, the Catholic third of the population has favoured the integration of Northern

Ireland in the Republic of Ireland. From 1921 to 1971 Northern Ireland was effectively governed by a local Parliament at Stormont. Since Protestants constituted two-thirds of the electorate, their party, the Ulster Unionists, could and did win every election. Catholics tried a variety of electoral tactics, sometimes voting for an Irish Republican Army (IRA) gunman serving a prison term; sometimes for Nationalist candidates favouring Irish unity; and often abstaining in order to emphasize their lack of consent to being governed by Stormont under the British Crown.

In 1968 a group of Ulster Catholics took to the streets to demonstrate against what they saw as a denial of their civil rights in Northern Ireland. One grievance was that Catholics did not have a fair share of jobs and patronage from a government controlled by an exclusively Protestant party. A second grievance was gerrymandering of electoral boundaries in towns such as Londonderry, depriving Catholics of political control where they were a majority in the electorate. While civil rights grievances in the American South were redressed by the courts, the United Kingdom has no written Constitution or Bill of Rights enabling ordinary people to challenge in the courts actions authorized by Parliament. The nearest court with any jurisdiction was on the border between France and Germany, the Strasbourg European Court of Human Rights. But its procedures have been too limited to operate effectively in Northern Ireland.

The impasse between the Unionist government and demonstrators in Northern Ireland was broken in an unexpected way. A counter-mobilization of Protestants led to violence in 1969 that brought the British government to Northern Ireland in an effort to maintain order. Optimistically, the British government diagnosed the problem as socio-economic deprivation, and sought to reduce political tension by boosting public expenditure in hopes of buying its way out of the problem. This did not work (McAllister and Rose, 1983). The focus of Catholic opposition shifted from demanding the rights of British citizens to the nationalist goal of unity with the Republic of Ireland. The Irish Republican Army used the fear generated by the violence of 1969 to mobilize armed forces within the Catholic community of Ulster and launch an insurrection against British rule. When the IRA started shooting British soldiers the British government could not claim to be neutral, and shot back. When the commitment of the British Army to defend Ulster appeared insufficient, illegal Protestant paramilitary groups mobilized, thus generating a three-sided armed conflict between the British Army and the local Royal Ulster Constabulary; IRA groups; and Protestant paramilitaries.

The result has been 20 years of civil war, in which more than 2,700 people have been killed in shooting and bombing incidents, and there have been tens of thousands of violent acts, such as the bombing of buildings and armed attacks on persons, causing injury and damage. The dead include hundreds of civilian bystanders as well as IRA and Protestant paramilitaries, British soldiers, and Ulster policemen and women. Given that the population of Ulster is only 1.5 million, the deaths are equivalent to more than 94,000 being killed in political disorder in Great Britain or more than 430,000 killed in the United States, totals greater than deaths in the American Civil War, and eight times the size of American casualties in Vietnam (Table 10.4).

Ordinary people in Northern Ireland do not want to be caught up in a civil war. However, try as one will, it is impossible for people to insulate their lives from the direct and indirect effects of government. When consent is absent, then small groups of political activists will seek to redress perceived grievances. When the courts are open, permitting a challenge to laws duly enacted by the majority, then civil and political rights may be secured by the rule of law, as the American experience demonstrates. But when courts are closed and voting is ineffectual – because of rigging the electoral system, the aggrieved being in a minority, or both – then

Table 10.4   *Deaths by Political Violence in Northern Ireland and British and American Equivalents*

| | Number of people killed | | | |
| | Northern Ireland | | Equivalent (cumulative) | |
	Annual	Cumulative	Britain	USA
1969	13	13	455	2,080
1970	25	38	1,330	6,080
1971	173	211	7,385	33,760
1972	467	678	23,730	108,480
1973	250	929	32,515	148,640
1974	216	1,145	40,075	183,200
1975	247	1,392	48,720	222,720
1976	297	1,689	59,115	270,240
1977	112	1,801	63,035	288,160
1978	81	1,882	65,870	301,120
1979	113	1,995	69,825	319,200
1980	76	2,071	72,485	331,360
1981	101	2,172	76,020	347,520
1982	97	2,269	79,415	363,040
1983	77	2,346	82,110	375,360
1984	64	2,410	84,350	385,600
1985	54	2,464	86,240	394,240
1986	61	2,525	88,375	404,000
1987	93	2,618	91,630	418,880
1988	93	2,711	94,885	433,760

Northern Ireland figure multiplied by 35 to adjust for British population size, and by 160 to allow for American population size.

Source: Calculated from data in Central Statistical Office, *Social Trends* (annual), updated.

minorities may turn to extra-constitutional protest. When the claims of the majority and minority are mutually exclusive – as in the clash of national identities in Northern Ireland – then there is no agreement about the object of consent. The lack of consent affects people in Northern Ireland, just as much as its presence affects people in Great Britain.

What do ordinary people want?

Ordinary people have many roles: in the course of a single day an individual can be a spouse, a parent, a son or daughter, a producer, a consumer, a friend, and even a citizen. Non-political roles are far more numerous than political roles, and ordinary people spend far more time in non-political than in political activities. That is why the priorities of policymakers are not the same as the priorities of ordinary people in everyday life.

From the underall position of ordinary people, the most important question is not whether politicians are satisfied with what government does but whether individuals are satisfied with their lives. A government could produce statistics that looked impressive in international league tables of economic strength or military power, but this would avail ordinary people little if the price of economic strength or military might was widespread popular dissatisfaction.

Eurobarometer surveys track life satisfaction among people by asking twice a year: On the whole, are you very satisfied, fairly satisfied, not very satisfied, or not at all satisfied with the life you lead? The great majority

Table 10.5 *Overall Life Satisfaction (percentages)*

		Satisfied			Dissatisfied	
	Total	Very	Fairly	Total	Fairly	Very
Denmark	96	60	36	3	3	–
Netherlands	93	45	48	6	5	1
Luxembourg	92	36	56	6	5	1
Britain	88	34	54	11	9	2
Germany	87	23	64	13	11	2
Belgium	84	29	55	15	11	4
Ireland	80	30	50	20	13	7
France	78	15	63	21	16	5
Italy	74	12	64	26	21	5
European mean	81	23	58	18	14	4
USA	80	n.a.	n.a.	19	n.a.	n.a.

Don't knows omitted.

Source: Calculated from *Eurobarometer* 29 (June 1988), pp. B1–11 and US Gallup Poll Report.

respond with an expression of satisfaction; satisfied Europeans outnumber the dissatisfied by a margin of four to one (Table 10.5). While ordinary people view their lives positively, they recognize problems. Those who say that they are very satisfied are less than half those reporting that they are fairly satisfied with their life. Those who say that they are not at all satisfied with their life are very few. Ordinary people are not divided into satisfied and dissatisfied; they are divided between those who are very satisfied and those who are fairly satisfied.

While political and economic conditions vary among member nations of the European Community, levels of life satisfaction show limited differences around the average of 82 per cent satisfied. Danes are at the top of the list; 96 per cent express satisfaction. While Italians are at the bottom of this European league table, this is not a sign of trouble, for three-quarters of Italians express life satisfaction. The gap between most and least satisfied has narrowed since surveys began in 1973. Insofar as national differences in life satisfaction are found, they are independent of national economic wellbeing. Germany, economically the most successful of European nations, ranks just at the median in life satisfaction, and the United States is very close to the average. The two countries where life satisfaction is relatively low – France and Italy – are at opposite ends of a continuum of relative affluence in Europe. Moreover, a high level of life satisfaction can be found on other continents, including Third World countries where surveys have been done (Cantril, 1965; Easterlin, 1974).

If levels of life satisfaction were significantly influenced by changes in economic conditions, as was often assumed a decade or two ago, then we would expect fluctuations in the economy to produce substantial fluctuations in the way in which ordinary people see their lives. All of the major economic indicators have shown substantial fluctuations since 1973. Growth rates in national economies have gone down and up in a jagged and often unexpected progression. Inflation rates have gone up dramatically and then fallen, and unemployment rates have tended to creep up.

Britain has been prominent among European nations in experiencing roller-coaster changes in the economy. In the 1970s growth rates slowed down and inflation and unemployment rose. In the 1980s inflation rates slowed down and growth rates subsequently picked up, while unemployment rose. If economic conditions determined life satisfaction, then we would expect that it too would show dramatic ups and downs, in keeping with the boom or gloom phase of the British economy.

In fact, life satisfaction in Britain has been remarkably steady and very high since it was first measured in 1973. Consistently, more than four-fifths of people surveyed report that they are satisfied with their lives. At no time has the measure of life satisfaction fallen below 80 per cent. Minor changes are primarily the result of sampling fluctuations rather than an indicator of any change in popular feelings. When trends in life satisfactions are compared with trends in major economic indicators, we see that while there have been substantial movements up and down in the economy, life satisfaction has been consistent, and consistently high for a decade and one-half (Figure 10.1).

Eurobarometer surveys emphasize that people have remained consistently satisfied with their lives, notwithstanding substantial fluctuations in the state of the economy since 1973. When the first Eurobarometer survey was taken then, 79 per cent of people in the Community reported that they were satisfied with their life. Fifteen years later in 1988, the proportion reporting satisfaction was 81 per cent. In the worst of the recession in 1975, the proportion satisfied remained as high as 75 per cent, and there has been remarkably little fluctuation in life satisfaction in particular nations, or in the average for the Community as a whole.

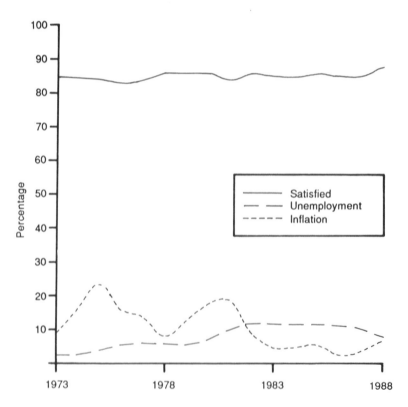

Figure 10.1   *Life Satisfaction in Britain Unaffected by Changes in Economic Conditions*

Percentage satisfied from *Eurobarometer* 29 (1988).

Insulation from politics. The explanation for a high level of life satisfaction is simple yet profound in its implications: the greatest concerns of individuals are substantially insulated from the macro-institutions of society. If we did a content analysis of what ordinary people talk about, we would find that talk about the weather, meals or sport was more frequent than talk about politics, and that phatic communication was more common than reasoned analysis of society's ills. Politicians and commentators who bemoan the low priority that ordinary people give to politics incidentally reveal how distant they are from the outlook of the ordinary people whom they claim to represent. Political insulation is different from political alienation. Alienation expresses a continuing and real concern – albeit negative – about the activities of government. Insulation expresses unawareness or indifference.

In a free society ordinary people have the right to be involved in politics – or not to be involved. Only a totalitarian regime would assert that people must devote their lives and thoughts to the good of the party, the state or the fatherland. A defining characteristic of a free society is that there are limits to the obligations of citizenship.

When surveys ask ordinary people to evaluate their satisfaction with different domains of life, the same pattern recurs: individuals report that they are most satisfied with their family, friends, the place they live, their health and their job, and least satisfied with those things for which major institutions of society are formally responsible, such as government, economic conditions, and law and order (Rose, 1984: Table 6.4). Individuals evaluate the life they lead positively because of the important satisfactions drawn from face-to-face relationships, and not from impersonal institutions of society.

Face-to-face relationships insulate or mediate between large-scale social institutions and individuals. This is particularly noteworthy at work, where money would be expected to be of most importance. Although people are paid for their work, money is not the only, or even the chief, satisfaction that is drawn from work. Within large factories and offices, individuals seek friendships and social satisfactions, and the morale of workers is important in any economic enterprise. Studies that ask individuals to evaluate their work situation consistently find a substantial level of positive satisfaction at all levels of pay, for work satisfaction tends to be based upon social psychological rewards rather than strictly material standard (cf. Table 9.3; *European Men and Women*, 1975, 65ff).

If people were motivated solely by money rather than by attachments to those around them and more general pride in nation, then many people would be prepared to leave their native country to seek better pay elsewhere. Notwithstanding the free movement of labour within the European Community, only a very small fraction of citizens emigrate. Deprivation must be as harsh as in the economically backward rural areas of the

Mediterranean lands to force people to uproot themselves for the sake of more money. Welfare states even encourage firms to move plants to less favoured sites to accommodate the desire of many unemployed to live within a community that is familiar and congenial.

Public policies provide private benefits that are important in nearly every household, but as previous chapters have shown, the state has no monopoly in providing income or goods and services important for wellbeing. The market and the household are important too. Insofar as government is part of the lives of ordinary people, it is through the delivery of private benefits, such as education, health care and social security. Social security is also an example of the limits of the state's role in everyday life. While public agencies provide an income to millions of people, government does not tell people how to spend the income they receive. In a free society, each household has the right to spend its money as it wishes.

While the concerns of ordinary people are central for many public policies, the activities of government are of limited concern to ordinary people. As long as politicians govern with consent and public agencies routinely deliver the services that they are obligated to produce, then ordinary people do not need to turn their mind to the challenge of governance. Individuals can enjoy the luxury of living in a free society by concentrating upon the satisfactions that can be gained from the face-to-face relationships of everyday life.

References

Advisory Commision on Intergovernmental Relations (ACIR), 1984. *Changing Public Attitudes on Governments and Taxes 1984*. Washington, DC: ACIR, S-13.

ADORNO, T.W., FRENKEL-BRUNSWICK, E., LEVINSON, D.J. and SANFORD, R.N., 1950. *The Authoritarian Personality*. New York: Harper.

ALLEN, William R., 1977. 'Economics, Economists and Economic Policy: Modern American Experiences', *History of Political Economy* 9, 48–88.

ALLISON, Graham, 1971. *The Essence of Decision*. Boston, MA: Little, Brown.

ALT, James, 1979. *The Politics of Economic Decline*. Cambridge: Cambridge University Press.

ATTICUS, 1988. *Sunday Times* (London), 10 July.

AUSTIN, Erik W., 1986. *Political Facts of the United States since 1789*. New York: Columbia University Press.

BANKS, Arthur S. and TEXTOR, Robert, 1963. *A Cross-Polity Survey*. Cambridge, MA: MIT Press.

BARNES, S.H., KAASE, M. et al., 1979. *Political Action: Mass Participation in Five Western Democracies*. London: Sage Publications.

BOGDANOR, Vernon and BUTLER, D.E., eds., 1983. *Democracy and Elections*. Cambridge: Cambridge University Press.

BRAYBROOKE, David E. and LINDBLOM, C.E., 1963. *A Strategy of Decision*. New York: Free Press.

BRITTAN, Samuel, 1975. 'The Economic Contradictions of Democracy', *British Journal of Political Science* 5, 2, 129–60.

BROWN, C.V., 1980. *Taxation and Labour Supply*. London: George Allen and Unwin.

BUDGE, Ian, CREWE, Ivor and FAIRLEY, Dennis, eds., 1976. *Party Identification and Beyond*. London: John Wiley.

BUTLER, D.E. and STOKES, Donald, 1969. *Political Change in Britain*. London: Macmillan.

CAMPBELL, Angus, CONVERSE, P.E., MILLER, W. and STOKES, D.E., 1960. *The American Voter*. New York: John Wiley.

CANTRIL, Hadley, 1965. *The Pattern of Human Concerns*. New Brunswick, NJ: Rutgers University Press.

CENTRAL STATISTICAL OFFICE, 1987. *Social Trends*. No. 17. London: HMSO.

CENTRAL STATISTICAL OFFICE, 1988. *Social Trends*. No. 18. London: HMSO.

CHARLES, Prince, 1981. 'Sayings of the Week', *The Observer* (London) 22 November.

COLLINS, Martin, 1987. 'Business and Industry'. In R. Jowell, S. Witherspoon and L. Brook, eds., *British Social Attitudes: the 1987 Report*. Aldershot: Gower, 29–50.

CREWE, Ivor, 1981. 'Electoral Participation'. In D. Butler, Howard R. Penniman and Austin Ranney, eds., *Democracy at the Polls*. Washington, DC: American Enterprise Institute, 196–215.

CSR, 1980. *A General Taxpayer Opinion Survey*. Washington, DC: Prepared for the Internal Revenue Service.

DAHL, Robert A., 1970. *After the Revolution?* New Haven, CT: Yale University Press.

DALTON, Russell, 1988. *Citizen Politics in Western Democracies.* Chatham, NJ: Chatham House.

DALTON, Russell, FLANAGAN, Scott and BECK, Paul, eds., 1984. *Electoral Change in Advanced Industrial Democracies.* Princeton, NJ: Princeton University Press.

DAVIS, James A. 1986, 'British and American Attitutdes: Similarities and Contrasts'. In R. Jowell et al., eds., *British Social Attitudes: the 1986 Report.* Aldershot: Gower.

DAY, Patricia and KLEIN, Rudolf, 1987. *Accountabilities: Five Public Services.* London: Tavistock.

DEAN, Tom and WARE, Alan, 1986. 'Charity–State Relations: a Conceptual Analysis', *Journal of Public Policy* 6, 4, 121–36.

DEUTSCH, K.W., 1963. *The Nerves of Government.* New York: Free Press.

DILNOT, A. and MORRIS, N., 1981. 'What do we Know about the Black Economy?', *Fiscal Studies* 2, 1, 58–73.

EASTERLIN, Richard, 1974. 'Does Economic Growth Improve the Human Lot?' In P.A. David and M.W. Reder, eds., *Nations and Households in Economic Growth.* New York: Academic Press.

EISNER, Robert, ed., 1981. 'Total Incomes in the United States: 1946 to 1976'. Gouvieux, France: 17th Annual Conference, International Association for Research in Income and Wealth.

EMERSON, Rupert, 1960. *From Empire to Nation.* Boston, MA: Beacon Press.

ETZIONI, Amitai, 1988. *The Moral Dimension: Toward a New Economics.* New York: Free Press.

European Men and Women, 1975. Brussels: Commission of the European Community.

FEREJOHN, J.A. and FIORINA, Morris, 1985. 'Incumbency and Realignment in Congressional Elections'. In J.E. Chubb and Paul E. Peterson, eds., *The New Direction in American Politics.* Washington, DC: Brookings Institution, 91–116.

FESLER, James W., 1949. *Area and Administration.* Tuscaloosa, AL: University of Alabama Press.

FLORA, Peter, 1983. *State, Economy and Society in Western Europe 1815–1975.* vol. 1. London: Macmillan.

FLORA, Peter and ALBER, Jens, 1981. 'Modernization, Democratization and the Development of Welfare States in Western Europe'. In Flora and Heidenheimer (1981), 37–80.

FLORA, Peter and HEIDENHEIMER, A.J., eds., 1981. *The Development of Welfare States in Europe and America.* New Brunswick, NJ: Transaction.

FOGARTY, Michael, 1985. 'British Attitudes to Work'. In M. Abrams, D. Gerard and N. Timms, eds., *Values and Social Change in Britain.* London: Macmillan, 173–200.

FRIEDMAN, Milton, 1953. *Essays in Positive Economics.* Chicago, IL: University of Chicago Press.

FURNHAM, A. and LEWIS, A., 1986. *The Economic Mind.* Brighton: Wheatsheaf.

GALLUP POLL. *Political Index*, monthly. London: Social Surveys Gallup Poll Ltd.

GERSHUNY, J.I., 1981. 'Changement des Modèles de Loisir, Royaume Uni, 1961–1974/5', *Temps Libres* 4, 115–34.

GERSHUNY, J.I., 1988. *Changing Times: the Social Economics of Post-industrial Societies.* Bath: University report to the Joseph Rowntree Memorial Trust.

GOODE, Richard, 1984. *Government Finance in Developing Countries.* Washington, DC: Brookings Institution.

GOODSELL, Charles T., 1985. *The Case for Bureaucracy.* 2nd edn. Chatham, NJ: Chatham House.

GRAZIA, Raffaele de, 1980. 'Clandestine Employment: a Problem of our Times',

International Labour Review 119, 5, 549–63.

GURR, T.R., 1970. *Why Men Rebel*. Princeton, NJ: Princeton University Press.

HADENIUS, Axel, 1985. 'Citizens Strike a Balance: Discontent with Taxes, Content with Spending', *Journal of Public Policy* 5, 3, 349–64.

HADENIUS, Axel, 1986. *A Crisis of the Welfare State? Opinions about Taxes and Public Expenditure in Sweden*. Stockholm: Almqvist and Wiksell International.

HAHN, Frank H., 1985. 'Recognizing the Limits', *Times Literary Supplement*, 2 December.

HARDING, Stephen and PHILLIPS, David, with FOGARTY, Michael, 1986. *Contrasting Values in Western Europe*. London: Macmillan.

HARGROVE, Erwin C. and MORLEY, Samuel A., eds., 1984. *The President's Council of Economic Advisers: Interviews with CEA Chairmen*. Boulder, CO: Westview Press.

HARROP, Martin, 1980. 'Popular Conceptions of Mobility', *Sociology* 14, 1, 89–98.

HEALD, David, 1986. 'Privatization as Theology', *Public Policy and Administration* 1, 2, 49–66.

HECLO, Hugh, 1981. 'Toward a New Welfare State?' In Flora and Heidenheimer (1981), 383–406.

HEIDENHEIMER, A.J., 1985. 'Comparative Public Policy at the Crossroads', *Journal of Public Policy* 5, 4, 441–66.

HELLER, Peter, 1981. 'Diverging Trends in the Shares of Nominal and Real Government Expenditure in GDP', *National Tax Journal*, 34, 1, 61–74.

HERMET, Guy, 1978. 'State Controlled Elections: a Framework'. In Hermet et al. (1978), 1–18.

HERMET, Guy, ROSE, Richard, and ROUQUIÉ, Alain, eds., 1978. *Elections without Choice*. London: Macmillan.

HIRSCHMAN, Albert O., 1970. *Exit, Voice and Loyalty*. Cambridge, MA: Harvard University Press.

HUNTINGTON, S.P., 1974. 'Post-Industrial Politics: How Benign Will It Be?' *Comparative Politics* 6, 2, 163–91.

JENKINS, Peter, 1987. *Mrs Thatcher's Revolution*. London: Jonathan Cape.

JOWELL, Roger and WITHERSPOON, S., eds., 1985. *British Social Attitudes*. Aldershot: Gower.

JUDGE, Ken, ed., 1980. *Pricing the Social Services*. London: Macmillan.

KARIEL, Henry, 1969. *The Promise of Politics*. Englewood Cliffs, NJ: Prentice-Hall.

KATONA, George, STRUMPEL, Burkhard and ZAHN, Ernest, 1971. *Aspirations and Affluence: Comparative Studies in the United States and Western Europe*. New York: McGraw-Hill.

KATZ, Daniel, GUTEK, Barbara, KAHN, Robert and BARTON, Eugenia, 1975. *Bureaucratic Encounters*. Ann Arbor, MI: Institute for Social Research.

KAVANAGH, Dennis, 1987. *Thatcherism and British Politics*. Oxford: Oxford University Press.

KAY, John, MAYER, Colin and THOMPSON, David, eds., 1986. *Privatisation and Regulation – the UK Experience*. Oxford: Clarendon Press.

KAYSEN, Carl, 1969. 'Model-Makers and Decision-Makers: Economists and the Policy Process'. In R.L. Heilbroner, ed., *Economic Means and Social Ends*. Englewood Cliffs, NJ: Prentice-Hall, 137–53.

KEENAN, A. and DEAN, P.N., 1980. 'Moral Evaluations of Tax Evasion'. Unpublished paper, Heriot–Watt University, Edinburgh.

KEY, V.O. Jr, 1966. *The Responsible Electorate*. Cambridge, MA: Harvard University Press.

KIEWIET, D.R., 1983. *Macroeconomics and Micropolitics*. Chicago, IL: University of Chicago Press.

LAWSON, Kay and MERKL, Peter, eds., 1988. *When Parties Fail*. Princeton, NJ: Princeton University Press.

LEA, S.E.G., TARPY, R.M. and WEBLEY, P., 1987. *The Individual in the Economy*. Cambridge: Cambridge University Press.

LEONTIEF, Wassily, 1985. *Essays in Economics: Theories, Theorizing, Facts and Policies*. New Brunswick, NJ: Transaction.

LINDBECK, Assar, 1976. 'Stabilization Policy in Open Economies with Endogenous Politicians', *American Economic Review* 66, 2.

LIPSET, S.M., 1960. *Political Man*. New York: Doubleday.

LIPSET, S.M., 1964. *America – the First New Nation*. London: Heinemann.

LIPSKY, Michael, 1980. *Street-Level Bureaucracy: Dilemmas of the Individual in Public Services*. New York: Russell Sage Foundation.

LITTLE, I.M.D. 1950. *A Critique of Welfare Economics*. London: Oxford University Press.

McALLISTER, Ian and ROSE, Richard, 1983. 'Can Political Conflict be Resolved by Social Change?' *Journal of Conflict Resolution* 27, 3, 533–57.

MACKIE, T.T. and ROSE, Richard, 1990. *International Almanac of Electoral History*. 3rd edn. London: Macmillan.

MANN, Michael, 1986. 'Work and the Work Ethic'. In R. Jowell, S. Witherspoon and L. Brook, eds., *British Social Atittudes: the 1986 Report*. Aldershot: Gower, 17–38.

MARSHALL, T.H., 1950. *Citizenship and Social Class*. Cambridge: Cambridge University Press.

MILLWARD, R. and PARKER, D., 1983. 'Public and Private Enterprise'. In R. Millward, D. Parker, L. Rosenthal, M. Sawyer and N. Topham, *Public Sector Economics*. London: Longman, 199–274.

MORIN, R., 1988. 'Still, our Families are More Important than our Jobs', *Washington Post National Weekly Edition*, 19–25 December.

MUELLER, Dennis, 1979. *Public Choice*. Cambridge: Cambridge University Press.

MUSGRAVE, R.A. and MUSGRAVE, P., 1980. *Public Finance in Theory and Practice*. New York: McGraw-Hill.

NELSON, Robert H., 1987. 'The Economics Profession and the Making of Public Policy', *Journal of Economic Literature* 5, 49–91.

NORDHAUS, W. and TOBIN, J., 1973. 'Is Growth Obsolete?' In Milton Moss, ed., *The Measurement of Economic and Social Performance*. New York: Columbia University Press, 509–32.

OECD, 1985. *Social Expenditure, 1960–1990*. Paris: OECD Social Policy Studies.

OECD, 1985a. *Measuring Health Care, 1960–1983*. Paris: OECD Social Policy Studies No. 2.

OLSON, Mancur, 1965. *The Logic of Collective Action*. Cambridge, MA: Harvard University Press.

PAGE, Edward, 1985. 'Laws as an Instrument of Policy', *Journal of Public Policy* 5, 2, 241–675.

PARRY, Richard, 1987. 'Public Employment in Britain in the 1980s'. Glasgow: University of Strathclyde *Studies in Public Policy*, 157, 3–29.

PEEL, Quentin, 1988. 'Gorbachev Fights the Flames', *Financial Times*, 26 November.

PETERS, B. Guy, 1985. 'The United States: Absolute Change and Relative Stability'. In Rose (1985b), 228–61.

PLAMENATZ, John, 1958. 'Electoral Studies and Democratic Theory', *Political Studies* 6, 1–15.

POWELL, G. Bingham, 1982. *Contemporary Democracies: Participation, Stability and Violence*. Cambridge, MA: Harvard University Press.

ROSE, Richard, 1965. 'England: a Traditionally Modern Political Culture'. In L.W. Pye and S. Verba, eds. *Political Culture and Political Development*. Princeton, NJ: Princeton University Press, 93–129.

ROSE, Richard, 1969. 'Dynamic Tendencies in the Authority of Regimes', *World Politics* 21, 4, 612–28.

ROSE, Richard, 1971. *Governing without Consensus: an Irish Perspective*. London: Faber and Faber.

ROSE, Richard, 1974. *The Problem of Party Government*. London: Macmillan.

ROSE, Richard, 1976. 'Disciplined Research and Undisciplined Problems', *International Social Science Journal* 28, 1, 99–121.

ROSE, Richard, 1976a. 'On the Priorities of Government', *European Journal of Political Research* 4, 3, 247–89.

ROSE, Richard, 1976b. 'On the Priorities of Citizenship in the Deep South and Northern Ireland', *Journal of Politics* 38, 2, 247–91.

ROSE, Richard, 1980. 'Misperceiving Public Expenditure: Feelings about Cuts'. In C.H. Levine and I. Rubin, eds., *Fiscal Stress and Public Policy*. Beverly Hills, CA: Sage Publications, 203–30.

ROSE, Richard, 1980a. 'Ordinary People in Extraordinary Economic Circumstances', in R. Rose, ed., *Challenge to Governance*. London: Sage Publications, 151–74.

ROSE, Richard, 1983. 'Elections and Electoral Systems: Choices and Alternatives'. In Bogdanor and Butler (1983), 20–45.

ROSE, Richard, 1983a. 'Two and One-Half Cheers for the Market in Britain', *Public Opinion* 6, 3, 10–15.

ROSE, Richard, 1984. *Understanding Big Government*. London: Sage Publications.

ROSE, Richard, 1984a. *Do Parties Make a Difference?* 2nd edn. London: Macmillan.

ROSE, Richard, 1985. 'From Government at the Centre to Nationwide Government'. In Yves Meny and V. Wright, eds., *Centre–Periphery Relations in Western Europe*. London: George Allen and Unwin, 13–32.

ROSE, Richard, 1985a. 'The Programme Approach to the Growth of Government', *British Journal of Political Science* 15, 1, 1–28.

ROSE, Richard, 1985b. *Public Employment in Western Nations*. Cambridge: Cambridge University Press.

ROSE, Richard, 1985c. 'Maximizing Tax Revenue while Minimizing Political Costs', *Journal of Public Policy* 5, 3, 289–320.

ROSE, Richard, 1985d. 'Getting By in Three Economies: the Resources of the Official, Unofficial and Domestic Economies'. In Jan-Erik Lane, ed., *State and Market*. London: Sage Publications, 103–41.

ROSE, Richard, 1986. 'Law as a Resource of Public Policy', *Parliamentary Affairs* Summer, 297–314.

ROSE, Richard, 1986a. 'The Dynamics of the Welfare Mix in Britain'. In R. Rose and R. Shiratori, eds., *The Welfare State East and West*. New York: Oxford University Press, 80–106.

ROSE, Richard, 1986b. 'Common Goals but Different Roles: the State's Contribution to the Welfare Mix'. In R. Rose and R. Shiratori (1986a), 13–39.

ROSE, Richard, 1987. *Ministers and Ministries: a Functional Analysis*. Oxford: Clarendon Press.

ROSE, Richard, 1987a. 'Steering the Ship of State: One Tiller but Two Pairs of Hands', *British Journal of Political Science* 17, 4, 409–33.

ROSE, Richard, 1987b. 'Learning to Understand Democratic Government Better'. In Peter Koslowski, ed., *Individual Liberty and Democratic Decision-Making*. Tuebingen: J.C.B. Mohr, 145–72.

ROSE, Richard, 1988. 'The Growth of Government Organizations: Do We Count the Number or Weigh the Programs?'. In C. Campbell and B.G. Peters, eds., *Organizing Governance, Governing Organizations*. Pittsburgh, PA: University of Pittsburgh Press, 99–128.

ROSE, Richard, 1988a. *The Postmodern President: the White House Meets the World*. Chatham, NJ: Chatham House.

ROSE, Richard, 1989. 'How Exceptional is the American Political Economy?' *Political Science Quarterly* 104, 1, 91–115.

ROSE, Richard, 1989a. *Politics in England*. 5th edn. London: Macmillan.

ROSE, Richard, 1989b. 'Privatization: a Question of Quantities and Qualities'. In Gerhard Fels and George M. von Furstenberg, eds., *A Supply-Side Agenda for Germany*. Hamburg: Springer-Verlag, 247–77.

ROSE, Richard and GARVIN, Tom, 1983. 'The Public Policy Effects of Independence: Ireland as a Test Case', *European Journal of Political Research* 11: 377–97.

ROSE, Richard and KARRAN, T., 1987. *Taxation by Political Inertia*. London: George Allen and Unwin.

ROSE, Richard and KAVANAGH, Dennis, 1976. 'The Monarchy in Contemporary Political Culture', *Comparative Politics* 8, 3, 548–76.

ROSE, Richard and McALLISTER, Ian, 1986. *Voters Begin to Choose*. London: Sage Publications.

ROSE, Richard and MACKIE, T.T., 1983. 'Incumbency in Government: Asset or Liability?' In H. Daalder and P. Mair, eds., *Western European Party Systems*. London: Sage Publications, 115–37.

ROSE, Richard and MACKIE, T.T., 1988. 'Do Parties Persist or Fail? The Big Trade-Off Facing Organizations'. In Kay Lawson and Peter H. Merkl, eds., *When Parties Fail*. Princeton, NJ: Princeton University Press, 533–60.

ROSE, Richard and MOSSAWIR, Harve, 1967. 'Voting and Elections: a Functional Analysis', *Political Studies* 15, 2, 173–201.

ROSE, Richard, and PETERS, B. Guy, 1978. *Can Government Go Bankrupt?* New York: Basic Books.

ROSE, Richard and Shiratori, Rei, eds., 1986. *The Welfare State East and West*. New York: Oxford University Press.

SAMETZ, A.W., 1968. 'Production of Goods and Services: the Measurement of Economic Growth'. In E.B. Sheldon and W.E. Moore, eds., *Indicators of Social Change*. New York: Russell Sage Foundation, 77–96.

SCHUMPETER, Joseph A., 1952. *Capitalism, Socialism and Democracy*. 4th edn. London: George Allen and Unwin.

SAWHILL, Isabel V., 1986. 'Reaganomics in Retrospect'. In J.L. Palmer, ed., *Perspectives on the Reagan Years*. Washington, DC: Urban Institute, 91–120.

SELDON, Arthur, 1977. *Charge*. London: Temple Smith.

SIMON, Herbert, 1979. 'Rational Decision Making', *American Economic Review* 69, 4, 493–513.

SMITH, Stephen, 1986. *Britain's Shadow Economy*. Oxford: Clarendon Press.

SNIDERMAN, Paul and BRODY, Richard, 1977. 'Coping: the Ethic of Self-Reliance', *American Journal of Political Science* 26, 3, 501–21.

SONG, Young-dahl and YARBOROUGH, T.E., 1978. 'Tax Ethics and Taxpayer Attitudes: a Survey', *Public Administration Review* 38, 5, 442–52.

STOETZEL, Jean, 1983. *Les Valeurs du Temps Présent*. Paris: Presses Universitaires de France.

SURREY, Stanley and McDANIEL, Paul, 1985. *Tax Expenditures*. Cambridge, MA: Harvard University Press.

SZALAI, Alexander, ed., 1972. *The Use of Time*. The Hague and Paris: Mouton.

TANZI, Vito, ed., 1982. *The Underground Economy in the United States and Abroad*. Lexington, MA: Lexington Books.

TANZI, Vito, 1988. 'International Coordination of Fiscal Policies', *Journal of Public Policy* 8, 2, 111–25.

THOMAS, J.J., 1988. 'The Politics of the Black Economy', *Work, Employment and Society* 2, 2, 169–90.

TITMUSS, Richard, 1970. *The Gift Relationship: From Human Blood to Social Policy*. London: George Allen and Unwin.

VICKERS, John and YARROW, George, 1988. *Privatization: an Economic Analysis*. Cambridge, MA: MIT Press.

VOGEL, Joachim, 1974. 'Taxation and Public Opinion in Sweden', *National Tax Journal* 27, 4, 499–513.

WALSH, Cliff, 1987. 'Individual Irrationality and Public Policy: in Search of Merit/Demerit Policies', *Journal of Public Policy* 7, 2, 103–34.

WARNERYD, K.E. and WALERUD, Bengt, 1982. 'Taxes and Economic Behavior: some Interview Data on Tax Evasion in Sweden' *Journal of Economic Psychology* 2, 3, 182–212.

WEAVER, R. Kent, 1988. *Automatic Government: the Politics of Indexation*. Washington, DC: Brookings Institution.

WEBBER, Carolyn and WILDAVSKY, Aaron, 1986. *A History of Taxation and Expenditure in the Western World*. New York: Simon and Schuster.

WEISBROD, Burton A., 1988. *The Non-Profit Economy*. Cambridge, MA: Harvard University Press.

WILDAVSKY, Aaron, 1985. 'Keeping Kosher: the Epistemology of Tax Expenditures', *Journal of Public Policy* 5, 3, 413–31.

WOLF, Charles, 1987. 'Market and Non-Market Failures: Comparison and Assessment', *Journal of Public Policy* 7, 1, 43–70.

ZETTERBERG, Hans and FRANKEL, Greta, 1981. 'Working Less and Enjoying it More in Sweden', *Public Opinion* 4, 4, 41–5.

Index